CU01046468

BEN NEVIS AND GLEN COE

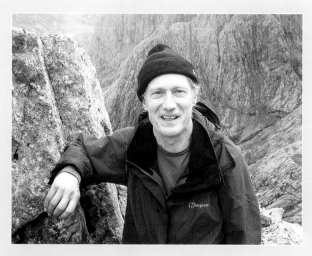

About the Author

Ronald Turnbull is seen here on the Ledge Route of Ben Nevis, a hill he first climbed, at the age of nine, by way of Tower Ridge. Bidean nam Bian followed a few months later. Since then he has learnt to enjoy also the smaller and less arduous mountains in between, while admitting that the particular pleasure of writing this book has been the four further revisits to Bidean.

He has won awards for his writing – the Outdoor Writers' Guild Awards for Excellence four times – and also for his walking – the Fell Running Association's Long-distance Trophy for a journey over all the 2000ft hills of Southern Scotland. His previous books for Cicerone include *The Book of the Bivvy*, on tentless travel, and *Walking in the Cairngorms*.

Photo: Ronald Turnbull, seen here at the half-way point on the Ledge Route, Ben Nevis (Route 9) (photo D McLean)

BEN NEVIS AND GLEN COE

by
Ronald Turnbull

2 POLICE SQUARE, MILNTHORPE, CUMBRIA LA7 7PY
www.cicerone.co.uk

First edition 2007
ISBN 13: 978 1 85284 502 5
© Ronald Turnbull 2007
Reprinted 2010 (with updates)

Sketch maps and photographs: Ronald Turnbull

A catalogue record for this book is available from the British Library.
Printed by MCC Graphics, Spain

Advice to Readers

Front cover: At the western end of the Aonach Eagach (Route 52)

CONTENTS

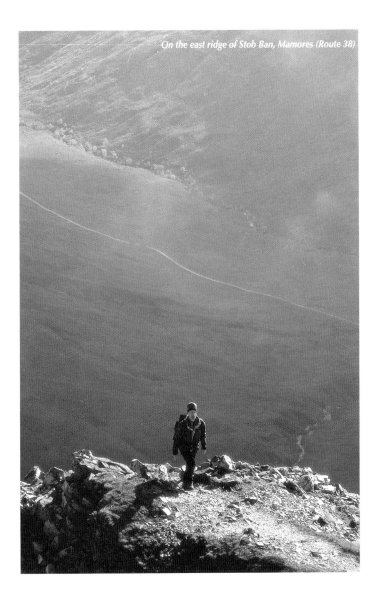

On the east ridge of Stob Ban, Mamores (Route 38)

N

Map Key

▢	ground above 1200m / 4000ft
▢	ground above 1050m / 3500ft
▢	ground above 900m / 3000ft
▢	ground above 750m / 2500ft
▢	ground above 600m / 2000ft
▢	ground above 450m / 1500ft
▢	ground above 300m / 1000ft
▢	ground above 150m / 500ft
▢	ground below 150m / 500ft

Contour intervals chosen to feature the Munro and Corbett levels at 3000ft and 2500ft

▲ Munro

△ Other summit of interest: on overview maps, the Corbetts

P Parking (typically at walk start)

▫ building

⌂ bothy or the CIC Hut, Ben Nevis (private)

♜ castle

⬭ loch

〜 river, stream

major road

minor road

unsurfaced track

 The route ◀ start ◁ finish (if different)

 Variants, and adjacent routes

Overview maps (pages 12–15)

estate boundaries (see access section)

 the through routes (long daywalk or backpacking)

53 route location

 town, village

Route symbols on OS map extracts

route 1
alternative route 1

route 2
alternative route 2

linking routes

 start point

 finish point

 start/finish point

 direction of walk

For OS symbols key see OS maps

Ben Nevis & Glen Coe
overview map, with through routes: **north**

to Gleann Cia-aig and Glen Garry

Great Glen Way to Inverness

Glen Scaddle to Glenfinnan

the Aonachs **13-14**

6

0   5 km

N

1

7-12

Fort William

Druimarbin

4

Ben Nevis

GLEN NEVIS

2-3

39

Loch Linnhe

GC/M WEST

the MAMORES

25-38

West Highland Way

Mam na Gualainn **41**

Loch Leven

Kinlochleven

Onich

Pap of Glencoe

51

Aonach Eagach

52

53

40

Ballachulish

Glencoe village

49-50

GLEN COE

59

Beinn a' Bheithir **47**

Bidean nam Bian

58-68

NTS

FC

48

56

Spean Bridge

GREY CORRIES /
MAMORE
EAST

△ **23**

△

15-22

the GREY CORRIES

Lairig
Leacach

Loch
Treig

▲
▲
▲
▲
▲
▲
▲

24

5

to Culra and
Dalwhinnie

40

45

Corrour

42

△

Glas Bheinn

44

46

△ Leum Uilleim

CORROUR

43

see overview map: South

Blackwater Reservoir

RANNOCH MOOR

Beinn a' Chrulaiste

△ **57**

to Rannoch
Station

55

54

Kings House

77

Buachaille Etive Mor

Ben Nevis & Glen Coe
overview map, with
through routes: **south**

Ballachulish

Beinn a' Bheithir
47 ▲ FE

see overview map: North

GLEN CRERAN

GLENCRERAN
70 ▲
Beinn
Sgulaird

Lismore

△ APPIN

Benderloch
△ Beinn Lora
100

Loch Etive

Connel

77

Taynuilt

Kerrera

Oban
99

Stob Coire nan Lochan and the top of its northwest ridge from Coire nan Lochan in early May. The continuous snow-strip is Broad Gully, Winter Grade I, offering a late-season axe-and-crampon route for the competent (Routes 61, 62).

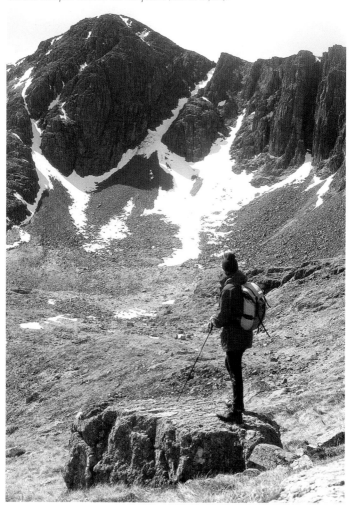

INTRODUCTION

'GLEN COE, GLEN COE, IT'S THE PLACE TO GO...'

The best of walking is ridge walking. Swoop downwards from the peak, level off along a rocky crest, then rise again to another summit; and then do the same thing again, four or five or even eight times over. Let the ridge sides drop steeply 900m to a green valley where a river gleams among the alder trees; and beyond the valley another steep ridge, and another, and the sea reaching silver-grey into the furthest west. For added interest let the ridge top be composed of three different sorts of stone. And you've started to understand why the area from Ben Nevis southwards to Glen Coe is some

of the finest mountain walking there is in the UK.

I put that 'some of' so as not to annoy the lovers of Snowdonia, or the English Lakes, or Skye, or Torridon. There's a lot more of Lochaber than there is of Snowdonia; it's one and a half times as large as Lakeland. It's a whole lot easier to get to than Skye. Still not convinced? In that case...

Follow me first onto one of the less celebrated summits, Ben Starav at the bottom of Glen Etive. Its long ridge (Route 73) is stony with moss, and leads into an easy scramble over blobby boulders of grey granite. But now, drop into the green valley on the left and enjoy another aspect of

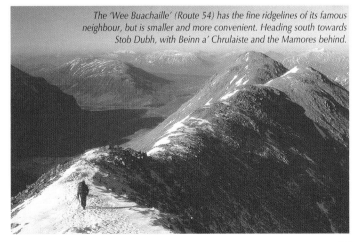

The 'Wee Buachaille' (Route 54) has the fine ridgelines of its famous neighbour, but is smaller and more convenient. Heading south towards Stob Dubh, with Beinn a' Chrulaiste and the Mamores behind.

Quartzite walking on the west ridge of Stob Coire Easain, Grey Corries (Route 15)

it all. Steep grass and granite slabs shut out the sky. Below the path, a gloomy ravine, with the flash of a waterfall. And at the valley foot, under green birch and dark pine, the cuckoo calls, and white water slides over granite that mysteriously is now coloured pink.

Next, let's visit Bidean nam Bian. The rocks now are volcanic, grey-blue andesite and pinky-grey rhyolite, all of it great to climb on if you're a rock climber. Enter Bidean up one of its three ravines, each with some of that great climbing rock hanging impressively overhead. It's steep, and it's gloomy, and it gets steeper, until all at once you emerge onto Bidean's ridge, with bright sky around you.

Granite and volcanic: the third rock is called quartzite. It's flat but cracked, like a city pavement after

earthquakes. Follow it along the Grey Corries, where its sharp edges will slash your boots, but its flat slabs give almost-easy walking above the precipices.

By now you're getting tired. So take a break; and come back in February or March. The eroded path along the Mamores is gone, and instead a snow edge swoops like a breaking wave, the snow crisp and crunchy for your crampons. In the clear cold air of a classic winter day, views are southwards over half a dozen ranges to the dome of Ben Lomond.

At the bottom of every steep-sided ridge there's a steep-walled valley. Some of those valleys contain the A82 (alas, how even lovelier would be Glen Coe without its busy road). But the others offer long through routes, with rugged paths and smooth

18

Landrover tracks. A comfortable track leads between the jaws of the Lairig Leacach, and down past small waterfalls while looking up at Ben Nevis and the Mamores. Then it's down a river whose alder-shaded bank has green levels for the tent. An even lonelier glen – but still with a good footpath – leads you to a lochan and bothy that are completely out of it. And however bleak the Blackwater, the last 4 miles, through a deep, steep glen of beautiful birchwoods, will leave you at Kinlochleven longing for the next really long walk with the big rucksack. Just as soon as your feet and shoulders have recovered from the first one.

OH, SIR HUGH MUNRO

An oddity of hillwalking in Scotland is that it takes place almost entirely above the 900m contour line. Sir Hugh Munro in 1892 listed the hills above 3000ft (914.4m) – after revisions there are currently 284 of them, of which 44 are in the area of this guidebook. Many hillwalkers are engaged in visiting these 284, and they are indeed worthwhile hills to visit. But the consequence is that the well-trodden ways and rebuilt paths are on these, rather high, hills. The lesser heights, of 914.3m and below, are largely pathless, and their lesser altitude usually means denser and tougher vegetation. Accordingly, the lower hills are interesting, and unfrequented; but they are not easy. The

less difficult of them, and the most interesting, are included here.

The 'standard routes' up the Munros are detailed in several existing guidebooks, including Steve Kew's *Walking the Munros Vol 1* (Cicerone). So, while I have described them here briefly, I have also sought out the more interesting ways around the back, the unfrequented corries, the more demanding rugged ridgelines from the less convenient car parks.

But on the finest of them all I've left the choice to you. Bidean is a hill to visit many times by many different routes; and so, in the south, is Ben Cruachan. The Mamores is one great ridge of many mountains: where you go up and come down depends on how much of it you want to do today. The Black Mount's great complex sprawl also deserves to be explored in detail.

For more serious scrambling, the area is inspiringly described in Noel Williams' *Scrambles in Lochaber*. My own copy is now extremely battered! Here I have included various tough walking routes involving rock, but just two of the easiest and most spectacular scrambles: the magnificent Ledge Route on Ben Nevis, and the Zigzags onto Bidean nam Bian (Routes 9 and 63). Here is also the harder, but unmissable, scramble of the Aonach Eagach ridge above Glen Coe (Route 52). If you like them as much as I do, get hold of Noel's book and take an extra fortnight off.

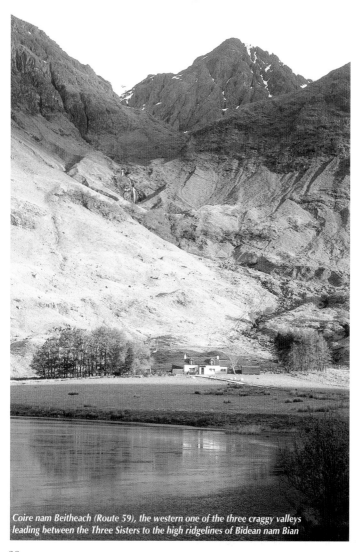

Coire nam Beitheach (Route 59), the western one of the three craggy valleys leading between the Three Sisters to the high ridgelines of Bidean nam Bian

The type of walk is indicated as follows:

Low level
Forest and riverside walks, below 600m

Mountain
Mountain walks above 900m

Mid level
Moorland and foothills, below 900m

Treks and through routes
Bothy or tent, or using rail/bus

WALKING CONDITIONS

For **low-level walking**, Scotland used to offer only the plod through the bog or the smooth and stultifying forest road through the spruce. The south of the area is still like that. However, Kinlochleven has an excellent little network of scenic paths; Glen Nevis has a more variable selection. Some are waymarked and signposted, some not; it's a good idea to carry a compass and keep a general idea of which way is the road and which way is vast and pathless wilderness.

The **mid-level hills** are more demanding. They tend to offer arduous half-days, somewhat tougher but less rockily rewarding than the higher ground. Chase after them though for good views achieved in solitude, or on a windy day or one with poor-quality soggy snow on the bigger hills.

On **mountains** of 900m and upwards, bare rocks and stones replace the clinging heather or grassy tufts. Or else you're on a path; popular ways lead to all the Munro summits. The high ground may be comparatively easy, but it is also serious. On the ridges of Bidean nam Bian you're several hours' walk from any shelter, and that walk will have to find its way down between crags.

Provided there aren't also strong winds, cloud just makes the Carn Mor Dearg Arête (Route 8) even more atmospheric

Fancy backpacking, but not sure how it all fits together? Worried you might pack too little gear into the big rucksack – or, even worse, too much? **The treks and through routes** are full-on in terms of big scenery, lochs and rivers, and real remote country. But at the same time they are fairly easy-going in terms of tracks and footpaths, and a couple of bothies just in case you did manage to lighten your pack by leaving behind the tent poles.

But let's be hopeful and suppose you remember the tent poles (and even the tent itself), get the weight below 25lb/12kg without leaving out anything that really matters, start early, and keep the speed sensibly low. Then Glen Coe and Glen Nevis could turn you from a boring Munro-bagger into a backpacker for ever.

Within the various sections, the through routes are described from south to north so as to get the bad

Long paths and tracks lead in among the mountains. The track alongside Loch Etive (Route 77) gives easy but rewarding walking.

weather beating on your back. In the northern part of the area, routes web in and out around Corrour station at the edge of Rannoch Moor. The overview maps on pages 12–15 let you link them into expeditions of up to a week.

These overview maps also mark deer-stalking estates. In Scotland there is a legal **right of access** to virtually all open country, provided that access is taken responsibly. In certain areas, reponsible access means – during three months of autumn – adapting your walking so as not to disturb deer stalking. Over Ben Nevis itself, and in Glen Coe, there is free access year-round; in places like Black Mount and Etive, where deer are hunted for sport, helpful phone lines or agreed routes are available. Full details are in Appendix 1.

WHEN TO GO

April is still winter on the summits, but low-level routes already offer good walking then and in May. The leaves are breaking and birds are at their noisiest. Low-level routes are also excellent in October as the birch leaves turn gold.

May and June are enjoyable at all altitudes. July and August can be hot and humid, with less rewarding views and midges infesting the glens. West Highland midges can be pretty grim; the trick is to keep moving, and when you stop, stop high.

Midges hang on until the first frost, normally some time in September. October often brings clear air and lovely autumn colours. In between times there'll be gales. As noted above, deer stalking (mid-August to mid-October) causes only

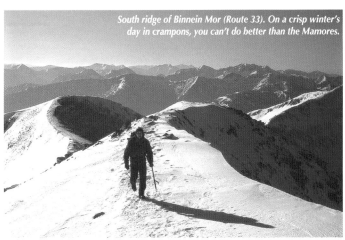

South ridge of Binnein Mor (Route 33). On a crisp winter's day in crampons, you can't do better than the Mamores.

WEATHER AND SNOW CONDITIONS

The most useful and accurate Internet forecast is at Mountain Weather Information Systems www.mwis.org.uk. This site has links to snow reports from various Fort William climbers and guides. The Sportscotland Avalanche Information Service issues forecasts of snow conditions and avalanche risk daily December– Easter at www.sais.gov.uk/latest_forecast; they have previously also had a free phone line.

A webcam for Ben Nevis is at http://visit-fortwilliam.co.uk/webcam/; for Glen Coe, see Buachaille Etive Mor (or not, if the cloud's down) at www.kingy.com.

minor disturbance to hillwalking in this area; with a little care and consultation, you can have hill days here during the stalking season more readily than anywhere else in Scotland (see Appendix 1).

Winter is a time of short days and often foul weather. Snow often lies on the high tops from December to April, with patches in the corries obstructing some routes even into June. Well-equipped walkers skilled in navigation and with ice axe love the winter most of all, for the wonderful crisp snow along the ridges of Bidean, the 100km views through the winter-chilled air.

SAFETY IN THE MOUNTAINS

In Glen Coe and Lochaber you're usually within a few hours of a road; but the downward ground may be steep with crags. Safety and navigation in the mountains is best learnt from companions, experience, and perhaps a paid instructor; such instruction is outside the scope of this book. Those experienced in smaller, less

steep hills will need some extra fitness and endurance, and the level of map expertise that enables you to get away safely when the headwind that's cutting you off from your descent route is also going to shred your map should you attempt to unfold it.

The international mountain distress signal is some sign (shout, whistle, torch flash or other) repeated six times over a minute, followed by a minute's silence. The reply is a sign repeated three times over a minute, followed by a minute's silence. To signal for help from a helicopter, raise both arms above the head and then drop them down sideways, repeatedly. If you're not in trouble, don't shout or whistle on the hills, and don't wave to passing helicopters.

To call out the rescue, phone 999 from a landline. From a mobile, phone either 999 or the international emergency number 112: these will connect you via any available network. Reception is good on most summits and ridges, but absent in places without direct sightlines to

Easy scrambling above the Zigzags of Gearr Aonach, Bidean nam Bian (Route 63), one of three scrambles that sweet-talked their way into this walking guide

Fort William, Glencoe village or the mast behind Kings House. Sometimes a text message can get through when a voice call can't. Lochaber police aren't yet equipped to receive text messages on 999, so you'll have to text a reliable friend.

Given the unreliable phone coverage, it is wise to leave word of your proposed route with some responsible person (and, of course, tell that person when you've safely returned). Youth hostels have specific forms for this, as do many independent hostels and B&Bs. You could also leave word at the police stations at Glencoe or Fort William.

Being lost or tired is not sufficient reason for calling the rescue service, and neither, in normal summer weather, is being benighted. However, team members I've talked to say not to be too shy about calling them: they greatly prefer bringing down bodies that are still alive...

There is no charge for mountain rescue in Scotland – teams are voluntary, financed by donations from the public, with a grant from the Scottish Executive and helicopters from the Royal Air Force and Royal Navy rescue services. You can make donations at youth hostels, TICs and many pubs.

MAPS

The mapping used on lower walks in this book is from the Ordnance Survey's Landranger series at 1:50,000 (enlarged in Routes 49 and 58). For high mountain walks, too, these maps were for about 40 years the only ones available, and are perfectly satisfactory: sheet 41 is Ben Nevis and Glen Coe with part of Black Mount and Glen Etive; the rest of Black Mount and Glen Etive, southwards to Ben Cruachan, are on sheet 50 (Glen Orchy) – annoyingly, the two sheets don't overlap.

The new Harveys Ben Nevis British Mountain Map, at 1:40,000 scale, covers the whole area as far south as Loch Tulla and the head of Loch Etive. Just 15 of the routes here (notably, Cruachan) aren't on it. It is beautifully clear and legible, marks paths where they actually exist on the ground, and is made of plastic so robust that one lightweight gear guru uses it as his groundsheet.

For detailed exploration of crags and corries and pathless boulder slopes, you will be helped by the extra contour detail at 1:25,000 scale. The two Harveys Superwalker maps 'Ben Nevis' and 'Glen Coe' score very highly.They cover much the same ground as the Mountain Map, and overlap conveniently, so that Kinlochleven is on both. Also at 1:25,000 is the Explorer series of the Ordnance Survey. These maps have excellent contour detail on the lower ground, but many of the summits are so obscured with crag-marks that the contour detail is almost illegible. Harveys also offer an A4-sized Ben Nevis summit map at 1:12,500. This is equivalent to the summit enlargement on the back of their 1:25,000 map but with the very useful addition of 100-metre grid lines for GPS users.

I'd suggest the Ben Nevis Mountain Map, with Landranger sheet 50 (Glen Orchy) for the far south around Cruachan. But for ambitious mountain explorations, the Harvey Superwalker is preferable.

COMPASS AND GPS

A compass is a very useful aid in mist, even if your skills only extend to 'north-west, southeast' rather than precision bearings. Magnetic deviation is about 4° west: to convert a map bearing to

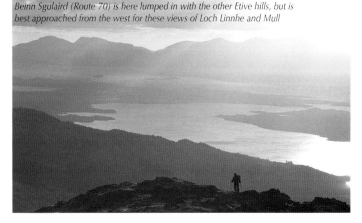

Beinn Sgulaird (Route 70) is here lumped in with the other Etive hills, but is best approached from the west for these views of Loch Linnhe and Mull

Sunscreen stop on the northwest ridge of Stob Coire nan Lochan (Route 61)

a compass one, add 4. No magnetic rocks have been found in this area; it's you that's wrong, not the compass!

GPS receivers should be set to the British National Grid (known variously as British Grid, Ord Srvy GB, BNG, or OSGB GRB36). GPS readings are normally good within 10m, and I have given 8-digit (10m accuracy) grid references at various tricky points, such as where you turn down off a ridge. I have recorded these on the hill, checking for plausibility against a 1:25,000 map afterwards. I have found GPS less reliable on steep slopes, such as the corries of Bidean, with a smaller sky in sight, and hopeless in the Nevis Gorge; such readings should be regarded with some caution. Somewhere on the gadget, if you press the correct buttons, you can find the degree of inaccuracy. The GPS readings are supplementary; this book is designed to be used without a GPS.

HOW TO USE THIS BOOK

A glance ahead into the book will show two different sorts of mapping. The **low-level** and **mid-level** routes have 1:50,000 mapping; this scale is large enough for use on the actual walk. The linear walks are on the overview maps here at the start; the mountain routes have similar hand-drawn sketch maps at a larger scale. The sketches are not sufficient for route-finding on the actual mountaintop. A full-sized walkers' map is needed so that you know not just the route you're walking, but also the bad-weather escape route which may take you into a different glen altogether.

Each of the **Munros** (3000ft/914m mountains) has its well-worn 'standard route'. That will be the quickest and most convenient – and fairly straightforward – route, but usually not the most interesting. I have

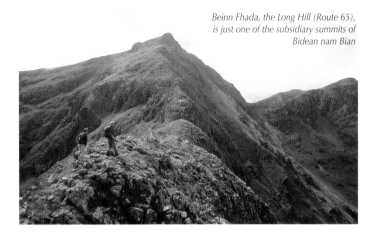

Beinn Fhada, the Long Hill (Route 65), is just one of the subsidiary summits of Bidean nam Bian

pointed out those routes in the pre-ambles, and they are listed in several guidebooks, including Steve Kew's *Walking the Munros Vol 1*. However, I've concentrated on what I consider the most rewarding routes for each hill. These may also be a little more demanding, as they seek out the steeper scenery and avoid the flat Landrover track.

But for the very finest hills I have left the choice to you. **The Grey Corries, the Mamores,** and the **Black Mount**; **Bidean** and **Ben Cruachan**: these are hills you will want to ascend lots of times, by many different routes, or ranges where only you can decide how much, once you're up, to do. For these I have given a **Summit Summary**, with the standard route and the adventure around the back, the slightly rocky scramble and the long, long walk in from somewhere else altogether.

Many of the mountain routes start off along one of the low or mid-level ones. Accordingly, the starts of high-level routes are marked (in green) on the 1:50,000 mapping of the lower ones.

The headers at the start of each walk should be pretty well self-explanatory. The walk-type icons are shown on page 21. The difficulty blobs are explained in the panel on page 30. The length blobs correspond with the **approximate times** in the main headers: one blob is up to 4 hours, two blobs up to 6 hours, with the full five blobs for walks of over 10 hours – those could also be enjoyed over two days using a tent or bothy. The approximate times are based on 1 hour for 4 horizontal km or for 400m of height gained, with extra time where the ground is particularly steep or rough. They'll be about right, including brief

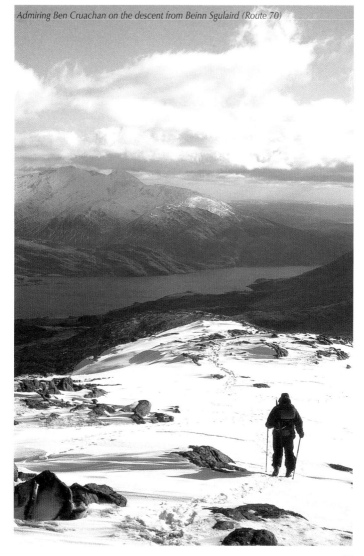

Admiring Ben Cruachan on the descent from Beinn Sgulaird (Route 70)

The **difficulty ratings** are on a rough scale of 1 to 5:

Clear smooth paths, with no steep sections

Small rough paths, some steep ground

Short steep climbs or long gentle ones, pathless ground with clear ridgelines

Some boulderfields, steep rough ground, navigation at the level of 'northwest, southeast'

Featureless plateau requiring compass bearings in mist or pathless forest; heather tramping; remote high ground; long steep rough ascents and descents; rocky ground and scrambling

snack stops, for a moderately paced party. (**Note** there are no length blobs in the Summit Summary routes as they are uphill only.)

On the treks and through routes, I've used the same 4kph calculation for the 'going time'. These walks can sometimes be done as day walks with a light pack. When done with a load, the calculated time should be considered to exclude lunch and other stops. The length in days supposes 8 hours of actual walking.

Where a bus or train can be used to link the two ends of a linear route, or to go up one route and come down another, I've noted this at the routes concerned. Other public transport information is in Appendix 2.

In old numbers, 600ft was a vertical distance, while 200yds was horizontal. I've used a similar convention, so that 600m is an altitude or height gain, while 600 metres (with 'etres') is along the ground. When going up or downhill diagonally, 'slant up left' means in a direction to left of straight up. So if straight up the slope is north, 'slant up right' would be northeast. I use 'track' (rather than 'path') for a way wide enough for a tractor or Landrover; the exception here is the Mountain Track on Ben Nevis, as this new name for the Pony Path appears on many maps and leaflets.

Finally, the 'standard route' up a hill is the convenient and well-trodden one featured in guidebooks like Steve Kew's *Walking the Munros*. Thus the Mountain Track is the 'standard route' up Ben Nevis. The Blackmount Ranger has determined that 90 percent of walkers would be content to be restricted to such routes and no others. If that figure drops as a result of this book, the Blackmount Ranger may not like it – but I shall be very pleased.

PART ONE

FORT WILLIAM AND GLEN NEVIS

Fort William is a prettier place than Aviemore (entry point for the Cairngorms) or Chamonix (entry point for Mont Blanc). This still doesn't make it very pretty. It is, however, very useful, with its supermarket and street full of gear shops, its hostels both independent and SYHA, its rail and coach links, and its charming little museum for a wet day.

For a slightly less wet day, or for a half-day, this section rounds up some walks that don't go up Ben Nevis. The highlight here is the Nevis Gorge (Route 2): the shortest walk in this book, but on its wide path possibly Britain's most spectacular stroll.

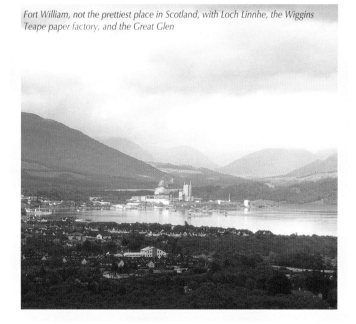

Fort William, not the prettiest place in Scotland, with Loch Linnhe, the Wiggins Teape paper factory, and the Great Glen

1 Cow Hill and Druimarbin

Length
■ ■ □ □ □

Difficulty
■ □ □ □ □

Start/finish	Fort William south end
	NN 098736
Distance	14km/8.5 miles
Ascent	500m/1700ft
Approx time	4.5hr
Max altitude	Druimarbin 287m
Terrain	Smooth paths

A gentle exploration of Fort William and lower Glen Nevis; but with a touch of mountain ground, plus Linnhe views, on Druimarbin.

Start at the car park at the Ballachulish end of Fort William. Follow the loch-side pavement back around the town to a roundabout with the old fort, start of the **Great Glen Way**, on the left. GGW waymarkers lead along tarred path to left of McDonalds, then through a warehouse area. Dogleg right then left among houses to a road bridge across River Nevis.

Cross, and ignoring a track beside the river, turn right up a fenced path beside houses for 300 metres. Keep ahead along Dubh MacDonald Road, then bear right to the **A82**. Cross into a street signposted for the Ben Nevis track, but after 100 metres turn right on a stone bridge over River Nevis. Turn left on pavement for 400 metres, until a track forks down left to another crossing of River Nevis, a metal footbridge.

Turn right to a small car park, where a good path continues ahead along the river. After 1.2km, cross a footbridge into the car park of the **Nevis Visitor Centre** (Ionad Nibheis). Pass along riverbank to left of the visitor centre, onto a path through trees to the Glen Nevis road. Continue for 50 metres, to a track opposite signed as the Peat Track to Cow Hill. Head up the track; as you enter trees, a gate on the right leads to a footbridge to the nearby burial ground, a place of not terribly antique gravestones and beech trees. Return to the Peat Track and continue up it.

At a forest road crossing, right is signed for Fort William, but keep ahead on the steep but good path for Cow Hill. At the top of the trees, keep ahead on the track to a track T-junction. Turn right, for 1.5km to **Cow Hill**. At the radio mast, keep ahead for a few steps for a view down onto Fort William. Return along the track to the track 'T', keeping ahead on the main track, which bends round to the right. Follow the track down to a road at the edge of Fort William.

Turn left up to a car park viewpoint and picnic place. Opposite this, go through a rusty metal gate. Head up, with a fence on the right to start with, to a second rusty red gate onto open hill. A peaty, heathery path leads uphill and follows the rounded crest to the trig point on **Druimarbin**, with a lovely view along Loch Linnhe.

Turn round – the views now are along the Great Glen – and head back to the road at the viewpoint. Turn left, downhill, past the end of the Peat Track and into Fort William. Keep ahead down Lundavra Road for 500 metres. Just after a bridge over a stream, at a waymark post, turn left down a tarred lane. After it recrosses the stream, turn right down steps then a tarred path. Keep ahead down Ashburn Lane to the A82.

Cross the main road and take paths past flowerbeds along the lochside, to the walk start.

2 Nevis Gorge

Length

Difficulty

to

Start/finish	Glen Nevis top car park
	NN 168691
Distance	3km/2 miles
Ascent	150m/500ft
Approx time	2hr
Max altitude	285m on upper path
Terrain	Choice: a wide smooth path, or a slippery scramble

The Nevis Gorge has high, steep slopes where 1000 pine trees cling to ledges between glaciated slabs. Below, the river rushes under house-sized boulders, and at its head is the 100m-high Steall waterfall.

A deservedly popular path leads up the gorge. It is smooth and engineered, but even so has warning notices because of the drops alongside.

However, two older and disused paths, one above and one below, offer slightly better views and a much wilder experience. The lower path, in particular, crosses damp and rather slimy rocks in an exposed position. All three options are given here: my preference is take the lower path up the gorge, and the high one back again.

Start along the big, level **main path** out of the car park end, with signs for Corrour, and another warning about exposure to come. This path leads straightforwardly up the wooded gorge side to the meadow below **Steall Falls**.

The two alternative paths are much less comfortable.

*   The **lower path** gives a more intimate acquaintance with the river below. Its untrodden rocks are damp and slippery; there are drops below; so the path in its current condition must be considered a mild scramble (Grade 1).

Nevis Gorge, Scotland's tribute to Nepal, is inappropriately not just the shortest but, because of its well-made path, one of the easiest routes in this book. Steall Falls are above.

About 400 metres from the car park, the main path becomes a gangway carved out of pink rock to cross a stream. In another 20 metres, just round a left bend, a small waymark points left along the main path. This is where the lower path forks down right.

The small path drops close above River Nevis. Then it ascends again on a ledge around a craggy slope. There are old iron posts and ringbolts. After its rocky section, the path ascends gently over large stones. It rejoins the main path at another small waymark, at the foot of a grey rock gangway on the main path.

- The **upper path** is very small and needs some care to follow, especially in reverse at the Steall end. It is rough but not rocky, and leads to a splendid little shelf below the crags of Meall Cumhann.

  About 400 metres from the car park, the main path becomes a gangway carved out of pink rock to cross a stream. It bends left, past the waymarker at the start of the lower path, then rises for 100 metres across a pitched section and then between sheep-sized grey boulders. As it levels, three stream culverts cross it in quick succession. The middle culvert is where the upper path forks up left. It slants gently uphill, but with a couple of little zigzags to look out for. It emerges onto open hill at a grassy platform below crags of Meall Cumhann (small cairn, NN 1751 6896).

  The path slants down, to left of a large boulder, then zigzags south down a spur with some birch trees, to join the main path just above the top of **Nevis Gorge**.

All three routes arrive in the meadow above the gorge, dominated by the high **Steall waterfall** on the right. At the meadow's end the path forks, the right branch leading to a bridge over the Water of Nevis marked 'dangerous bridge' and consisting of three steel cables. According to your temperament, this crossing is either terrifying or terrific. It is not necessary – return is by the same side of the river – but it does let you reach the foot of the Steall Falls by a muddy path.

Return is by any of the three paths. Below is given the upper path, as its start is not clear. Should you cross the wire footbridge and find you prefer not to come back over, there's also a descent by the south side of the river. Meanwhile, those unsatisfied by Scotland's finest 2-mile walk explore Meall Cumhann on the following Route 3.

A good path, albeit with drops on the right, leads up Nevis Gorge. In five more steps the front walker will reach the branch-off for the slippery and exposed lower path.

• **Upper path (return)** From the Steall meadow, the path dips for 30 metres to the first trees at the entrance of the gorge. Immediately before this short descent, turn uphill, right, towards a stone terrace ruined among the bracken. From the left-hand end of this, the path heads up left in its first zigzag. Once found, the zigzags rise north up a spur with a few birch trees, towards a boulder visible on the skyline. The viewpoint terrace is just above.

Steall Falls

Contour forward for a few steps to find the beginning of the descent path. It is small but clear as it slants down through the wood to join the main path.

- **South riverside** Across the three-wire bridge, head downstream above a rocky knoll, then find a small path along the riverside meadow. Just upstream from the gorge entrance, the path turns left, and climbs a steep grass slope in two zigzags to a wide shelf of grass and glacier-smoothed rocks.

  Head northwest across the rocks, with an ancient deer fence on the left. At the shelf end, follow the fence down to the right into a grassy wooded gully. There are traces of a rough, steep path. In steep woodland below, keep downhill near the fence (avoiding steeper ground on the left). As the ground gets less steep there is a small rough path just above the fence.

  As the fence joins the river, pass through it to find a well-used path. Follow this downstream along beautiful riverbank, with river roar drowning any traffic sounds from the other side. Just before the path suddenly becomes well made, cross a footbridge on the right to join the road. Head up right for 1.2km to the car park, taking care as the road has blind corners and is busy.

3 Meall Cumhann

Length

Difficulty

Start/finish	Glen Nevis top car park NN 168691
Distance	6.5km/4 miles
Ascent	600m/2000ft
Approx time	3.5hr
Max altitude	Meall Cumhann 698m
Terrain	Rough hillsides

If Nevis Gorge on its own isn't magnificent enough, take in this viewpoint 500m higher up. Meall Cumhann (Hill of the Gorge) is a fine little top in its own right, and if you can bring yourself to turn round has views eastwards up Glen Nevis as well as down onto the gorge and across to Steall Falls.

Start along Route 2 to the meadow below **Steall Falls**. After playing around on the wire footbridge (but returning to the original side), take the path fork that continues up Glen Nevis. After 1km, just before a footbridge, turn up left into **Coire Giubhsachan**, on a rough path to left of its stream. After 1.5km it reaches a flat, boggy section of valley. Here turn up left, slanting right to avoid outcrops, to the summit of **Meall Cumhann**.

Head north along a fine little ridge and down to Bealach Cumhann col. Head southwest, slantwise down a steep slope towards the long waterslide of **Allt Coire Eoghainn**. The slabs of the waterslide itself are smooth and slippery, and there have been accidents there. A path runs down on the near side of the waterslide, to the car park.

4 Down Glen Nevis

Start	Glen Nevis lower falls
	NN 145683
Finish	Fort William station NN 104742
Distance	11.5km/7 miles
Ascent	Nil
Approx time	3hr
Max altitude	Upper fall 55m
Terrain	Good paths
Transport	Highland Country Buses service 42

Length

Difficulty

The Glen Nevis road hardly intrudes on this at all, and enables an outward journey on the Glen Nevis bus – that's unless you make it the second half of the walk from Corrour station (Route 5) or a backpack trek from Kinlochleven, Rannoch, or elsewhere.

Start by turning right out of the car park, to cross two bridges, under the second of which are the Lower Falls. Beware of inaudible traffic coming round the blind bends. A stile on the left merely allows photographers to get their vantage – pass it to a track just beyond. Follow this past **Polldubh** cottages, to find a faint path. After 400 metres along the foot of the hill slope, the path joins the river; then follows it downstream, past the square wooded enclosure of an old burial ground. After crossing

Map continues p.42

41

the two branches of the **Red Burn** (no footbridges), you reach a long bridge on the left that would lead to the **youth hostel**.

Keep going on a good path still to right of the stream. Pass another bridge into the car park at **Nevis Visitor Centre**. After another 400 metres the path is about to join the Achintee Road.

To avoid this, fork left on a muddier path, still along-side the river, to join the road further down. After 200 metres cross a green footbridge over the River Nevis, then turn right to join the pavement of the Glen Nevis road. At the roundabout by the Nevis Bank Hotel, turn left to the town centre.

5 Corrour Station to Glen Nevis

Start	Corrour station NN 355664
Finish	Fort William station NN 104742
Distance	33.5km/21 miles
Ascent	150m/500ft
Approx time	2 short days (9hr going)
Max altitude	Tom an Eite 375m
Terrain	Small, rough paths
Transport	Train (Scotrail) Fort William to Corrour. No road access to Corrour
Sketch map	See overview map (page 12)

Length

■ ■ ■ ■ ☐

Difficulty

■ ■ ☐ ☐ ☐

The long valley starts at Corrour, a place reached by railway but by no road, with a B&B and a youth hostel, and runs for 30km between two of Scotland's highest mountain ranges. Along the way it passes a couple of handy bothies. At last it emerges round the back of Ben Nevis by a huge waterfall and a gorge: this is where, if anywhere, Scotland becomes Himalayan.

While it's the last day of long backpack trips from almost anywhere, the early train (7.45am) from Fort William lets you do this as a day walk. Route 4 allows you to walk the riverside for those last 10km, but you may prefer the road, where any passing car will be a climber or walker and might offer a lift even to the muddy. (You can't phone for a taxi on your mobile; mobiles won't work.)

- **Start** from **Corrour station** on the west side of the railway, where a rough and often soggy track runs beside the railway line. After 2km, the firm new track from Loch Ossian emerges from under the railway. Or else, for clean feet and legs, head east from the station to the track around Loch Ossian.

- **Start** from **Loch Ossian youth hostel** by turning right on the track towards Corrour station, then right on a side track at a waymark arrow. In 200 metres the track bends left; at once, turn off left on a rugged old track. After 400 metres this joins a much newer one, running west to pass under the railway in the bed of a stream.

Note If you are heading for Staoineag bothy, and if the river under the bridge is in spate, don't cross but head upstream to left of the river.

Staoineag Bothy, a possible overnight point on the way down Glen Nevis, though the river crossing can cause problems

Follow the track down to **Loch Treig**, and then around it; at the foot of Gleann Iolairean it reverts to its rough state. The track ends at Abhainn Rath near **Creaguaineach Lodge**. ◄ Cross the slippery wooden bridge and turn left upstream, on a path that's sometimes a delight on firm green riverbank and sometimes less pleasant. After 2km you pass the charmingly situated **Staoineag** bothy on the opposite bank; with normal summer water levels you can cross to it on large stones. The better path continues to right of the river. After another 3km the valley floor levels, and the path bears away from the river across bog to visit **Meanach** (Meannanach) bothy (see Route 45). It regains the riverbank opposite Luibeilt.

The OS map marks the path continuing on the southern bank of Abhainn Rath. However, the crossing

In Glen Nevis below Sgurr a' Mhaim

can be awkward, and I've always kept my feet dry and stayed on the path on the northern bank. After 2.5km, the river turns up in front of you, so now you must cross it to the small landmark knoll **Tom an Eite**. The best crossing is 100 metres north of the knoll (NN 242695; 15km, 4hr).

A new path heads downstream then turns right, passing immediately to left of Tom an Eite. The path is clear, and mostly not boggy, as it heads down to right of a small stream that gradually develops to become the **Water of Nevis**.

After 7km you emerge onto the level meadow with the high **Steall Falls** on the opposite side of the river. Here the three-strand wire bridge across Water of Nevis does not need to be crossed (Steall hut, on the further side, is a private and locked club hut). Continue to right of the river, into the narrows at the top of **Nevis Gorge**.

▶ The path now is very well built, but with steep drops on the left to the roaring river: in the dark this section is spectacular. After 1km the path reaches the car park at the top of Glen Nevis.

Route 2 for exciting side-paths here.

From the Lower Falls, Route 4 offers a riverside alternative, which is delightful if you have the energy.

From here it's 10km of tarmac to Fort William, or 7km if you cleverly booked into Glen Nevis youth hostel. After 1km you can take a footbridge onto a good path to left of the river. ◄

6 Caledonian Canal

Length
■ □ □ □ □

Difficulty
■ □ □ □ □

Start/finish	Fort William, old fort NN 103742
Distance	14.5km/9 miles
Ascent	30m/100ft
Approx time	3.5hr
Max altitude	Neptune's Staircase 33m
Terrain	Smooth paths and pavements

A flat walk at Fort William? Well, you only need the cloud to rise 35m to enjoy this one. It explores the seaside, the canal side and a ruined castle, as well as some less interesting back streets of Inverlochy and Caol. The surprise bonus is the underwater section at the halfway point.

Start at the old fort, which is on the shoreline at a roundabout 100 metres west of Fort William station. A stone marks the start of the **Great Glen Way**; and GGW markers will guide for the first part of the walk. Follow them along pavement north to a second roundabout, and take a tarred path to left of McDonalds. It runs through scrubby industrial waste ground, then to left of the shinty pitch. At a housing estate, dogleg right then left to a disused road bridge.

Across it, the path on the left is signposted GGW. It runs around a wood to the shoreline by the tidal **River Lochy**. Follow the path next to the river, then through a wood, then again alongside the river past a football pitch. At the field end the path heads right but keep ahead to a narrow footbridge over a tailrace, then to a stile beside a long footbridge beside the railway – Soldiers' Bridge.

▸ Cross Soldiers' Bridge, and turn left along Glenmallie Road. The street runs down by River Lochy, then turns right into **Caol**. The first street left is sign-posted GGW. At its end, take a gravel path alongside the salt waters of Loch Linnhe towards the imposing (but scarcely attractive) Wiggins Teape factory. After a football pitch, a footbridge crosses an overflow stream out of the **Caledonian Canal** and rises to its towpath.

Now the GGW turns right, but turn left to the canal's end, and cross the lock gate between salt water (left) and fresh (right). Turn back along the northern towpath for 1km to the bridges at **Banavie**. Take a level crossing beside the railway's swing bridge, then cross the road, and go up steps alongside **Neptune's Staircase**. Continue along the towpath for 1km around a right-hand bend. Now a track forks down left to the base of the canal banking. Pass under the canal by a dripping tunnel, and turn

Before crossing Soldiers' Bridge, take the track on the right under the railway to visit **Old Inverlochy Castle**.

Neptune's Staircase, a challenging and strenuous ascent – but only if you're a boat on the Caledonian Canal

up right to a path along the wooded canal bank. Soon it returns via a grey field gate to the towpath.

Turn left along the southern towpath, passing a tearoom alongside Neptune's Staircase. GGW markers divert left, but you can simply cross the road and railway ahead. Follow the towpath for another 1km. With Loch Linnhe visible ahead, turn down left on a broad path to join a street near its end. From the street end, cross grass between houses (left) and a football pitch (right), to rejoin the outward route alongside **Loch Linnhe**.

PART TWO

BEN NEVIS AND THE AONACHS

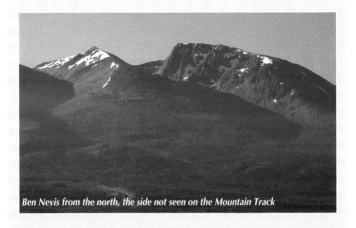

Ben Nevis from the north, the side not seen on the Mountain Track

Ben Nevis is a hill of two halves – except that the northern half has been carried away by a glacier and isn't there. Instead there's the hollow of the Allt a' Mhuilinn burn, and the biggest crag in Britain.

The very popular Mountain Track, on the mountain's western side, misses all that. It's a harsh trudge on a stony path, and Ben Nevis being the biggest, it's the harshest trudge in all UK hillwalking. If you enjoy the Mountain Track, then every one of Scotland's remaining 283 hills will be even better! Round the back, however, there's the Carn Mor Dearg Arête. Not quite a scramble, it's a spectacular granite ridge, with an outstanding view of the northern crags. Meanwhile the Ledge Route, which is a scramble (albeit a fairly easy one), gets right in among those crags.

On either of those routes, the sudden arrival at the summit, with its crowds, its cairns, and its litter, comes as a horrid shock – so avoid the top altogether. The Half Nevis takes you instead into the fine northern valley; and Meall an t-Suidhe, as a stand-alone or as a side-trip on the descent, has views of Loch Linnhe better than you get from the big Ben itself.

BEN NEVIS ROUTES

7 Ben Nevis by the Mountain Track
8 Carn Mor Dearg Arête
9 Ledge Route
10 Half Ben Nevis (CIC Hut)
11 Meall an t-Suidhe
12 Carn Mor Dearg East Ridge

7 Ben Nevis by the Mountain Track

Start/finish	Achintee NN 126730
Distance	
(up and down)	14.5km/9 miles
Ascent	1300m/4400ft
Approx time	7hr
Max altitude	Ben Nevis 1344m
Terrain	Path well built below, then stony

Length
■ ■ □ □ □

Difficulty
■ ■ ■ □ □

Even for experienced hillwalkers, the ascent of the Mountain Track, from barely above sea level to Scotland's highest point, is tough and tiring. As hillwalks go, it's not wonderful; relentlessly uphill for 1200m on going that becomes stony, and with no view at all of the mountain's exciting northern side. The summit is in cloud more often than not. Still, Ben Nevis has to be done, and this is the convenient way to do it.

Less experienced walkers should bear in mind that on the summit the weather will usually be two clothing-layers colder than at the start. Next, that for sore legs rather steep downhill is almost as arduous as up. On any summer evening you'll see half a dozen damaged walkers limping down in the last of the daylight – though injuries requiring rescue number only a dozen a year (out of 100,000 ascents).

A more serious problem can be the leaving of the summit. The path is unclear on the stony plateau, and doglegs between crag drops. Mostly, the way down is obvious because of the other walkers coming up; but the slowest person up, who may also be injured and exhausted, has no such guide. It's worth picking up one of the detailed summit maps handed out in Fort William's shops and information outlets or online at www.mcofs.org.uk ('Ben Nevis navigation'). Compass bearings and GPS references are also in a box below. There is an emergency shelter on the summit; if the Mountain Rescue is alerted to your non-return, this is the first place they'll look. Mobile phone coverage on the upper Mountain Track is good.

Alternative start points are at the **Nevis Visitor Centre** (NN 123730) or informal roadside parking near **Glen Nevis youth hostel** (NN 128718). The youth hostel is shortest, but gives a steep stone-surfaced descent right at the end when you really don't want it.

Start from the road end at **Achintee**. At the car park end, ignore a small stile but take a gate onto a track, to a signpost just ahead. Now the wide, well-built path slants up the side of Meall an t-Suidhe, with a couple of zigzags and crossing two little aluminium footbridges, into the hollow of the lower Red Burn. At the top of this it makes a zigzag to the left to arrive on the halfway plateau above **Lochan Meall an t-Suidhe** (the Halfway Lochan). ◄

Turn off here for Route 11, Meall an t-Suidhe.

The wide path slants uphill northeast above the lochan. After 400 metres the path ahead is blocked by a wall-like cairn to ensure that walkers for Ben Nevis summit make the sharp right turn here. ◄

Keep ahead for a nicer walk altogether, the Half Nevis Route 10.

After this sharp right turn, the path slants back across the hill to cross the **Red Burn** below a waterfall, and rises in wide zig-zags. From here it becomes stony and unreconstructed. As the slope starts to ease at 1100m, unseen drops into **Five Finger Gully** are on the right; occasional glances backwards will help memorise the path line for the descent. At 1200m the slope eases further, and the path runs just south of east to a steepening, **MacLean's Steep**. At this point you become aware of the tops of the great northern crag nearby on the left.

GETTING OFF BEN NEVIS

NN 1668 7128 Nevis summit
Southwest 150 metres to
NN 1658 7117 Turning point opposite Gardyloo Gully
285° (just north of west) 400 metres to
NN 1625 7125 Top of MacLean's Steep
Same bearing 285° (just north of west) 500 metres to
NN 1572 7137 Top of zigzags (you have now avoided Five Finger Gully)
Down path, or else:
285° (just north of west), directly downhill, to
NN 1467 7165 Mountain Track at foot of zigzags
Path, north, 200 metres to
NN 1474 7186 Path crosses Red Burn

Using **compass** alone, the bearings are:

From the summit to clear the head of Gardyloo Gully: pass to right of the observatory ruins, bearing 234° (roughly southwest) for 150 metres (roughly 100 double steps).

Thus having passed to left of the head of Gardyloo Gully: take a careful bearing 285° (slightly north of west) for 400 metres to the top of MacLean's Steep, and the same bearing for another 500 metres to the top of the zig-zags. If the zigzags are invisible (for example under fresh snow) the same bearing, which should be directly downhill, will eventually lead down steep soggy grass into the lower hollow of the Red Burn.

Bearings are magnetic 2006: subtract 1° for every six years after 2006.

Helicopter rescue on the Mountain Track – about a dozen injured walkers get lifted off each year

The path, marked by some cairns but still not very clear, continues in the same direction to pass the head first of Tower Gully (with a small pinnacle on its left wall) and then of Gardyloo Gully. It bears left beyond, to the **summit** with its observatory ruins, shelter, large cairn and trig point.

You may now refer to this hill as 'The Ben'.

In normal conditions, the **descent** is easily made by passing the stream of people coming up. In mist (or if you happen to be the tired and damaged last person up) it requires care. In a winter (or spring, or autumn) white-out, this can be a life-threatening place. In falling snow it may be impossible to see cliff edges until you're already standing on the unstable and overhanging snow cornice. For such situations was the summit shelter provided.

From the **summit cairn** head past the memorial cairn to the top of Gardyloo Gully that falls to the right, and turn half-right (see bearings in box above) on a wide path which is cairned, and clear enough in snowless daylight. After 400 metres is the top of **MacLean's Steep**. In mist, take the direct downhill path (north of east) rather than the gentler zigzag leading out left, as the latter path flirts with top of **Five Finger Gully**.

In another 500 metres you reach the cairn at the top of the zigzags (see GPS ref in box above). The well-built but now very stony path descends in broad sweeps, the last one heading rightwards to cross the **Red Burn**. In another 600 metres you reach the wall-like cairn blocking the onward path above the **Half-Way Lochan**. ▶

Turn sharp left, now on a well-reconstructed smooth path. It leads over the plateau edge to a zigzag, then down right, around the flank of Meall an t-Suidhe. Just after another small zigzag is the junction with the path down left for the footbridge to the **youth hostel**, or keep ahead for the gentler descent to **Achintee** car park. Just before that one, a signpost points down left for the car park at the **Nevis Centre**.

For the North Face car park, continue now on Route 8; or a crossing of Meall an t-Suidhe on Route 11.

8 Carn Mor Dearg Arête

Start/finish	North Face car park at Torlundy NN 145764
Distance	
(up and down)	16.5km/10.5 miles
Ascent	1500m/4900ft
Approx time	8hr
Max altitude	Ben Nevis 1344m
Terrain	Hill paths and a bouldery arête

Length
■ ■ ■ ■ □ □

Difficulty
■ ■ ■ ■ ■

The Pony Path, now renamed the 'Mountain Track', misses out all the exciting side of the mountain. The route by Carn Mor Dearg ('carn more jerrack', big red stonepile) and its arête gives all the excitement you want (and if there's a wind or some old snow, rather more excitement than that). It's more of a clamber than a scramble, over a ridge of granite blocks. The slopes on either side are steep, and ahead is the whole of the magnificent northern crag. Or else it's misty, which is even more atmospheric.

This grander route is usually started from Glen Nevis. (Start as Route 10, Half Nevis; arriving at Allt a' Mhuilinn, cross the stream and slant up left to join the rounded crest running up east to Carn Beag Dearg.) But this start from **Torlundy** keeps you mostly off the Mountain Track, and gives a gentler ascent of Carn Mor Dearg.

On the Carn Mor Dearg Arête, with the Northeast Buttress of Ben Nevis (photo of Oliver Turnbull by S. Warren)

At Torlundy 3km northeast from Fort William, turn right off A82, signed 'North Face Car Park'. Cross a narrow rail bridge, then turn right onto a track to the car park.

Start along the track, then on a wide path signed for Allt a' Mhuilinn. It rises to cross the former aluminium tramway. A wide new path slants up through the plantations, roughly south. (The older route by the old tramway and Allt a' Mhuilinn is prettier but is now disused and overgrown.)

The path winds up through woods to meet a track. Keep on up the track, ignoring a side-track on the right, and as it bends left, cross a ladder stile ahead. A well-built path leads up to the left of **Allt a' Mhuilinn** stream, with great views of crags ahead. After about 1km a small path forks off left to climb the broad spur of **Carn Dearg Beag**. It does not actually visit this first top but skirts to its right, running high along the slope opposite the great northern crags on Nevis.

Far below you may see the CIC Hut; directly above it the path turns uphill to the crest of the ridge, then turns right and soon reaches the summit of **Carn Dearg Meadhonach**. Down left you can see the top tower of its east ridge, a rather scrappy scramble.

A brief dip and rise lead to **Carn Mor Dearg**. One clear sharp ridge runs down left (Route 12, for the Aonachs); the one for the arête is equally clear, forking right, slightly west of south.

The **CMD Arête** is narrow but well trodden. The crest becomes a line of piled boulders, which can be crossed without hands for the first two thirds of the way. As the ridge bends right, southwest, and starts to rise, the final crest will require handholds, but there's a small path down on the left.

Where the crest joins the main mountain there is a marker for the abseil posts into Coire Leis. A few more steps and the rock changes from the pale granite to darker volcanic andesite, with a broad boulderfield rising ahead. Head up beside the fierce drop on the right that's the top of Northeast Buttress (snow here may form cornices along the right-hand edge), to join the crowds among the various junky structures at **Nevis summit**.

From the summit, **descent** is obvious in normal conditions. Using the arriving people as live waymarks, pass left of the head of Gardyloo Gully and then bear right, just north of west. In mist (or worse mist and snow) getting off the plateau is more serious as there are sudden gully tops, with snow cornices, both to left and right, and a dogleg course is required. ◄

For precision bearings, and grid refs for GPS, see Route 7.

Once over the rim of the plateau, the **Mountain Track** zigzags down a broad, steep slope. (Old snow in the hollow of the Red Burn, over on the right, can give easy descent, but stay in control as there's a waterfall lower down). The path takes a final 'zag' to the right, to cross the **Red Burn** below its waterfall. After another 500 metres the Mountain Track turns sharply back left, with a cairn ahead blocking the onward route. ◄

Here you could switch to Route 11 below – the crossing of Meall an t-Suidhe.

Keep ahead, past the blocking cairn, on a newly rebuilt path that runs down to the outflow of **Lochan Meall an t-Suidhe**. Do not cross this stream, but descend rough grass to right of it. Posts mark a faint path used by quad bikes.

Join a ruined deer fence down to the **Allt a' Mhuilinn**. Cross this at a metal mesh barrier below a deer fence, to join the track used for the ascent just above its ladder stile. If the stream is too full, there's a track bridge 200 metres downstream.

Descent from Nevis to CMD Arête Head southeast, down quite steep stonefield, with the way well trampled. If heading northeast down a narrowing ridge, this is the top of Northeast Buttress! Contour off right.

Approaching Carn Mor Dearg along its Arête

A spur descends bending left (east) to the stony cairned col at the start of the CMD Arête (NN 1708 7098, 1150m). The ridgeline is slightly uphill, the rock changes to rounded granite boulders, and a metal triangle marks the top of some abseil posts down left into Coire Leis.

Scramble along the ridge, cross **Carn Mor Dearg** to Carn Beag Dearg, and drop northwest down grassy slopes to join the Allt a' Mhuilinn.

9 Ledge Route

Start/finish	North Face car park at Torlundy NN 145764
Distance (up only)	7km/4.5 miles
Ascent	1100m/3600ft
Approx time up	5.5hr
Terrain	Scramble Grade 1 on ledges and ridge

Length

■ ■ ■ □ □

Difficulty

■ ■ ■ ■ ■

(scramble Grade 1)

This is just magnificent. The scrambling reaches Grade 1 only at a couple of points, but the route is still serious because of its length and situation. It is fairly easy to find and follow, even in mist. However, snow lingering often to midsummer in Number 5 Gully requires a diversion – (left of Moonlight Gully Buttress, not described here) which is rather trickier to find – or an ice axe, plus possibly crampons. Snow can be observed from the CIC Hut, or in advance on the Internet (webcams, see Appendix 2).

For confident scramblers it's a feasible descent route, *provided* you start from the correct cairn on Carn Dearg – coming from Ben Nevis it's the second one, at 1214m (NN 1585 7210).

Start as for Route 8, onto and up the path beside **Allt a' Mhuilinn**. This path is well built to the 500m level, and after that is still comfortable up to the stream junction below the **CIC Hut**. Cross one stream to reach the hut.

From here, the way up ahead into Number 5 Gully should be visible. Directly opposite the hut, ascend a

An exposed moment
on the Ledge Route;
the lower-left
scrambler is on the
easier alternative

An exposed moment on the Ledge Route; the lower-left scrambler is on the easier alternative

steep bank above the stream onto the toe of a long slope
of gentle slabs. These can be walked up, with perhaps a
little scrambling if wet. The slabs run up to big boulders
at the foot of the imposing **Carn Dearg Buttress**. Here
turn left up the crag base, then straight up on rough scree
paths alongside the crag, into **Number 5 Gully**.

Clamber up the bouldery gully bed with stream for
100 metres. Now above, the gully steepens, divides, and
becomes gently rocky; don't continue up it, but head to
the right up a grassy terrace onto a gentle but somewhat
exposed slab. This is ascended on the footholds provided
by a crack slanting right.

At its top, follow a small path to the right along a
grass ledge, with big drops below, for 30 metres. Now
a grassy groove slants back up left; the groove itself is
eroded to loose stones, so the easy scrambling on its left
is preferable. After 30m of ascent you emerge at the top
of the groove, and look down a steep slope back into
Number 5 Gully.

Turn right up the ridgeline formed by the slope top,
to pass to right of a tottery rock pillar, to a stony ledge
with a viewpoint boulder.

Head straight up the ridgeline above, which is bouldery with easy scrambling. After 100 metres or so, the
ridgeline has a vertical wall dropping on its left. Gradually

you are forced nearer to the brink of this wall as the ridge-line narrows. This narrowing ends with a drop to a small notch. The **obvious way** is to follow the narrowing arête to its very end, becoming somewhat exposed, to descend down right, into the notch; but there are easier ways.

- **Harder than the notch drop but less exposed** 5 metres before the notch, take a groove down right: steep, but with good well-worn holds. Reach the gravel gully below the notch.

- **The easiest option** 10 metres before the notch, descend to the right to find a narrow ledge with good handholds, traversing right, to the foot of the steep groove just described.

Continue up the blocky bouldery ridge. Rocky steepenings can be avoided on the right if desired, but always return to the crest. The crest levels, then a final tower is scrambled direct, good Grade 1, with a photogenic little arête to finish, or else bypassed on the left.

This fine finish to the Ledge Route can be bypassed by a path beyond the scrambler

Strictly, this is 'Carn Dearg North' as Nevis has two tops called Carn Dearg. A shelter marked on old maps here has been removed.

Arrive on the plateau at the 1214m cairn on **Carn Dearg**. This is the main cairn but not the main summit. Pass south around the head of Number 5 Gully, to the higher but less cairned 1221 summit. ◄

Descend south around the plateau rim – the Mountain Track is visible to the right with its procession of folk. Pass the head of **Number 4 Gully** (which has a cairn with marker post), then ascend gently to pass the head of **Number 3 Gully** (which has a pinnacle in the top and a view down to CIC Hut), then trend right to join the **Mountain Track** just below MacLean's Steep. Follow it past the head of Gardyloo Gully to **Ben Nevis summit**.

What next? Simplest is to descend the top part of the **Mountain Track** then past Lochan Meall an t-Suidhe's outflow (Route 8). You could incorporate **Meall an t-Suidhe** (Route 11). More ambitiously, go down by way of the **Carn Mor Dearg Arête** (end of Route 8).

10 Half Ben Nevis (CIC Hut)

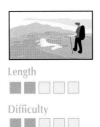

Length

■ ■ □ □ □

Difficulty

■ ■ □ □ □

Start/finish	Glen Nevis Visitor Centre NN 123730
Distance	17.5km/11 miles
Ascent	700m/2300ft
Approx time	6hr
Max altitude	Ben Nevis (CIC) Hut 670m
Terrain	Paths, rough for 4km

Half Ben Nevis actually gives you more of the mountain, as it takes you into the grandeur of the northern corrie. It also includes 3km of the Nevis riverbank, as well as some less lovely back corners of Fort William. Walkers halfway up the Mountain Track who can't face another 600m of straight 'up' can switch into this route, with its much better balance of pleasure and effort. ('CIC' stands for Charles Inglis Clark, a climber who died in World War I.)

Up Allt a´ Mhuillin towards the CIC Hut and the northern crags

Start at the
Visitor Centre. At the downstream end of the car park
cross the footbridge signed for Ben Nevis and turn
upstream, but where the Mountain Track turns off left,
continue along the riverside. In 1.5km you reach the
footbridge to Glen Nevis youth hostel. Don't cross it, but
turn up left on the rebuilt path that climbs steeply beside
a plantation to join the **Mountain Track**.

Turn right, uphill. The wide, well-built track slants up the side of Meall an t-Suidhe, with a couple of zig-zags and crossing two little aluminium footbridges, into the hollow of the lower Red Burn. At the top of this it makes a zigzag to the left to arrive on the **halfway plateau** above Lochan Meall an t-Suidhe.

The wide path slants uphill northeast above the lochan. After 400 metres, the path ahead is blocked by a wall-like cairn to ensure that walkers for Ben Nevis summit make the sharp right turn here onto a rough, stony path. But keep ahead past this cairn on the smooth rebuilt path. As it bends down left towards the outflow of Lochan Meall an t-Suidhe, fork off right on an unbuilt path. This bends around a spur, and becomes rugged as it contours into the valley of **Allt a' Mhuilinn**.

As you reach the stream, your eventual descent path is opposite, but continue upstream for 600 metres through scenes of increasing grandeur to the Ben Nevis hut, formally the Charles Inglis Clark or **CIC Hut**. ▶

Cross the stream 100 metres below the hut, and head down the rugged path to its right (east). The going gets easier as you leave the mountain corrie. After 3km, a wide ladder stile leads to the corner of a forest road. After 200 metres follow the road left over a bridge. This contours south-west for 1km, with fine views, until you can take a side-track down to the right.

If in Austria, the hut would serve gassy beer and herbal tea on red-chequered tablecloths. Being in Scotland, it is owned by the Scottish Mountaineering Club and is locked up.

At the slope foot it joins another track. Turn left for 200m, under power lines, until an overgrown stony path turns off right (NN133752). It is signed for 'the Distillery'. It leads to a stream, and follows its left bank, under the railway. Then it runs along to the right of a whisky shed. Head out though the **distillery**'s main gate to the A82.

Cross the A82 but not the Lochy Bridge ahead; instead turn sharp left onto a well-made path between the golf course (left) and the River Lochy (right). At a car park, bear right along the riverbank to **Old Inverlochy Castle**. Turn left, pass through the castle and back to the riverbank.

Ahead, a lane takes you under the railway. Just past the end of the long Soldiers' Bridge (footbridge) take a stile on the right, to a narrow bridge over a tailrace stream. Cross grass to join the smooth gravel path of the **Great Glen Way**. It runs near the wide, tidal river, then through woodland; then is again beside the Lochy for 400 metres. Finally it bends left around a wood to a tarred street.

Turn left for a few steps, ignoring a rough riverside track to find a gravel path alongside houses. After 300 metres it drops to join Dubh MacDonald Road. At this street's end, turn right in Earl of Inverness Road to the **A82**.

The street opposite is signed for Ben Nevis. Follow it for 100 metres, then cross a stone bridge on the right. Turn left, up Glen Nevis, and follow the pavement for 500 metres until a track forks off left to another footbridge, a green-painted metal one. Recross the **River Nevis** and turn right, upstream. In 300 metres the street bears left; here keep ahead on a riverside path. After 1km it brings you to the footbridge at the **Visitor Centre**.

11 Meall an t-Suidhe

Start/finish	Glen Nevis Visitor Centre
	NN 123730
Distance	
(for circuit)	14.5km/9 miles
Ascent	700m/2300ft
Approx time	5.5hr
Max altitude	Meall an t-Suidhe 711m
Terrain	Paths, grassy hillsides

Length
■ ■ □ □ □

Difficulty
■ ■ ■ □ □

As an alternative to visiting the northern corrie on Route 10, you can top out on Meall an t-Suidhe, a hill half as high as Ben Nevis but with rather better views as it's not only out of the cloud but also closer to the rest of the scenery. It's pronounced and sometimes spelt Melantee, the Hill of the Seat. The summit is grassy and peaceful and it is indeed comfy to sit down on. It can be done when you change your mind halfway up the Mountain Trail, or as a warm-down summit when descending the Ben towards the North Face car park (adding 1.5km, 150m, and 40mins to the descent from Ben Nevis).

- **Meall an t-Suidhe circuit** Start as for Route 10 from the Nevis Visitor Centre, and follow the Mountain Track until it levels onto the halfway plateau. At once turn off left.

- **Descending from Ben Nevis** Come down the zigzags of the Mountain Track and across the Red Burn, and at the obstructing cairn turn back left (all as Route 7). Before the path drops off the edge of the plateau, turn off right.

Cross grassland past the head of **Lochan Meall an t-Suidhe** to cross the trickle flowing out of the loch (a proper stream flows from the other end, which is accordingly the foot of the loch.) Head up the grassy and

Meall an t-Suidhe (Melantee), the Hill of the Seat, a great place to lounge around on and look along Loch Linnhe

somewhat wet slope beyond, then turn right along the rounded crest, which dips then rises to the cairned summit of **Meall an t-Suidhe.**

Descend northeast, on a rounded spur, with a small path vanishing. At the spur foot continue northeast, crossing a stream then following it down, to find the metal posts of an old deer fence (marked on Harveys map). A small path and quad-bike wheelmarks run alongside this. Follow it down north, to reach the **Allt a' Mhuilinn** at the 300m contour. Cross the stream at the metal grating underneath a deer fence, to reach a ladder stile on the upward path – or if the stream is full, continue downstream for 150 metres to a bridge.

Head down the track and path to the **North Face car park**, if that's where you started, or else switch back into Route 10 through Fort William for the **Nevis Visitor Centre**.

12 Carn Mor Dearg East Ridge

Start/finish	End of public road, Glen Nevis NN 167692
Distance (to Nevis summit)	7 km/4.5 miles
Ascent	1100m/3600ft
Approx time up	4.5hr
Terrain	Small paths, grassy ridge, stony plateau

Length
▮ ▮ ▮ ▯ ▯

Difficulty
▮ ▮ ▮ ▮ ▯

This sharp and stony ridge is used by those ambitiously linking the Aonachs with Carn Mor Dearg (combining Routes 8 and 14), or the even more ambitious joining Nevis with the Grey Corries in one over-the-top hill day. It's also a logical descent for anyone who ascends Nevis from the south, via Coire Eoghainn and Carn Dearg South (1020m) – only the fourth-best Nevis route, not included here.

Start from the far end of the car park, where a wide smooth path is signed for Kinlochleven and other distant places. ▶ At the head of the gorge the path emerges suddenly into a narrow meadow; above on the right are the spectacular **Steall Falls**. Keep to left of the river for 1km to a small footbridge over **Allt Coire Giubhsachan**. Before this, turn up left on a rough path, and follow the stream up to the col at the head of **Coire Giubhsachan**.

Turn up left, on a fairly steep rocky spur with a rough path. The spur narrows attractively in its upper part, to the summit of **Carn Mor Dearg**. Continue on Route 8.

See Route 2 for an exciting scrambly diversion off this path.

13 Aonach Beag from the Back

Start/finish	End of public road, Glen Nevis NN 167692
Distance	14.5 km/9 miles
Ascent	1350m/4500ft
Approx time	7hr
Max altitude	Aonach Beag 1234m
Terrain	Small paths, grassy ridge, stony plateau

Do the ethics of Munro-bagging allow the Nevis Range gondola? Do you even want to, if it means a trudge up Aonach Mor under the chairlifts, and a simple plateau walk to Aonach Beag? For more mountain fun, take the back way, by Glen Nevis. You'll come through the magnificent Nevis Gorge, and pass the Steall waterfall. You'll go between great mountains, and head up Aonach Beag by the way that actually feels like the seventh highest in the land. Then you'll descend by the grim and granitty bealach beside Carn Mor Dearg. (If you don't despise the gondola, there's a nice way up Aonach Mor on that side as well – see Route 14!)

Start from the far end of the car park, where a wide smooth path contours through beautiful woodland above the **Nevis Gorge**. At the head of the gorge the path emerges suddenly into a narrow meadow – this was a lochan until the river broke through the rock bar at the top of the gorge. Above on the right is the spectacular **Steall waterfall**. Keep to left of the river, and after 1km cross a small footbridge over **Allt Coire Giubhsachan**. Straight after the footbridge, strike left (northeast) on a small path to right of Allt Coire nan Laogh stream, then up a steepening grassy hillside to a shoulder at 800m. A gentler ridge leads up east, to the minor top **Sgurr a' Bhuic**.

Now the going gets more interesting, as well as rather more horizontal. Head northeast, along the top of

Routes 13 and 14
**Aonach Mor
Aonach Beag**

GLEN SPEAN

A82

finish

start/finish

14

8

17

**Aonach
Mor**

Coire an Eoin

16

The Grey Corries

7

Carn Mor
Dearg

**Aonach
Beag**

13

Ben Nevis

15

Sgurr
Choinnich
Mor

5

start/finish

Meall
Cumhann

GLEN NEVIS

N

0   1   2
km

The Mamores

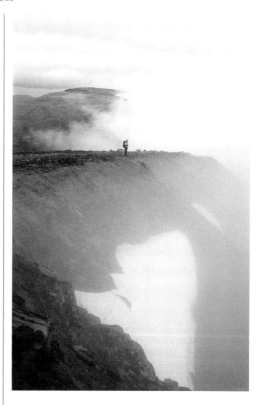

steep rocky slopes falling to the right. The ridge drops to a col at 895m, then rises to a corner above steep spurs descending east and north. The ridgeline turns left, first west then northwest, to the summit of **Aonach Beag**. The view across the Carn Mor Dearg Arête to the great north face of Ben Nevis is compelling.

Follow drops on the right north for 150 metres, then head down northwest on rough path to a col. Now a broad slope of short grass, with a path, leads gently upwards for 1.2km to the summit of **Aonach Mor**, the lowest of Scotland's nine 4000ers.

Now you need to find the descent point for Bealach Giubhsachan, the pass 300m below. In clear weather, return southwards down the gentle grassy plateau, looking for a small path soon forking off right. In mist, the easiest way is to follow the top of the steep slope that forms the right (west) edge of the grassy plateau. Where this edge bends back to the left (NN 1915 7219) is the top of a zigzag path heading directly down the steep slope below. This slope can hold steep, hard snow, even into early summer. If you're unhappy about that, or if you fail to find the drop-off point, it's safest to retrace the outward route over Aonach Beag. This only adds 30 mins to the walk.

Having found the steep little path, descend it. The gritty granite soil is fragile here, so stick to the zigzags; any short-cutting will worsen the erosion. At the bottom, the deep and wide pass **Bealach Giubhsachan** has a few little pools.

Descend to the left (south) into **Coire Giubhsachan**. A small path forms to right of the stream. If time or energy are short, this path leads right down to the Glen Nevis path, passing some waterfalls low down. However, the more interesting continuation heads out to the right at about the 600m contour, to the col Bealach Cumhann. Turn left up a gentle ridge of grass and rock to **Meall Cumhann**'s summit.

Meall Cumhann means the Hill of the Gorge; and indeed, the Nevis Gorge is directly between your toes. However, the horizontal views are equally spectacular: along lower Glen Nevis to Loch Linnhe, and up upper Glen Nevis between the great hill walls of the Aonachs and the Mamores.

Return north to Bealach Cumhann, and slant down across a fairly steep and pathless slope towards the long waterslide of the **Allt Coire Eoghainn**. Beware of the waterworn slabs alongside the watersplash, the site of accidents. A small path runs down the near side of the stream to the car park.

14 Aonach Mor by Gondola and Stob an Cul Choire

Start	Gondola top station NN 187756
Finish	Same, or gondola foot NN 172774
Distance (to gondola top finish)	13.5km/8.5 miles
Ascent	850m/2800ft
Approx time	5.5hr
Max altitude	Aonach Beag 1234m
Terrain	Pathless but comfortable, with a steep grass ascent to the plateau
Transport	First gondola 9.30am summer, 8am winter (depends on weather); last down, 6.00pm

Aonach Mor is odd as being the 4000er that wasn't. When hills were meas-ured imperially, Aonach Mor was 3999ft. It was only when they remeasured it in metric that it rose to 1221m, which is 4006ft. The names also are con-fused, in that Aonach Mor, the Big Ridge, is 13m lower than Aonach Beag, the Small Ridge. But in a sense they are both small hills, as the Nevis Range gondola lifts you up and over the unexciting spruce to visit two 4000-footers with a total climb of less than the 3000ft. So it creates what is rare here, a real mountain walk in under 6 hours.

Mountain walks don't have to be severe and strenuous, but they are supposed to be fun; and for me, up and down Aonach Mor under the ski tows isn't. But there's a splendid side-ridge where instead of looking up at dangling metalwork you look down from a great height on deer. Cul Choire is the Back Corrie, a name that invites any adventurous hill-goer.

Park at the Nevis Range bottom station and take the gon-dola up. **Start** underneath the Great Glen Chairlift out left, only very slightly uphill. (On some summer weekends you can ride this first kilometre of the walk as well.) Pass a café hut and carry on contouring into the valley of **Allt Choille-rais**. Cross the stream and slant left up the slope beyond onto the north ridge of Tom na Sroine. Go up the ridge, which becomes more defined with drops on the right. ▶

Cross the hummocky top of **Tom na Sroine** (918m, a Munro Top) and continue south along a pleasant ridge, with big drops now on the left to Allt Coire an Eoin. ▶ The ridge curves right – follow the crest or use a grass path down right – to a second Munro Top, **Stob an Cul Choire**. On the left now is the rocky face of Aonach Beag, with its classic North-East Ridge showing well (Diff, with pinnacles, popular in winter with those undiscouraged by the long walk in).

A rocky but not difficult ridge leads down west to a col. The slope ahead looks intimidating but is OK. Fairly steep grass heads straight up towards a tower of reddish granite. Either head up this grass, or find some easy, scrappy scrambling (Grade 1) immediately to the right.

Once at the base of the reddish tower, head round to its right, then slant back up left to reach its top. Now a small zigzag path heads up the spurline, reaching the plateau about 50 metres east of Aonach Mor's summit cairn. (**In descent** The spur top is only visible from the plateau edge, so in mist take a bearing from Aonach Mor's cairn or use the GPS reading: NN 1944 7295.)

From **Aonach Mor** summit, a path runs south down the grassy plateau. ▶ The main path descends gently south to the narrow neck joining Aonach Mor to Aonach

Across the valley is the black-run area of the Nevis Range ski slopes.

Schist (grey, flaky) interchanges with Nevis outer granite (rounded lumps, pinkish where unweathered). On the right, now, you are opposite the winter climbing ground of Coire an Lochan.

Ignore a much smaller path soon forking off right (descent towards Bealach Giubhsachan, Route 13).

On Stob an Cul Choire, approaching Aonach Mor

Beag. It heads on up through rocks, then becomes a scree path with drops on the left. At the slope top the drops are also ahead. Turn right alongside them, over stony ground without path, for 150 metres to the smallish cairn of **Aonach Beag**. There's a very fine view across Carn Mor Dearg and its arête to Ben Nevis, which looks like a pointy crag mountain from here.

Return to **Aonach Mor**. Continue ahead with steep drops on your left, north to a very slight rise and then downhill roughly northwest. Pass the top of a ski tow and then of a chairlift. At a levelling 650m, you reach a well-built path leading to **Meall Beag** just ahead. ◄

Meall Beag means, simply, Small Hump.

After visiting the viewpoint, you could head back along this path to the gondola top station. However, if the gondola has closed or you just fancy a stroll, from Meall Beag head on northwest down pathless ridge, zig-zagging carefully down a steep descent, then heading down left to join a rough path alongside **Allt Daim**. It runs down to an intake, with a footway across a dam and a track beginning beyond.

Note The mountain bike path under the gondola is closed to walkers during biking hours, and unattractive at any time.

The track recrosses the stream at another dam and enters forest. Immediately bear right and follow a track down northeast for 1km to another junction. Here turn left, curving downhill. The third turning left, a mountain-bike path, short-cuts a bend in the track. At its foot continue to a horizontal track below, where you turn right to the car park at the **gondola foot**. ◄

On Stob an Cul Choire, with Aonach Beag behind

PART THREE

GREY CORRIES
AND SPEAN BRIDGE

*Sgurr Choinnich Mor on the Grey
Corries main ridge (Route 15)*

Quartzite is quite different. It's not the usual rocky grey, but a pale yellowish-white that under sunlight shows an evil gleam. It's not lumpy but flat and smooth, and when it breaks it breaks in sharp edges and cubes. The three grey corries are flat-bottomed and green (quartzite is relatively rich in minerals), but rise to bleak fields of blocks and boulders. The tops of the corries are fringed with crags, and the hill range that takes its name from them is a long wiggly ridge. The rock underfoot is sometimes smooth as a pavement, but the sharp edges will slash your gaiters.

Rising between a wide, dreary spruce wood in the north and the remote top end of Glen Nevis to the south, the Grey Corries are slightly awkward to get at. This adds a certain solitude to their other excellent qualities. To make things even more strenuous, you really want all of this ridge, from

(Continues p. 79)

summit summary
Grey Corries

Sgurr Choinnich Beag in the west right along to Stob Coire na Ceannain. So make an expedition of them, using handy bothies to east and south. Make it more than an expedition by adding Ben Nevis, Carn Mor Dearg, and both of the Aonachs – a big hill day that even so is just the first half of the ultimate in such things, Tranter's Walk around the Nevis Watershed.

SUMMIT SUMMARY

Grey Corries

The routes are described, and measured, to the summit of Stob Coire Claurigh. Though overshadowed by its big neighbours to the west, it's actually Scotland's 15th-highest (1177m/3862ft). Route 15 follows the entire main ridge westwards; Routes 16–18 join that ridgeline from the north.

Sgurr Choinnich Mor from the east (Route 15)

GREY CORRIES ROUTES

15 Grey Corries Ridge
16 Coire an Eoin
17 Stob Coire Easain North Ridge
18 Stob Coire Claurigh North Ridge
19 Cul Coirean
20 Lairig Leacach and Lochan Rath
21 Lairig Leacach to Stob Ban
22 Meanach bothy to Stob Ban

15 Grey Corries Ridge

Difficulty
▨ ▨ ▨ ▨ ▢

Start	Aonach Beag summit NN 197715
Distance	8.5km/5.5 miles
Ascent	900m/3000ft
Approx time	
end to end	4.5hr
Terrain	Mostly pathed, but with scrambling, boulderfields, and very steep descent off Aonach Beg

If you like your ridges rocky but not scrambly, this is the place to be. For the seriously ambitious, the description begins at Aonach Beag, with various side-routes joining in as we go along.

From **Aonach Beag** descend following big crag drops on the left, first south, then east over a minor hump. After another 500 metres the ridge turns sharply right, south-east, steepening down to the ridge corner at GR 207708.

A steep zigzag path leads down to a narrow rib, then down a grassy gully on the right; then keep down to right of broken quartzite outcrops to the wide col at the head of **Coire Bhealaich**. However, if the steep spur is snow-covered, an easier descent can be made from the col north of Sgurr a' Bhuic, turning down a gully then contouring left to the wide col.

A small path leads up grass to the top of **Sgurr** *Route 16 joins here.* **Choinnich Beag**. ◄ The path continues on pleasant grass through a col and up **Sgurr Choinnich Mor**.

Descend a sharp grass ridge northeast. It levels, then drops steeply with a small path. The south ridge of Stob Coire Easain is quartzite slabs and stones, one of the best parts of the ridgeline. **Stob Coire Easain**, though named on *Route 17 joins here.* Landranger, is not the local Munro. ◄

Head down southeast, over stones and small quartzite outcrops. The ridge of rocks and stones rises to **Stob**

Coire an Laoigh (1116m, a Munro but unnamed on older Landranger maps). Here the ridge turns northwest, over three more minor tops and much pleasant rocky ground. In mist, at the first of these tops, **Caistell**, careful compasswork is required to avoid a wrong ridge northwards; at the second, **Stob Coire Cath na Sine**, the main ridge itself turns north; at the third, **Stob a' Choire Leith**, again you must avoid a wrong ridge northwards. In clear weather just enjoy the ridge and its views all the way to **Stob Coire Claurigh**.

Below Sgurr Choinnich Beag at the western end of the Grey Corries ridge, looking back towards Aonach Beag

Heading east along the Grey Corries ridge towards Stob Coire Claurigh

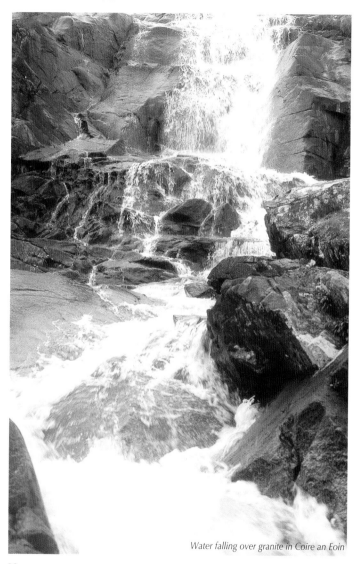

Water falling over granite in Coire an Eoin

16 Coire an Eoin

Start	Forest edge above Corriechoille NN 255788
Distance (to SC Claurigh)	18.5km/11 miles
Ascent	1450m/4800ft
Approx time up	8.5hr
Terrain	Pathless rough valley, with quad-bike wheelmarks higher up

This rock-ringed, empty corrie under the Aonachs sees far more deer than people. Being pathless, it's rather tough uphill, but makes a good, wild descent route; survey ahead from Sgurr Choinnich Beag to work out the best line. The valley is bog and bare rock – walk the rock rather than the bog.

Most routes on the range start from Corriechoille, at its northeast corner. Above the farm where the smooth gravel track enters the forest are concessionary pull-offs for about eight cars. Park with care, as timber lorries use the track.

All other spaces along this road and track are marked 'no parking' until you get back to a couple of pull-offs at the **Cour bridge** (NN 248811); this adds 3km and 120m, about 2hr to the return journey. Before that, the car park at **Coille Anachain** adds another 2km (add 1hr for a return journey). ▶

The route could also be started, ideally with bike, from Spean Bridge station.

To **start** with, the old tramway is rough but quick, with some views; the forest road is trouble-free but dull, and might be preferred by weary descenders.

- **Tramway** Directly opposite the parking pull-in, the green track of an old railbed contours west across grassland, marked with occasional wooden sleepers. In places this track is swampy, but the mire is only a couple of inches above a hard surface. After

1km the path enters forest. There are wide views downhill over the Great Glen for the next 10 years until replantation grows. After 1.5km in the trees, cross a ladder stile to arrive on a forest road. Turn down right for 200 metres, then sharp left across the top of a large quarry.

- **Forest road** Take the track back towards Corriechoille for 800 metres, and turn left ('Spean Bridge') into plantations. After 2.5km, ignore a smaller track down right (again 'Spean Bridge') and follow the main track uphill for another 700 metres, then bending right around the top of a quarry.

Either way, cross the Cour stream and keep ahead under mature larches. The track crosses **Allt Coire nan Eoin**, emerges from plantations, and ends near an intake dam (2km from the quarry).

Follow a concrete culvert left, and cross the stream above its dam. Head up to some small waterfalls, and take the bare rock of a seasonal water channel to left of the stream, to the foot of a larger fall (NN 224757). Above the fall, continue to left (east) of the stream, sometimes on grassy banks or bare rock but mostly rather rough, until the stream bends left past the rocky knoll **An Guirean** into a wide, wet valley.

Follow the left edge of the level ground, finding traces of quad-bike track, to cross the river at a pebbly ford (NN 2203 7455). Here is the start of a helpful quad-bike track that sweeps out right then back to the river at a solitary birch below two fine pools (NN 2213 7429). The track runs south up a spur with grey schist boilerplates, to pass a small cairn at 470m (NN 2186 7343). It gently descends to the valley floor at the foot of **Creagan na Gaibhre**. Here the track is lost. Cross the spur foot to a clump of boulders from a rockfall (NN 2161 7243), marked on Harvey map and visible, for descenders, from the hills above.

Cross the stream coming out of An Cul Choire to head southwest along the top of a river-moulded moraine hump. Cross a smaller side-stream, then go up a spur of schist boilerplates to right of the main stream (the one out of Coire Bhealaich). At about 700m, cross that stream and head up a spur of bare rock slabs that now are of whitish quartzite. A low crag at half-height is bypassed on either side. At the top of the quartzite slabs, below the final steepening of Sgurr Choinnich Beag, contour to the right (south) for 400 metres, to reach **Choinnich Beag**'s southwest ridge at the foot of its steep section (800m, NN 2174 7055; so far 10.5km/6.5 miles with 550m/1800ft of up, about 4hr).

Continue along the whole of the main ridge (see Route 15).

17 Stob Coire Easain North Ridge

Difficulty
■ ■ ■ ■ ☐

Start	Corriechoille NN 255788
Distance (to SC Claurigh)	10.5km/6.5 miles
Ascent	1200m/4000ft
Approx time up	5.5hr
Terrain	Steepish pathless grass, then pathed ridge

The gentle ridge is another great descent, after achieving most (but not quite all) of the Grey Corries ridgeline. Uphill, it's a bit of a trudge.

Start as Route 16 – note possible parking problems above Corriechoille. If using the **tramway**, then at its end turn up left on forest road. If using the drier but longer **forest road option**, then at the quarry bend (NN 238771) keep ahead up the smaller forest track.

The track runs above **Allt Choimhlidh** stream, to a concrete culvert leading to an intake dam. Cross a ladder stile onto a rough path down to the little reservoir. Cross above it onto a steep grass slope with an eroded little path.

Stob Coire an Laoigh and Stob Coire Easain from the east

Now it's just a long slog up a grass slope. Helpful quad-bike wheelmarks are easier to find when descending the route. At 750m a definite ridgeline starts to form, and at 850m you're on a very enjoyable ridge with great views of quartzite across the Grey Corries to Stob Coire Claurigh. The ridge underfoot, though, remains schist almost to the summit cairn of **Stob Coire Easain**.

Before the summit, a path passes left below crags, then climbs scree to the col west of Stob Coire Easain. But if you like hills, why skip SCE – which is a nice one? And if you don't like hills, what are you up to attempting 284 of them?

At the summit, turn left along the main ridge (Route 15); or turn right, cross Sgurr Choinnich Mor, and descend Route 16 (8hr circuit, 18.5km/11.5 miles, 1150m/3800ft of ascent).

18 Stob Coire Claurigh North Ridge

Difficulty

Start	Corriechoille NN 255788
Distance up	5.5km/3.5 miles
Ascent	1000m/3300ft
Approx time up	4hr
Terrain	Ridge grassy then stony with path

The easiest route, recommended for descent for its gentle grass and north-ward views.

Start as Route 16 – note possible parking problems. Head south up the track to the gate at the top edge of the forest, and once through it, turn off right alongside the forest fence. Ascend beside the fence for 1km, to its corner, then head straight up grass slopes south. The wide ridge leads up to **Stob Coire Gaibhre** (inconvenient to bypass in mist, and with fine views if mistless).

A small path follows the steep edge southwest across a col, then disappears. Head up the ridge, with drops on the left, passing to left of a stony ridgetop hollow to the minor top where the ridge joins from Stob Coire na Ceannain. Ahead the ridge sharpens: bypass on the right, or cross, some little quartzite towers to the summit of **Stob Coire Claurigh.**

In descent Head down north over or around some little quartzite towers and along the right-hand rim of a strange stone hollow to the little North Top. Head down northwest on a ridge that's stony then grassy, before a steeper descent leads into a slight col. A small path leads right, to **Stob Coire na Gaibhre**.

Descend broad slopes north. A short stretch of path rounds the head of Allt Coire na Gaibhre. Carry on north down broad slopes. Resist temptation to slant down right towards the top of an invisible crag (**Ruigh na Gualainn**), instead easing left to join the top edge of forest. Follow the forest fence down northeast to join the Lairig Leacach track.

19 Cul Coirean

Start	Corriechoille NN 255788
Distance up	9.5km/6 miles
Ascent	1000m/3300ft
Approx time up	5hr
Terrain	Pathless hillside and ridge

A remote and indirect route onto the splendid sub-summit of Stob Coire na Ceannain, the true start of the Grey Corries Ridge.

See Route 16 for parking issues at Corriechoille. Even from the parking spaces at the track top, a bicycle to Lairig Leacach bothy knocks about 2hr off the journey, most of the saving being on the return.

Start up the track, passing through a gate into forest being felled – if a lorry is loading, wait for a signal from the operator. After 1.3km pass out again by another gate with a kissing gate alongside. The track continues through the beautiful **Lairig Leacach** (Lairig means pass) to the small **Lairig Leacach bothy** (6km, 300m, 2hr).

Turn upstream behind the bothy on a peaty path that stays close to, and to right of, **Allt a' Chuil Choirean**, with waterfalls heard below. The path stays to right of the stream, to a stream junction, where the bigger stream tumbles down in waterfalls out of **An Cul Coire**.

Turn right, up this stream, through quite deep heather at first. As the ground steepens, a sheep or deer path is alongside the stream, initially on its right (east) side. Pass lots of little waterfalls, and small ravines colourful with roseroot and cranesbill. A crag outcrop defends the corrie above. Follow the stream up to left of this crag, then strike up onto its top, and cross the corrie's rim onto the ridgeline beyond. This runs up north, then west, onto **Stob Coire na Ceannain**.

A sharp little ridge runs to the north top of Stob Coire Claurigh. Turn up left, around the rim of a strange stone hollow reminiscent of limestone country in Europe, following the ridgeline with big drops on the left. Bypass or cross some little quartzite towers to the summit of **Stob Coire Claurigh**.

20 Lairig Leacach and Lochan Rath

Start	Corriechoille NN 255788
Distance	9.5km/6 miles
Ascent	1000m/3300ft
Approx time up	5hr
Terrain	Small rough paths

Difficulty

A beautiful route of ravine and ridge, and one that cleverly avoids any steep climbs.

Start by following Route 19 to **Lairig Leacach bothy** (2hr).

Turn upstream behind the bothy on a peaty path that stays close to, and right of, **Allt a' Chuil Choirean**, with waterfalls out of sight below. The path stays to right of the stream, crossing the sidestream from the Cul Coirean, to a stream junction at NN 271731. ▶

Bear left across grass below the quartzite slabs and then below the ravine that bounds them on the left, onto the wide spur beyond. The path reforms, heading up the left side of this spur, then up right, onto its crest. It keeps up the spur to 800m, where it turns right and contours across the rock-floored terrace between the middle and the uppermost of the Giant's three Stairs, to reach the col beyond. This is the lowest point between Stob Ban and Stob Coire Claurigh.

Just ahead now is the stack of quartzite slabs and crags that make the **Giant's Staircase** scramble (Grade 2, very enjoyable, see *Scrambles in Lochaber*, Appendix 3).

*Heading up Coire
Claurigh towards
Stob Ban*

Keep ahead (north) across the col, past its small pool
Lochan Rath, and head straight up the grassy slope to
Stob Coire Claurigh.

Note Those based at Lairig Leacach bothy could turn
left at the col, reversing Route 21. Steep scree path
leads up Stob Ban. Take a small path down the ridge
east, then northeast. The 2.5hr circuit of 5km/3 miles
with 500m/1700ft of ascent turns Stob Ban from a
nuisance Munro into a handy evening outing.

21 Lairig Leacach to Stob Ban

Difficulty

Start	Corriechoille NN 255788
Distance	10km/6.5 miles
Ascent	1200m/4000ft
Approx time up	5.5hr
Terrain	Track and path, rough off Stob Ban

This route is gentle onto Stob Ban, and harsh off it, so more comfortable in
reverse.

Start by following Route 19 to **Lairig Leacach bothy** (2hr).

Just beyond the bothy, a new footbridge crosses Allt a' Chuil Choirean. Follow the good stalkers' path beyond for 200 metres, to turn off up the spur of Stob Ban. A path passes along the right-hand (northwest) slopes of the minor knoll at 770m, then follows a pleasant ridge to the summit of **Stob Ban**.

Descend northwest on a scree path, becoming loose and steep down to the col above Coire Rath. Pass the pool there, **Lochan Rath**, and head straight up the grassy slope opposite to **Stob Coire Claurigh**.

22 Meanach Bothy to Stob Ban

		Difficulty
Start	Meanach bothy NN 266685	■ ■ ■ ■ □
Distance	4.5km/3 miles	
Ascent	600m/2000ft	
Approx time up	3hr	
Terrain	Pathless but grassy up Stob Ban, then rough stony descent	

A pathless but reasonably comfortable line, used to link Grey Corries with Mamores on Tranter's Walk, or as an end-of-day descent to the bothy.

Meanach (Meannanach) bothy is reached from Glen Nevis or Corrour station (Route 5), from Corriechoille (Route 24), or from Kinlochleven (Route 45). **Start** from the riverbank opposite Luibeilt, taking the stalkers' path up beside **Allt nam Fang**. At a stream junction at 500m, leave the path and follow the main Allt nam Fang upstream, due north. Its grassy banks give a way up through the heather, onto open grass high on the side of **Stob Ban**.

Reach Stob Ban's south ridge at about 900m and follow it to the summit. Continue as Route 21 to Stob Coire Claurigh.

23 The Innses

Start/finish	Above Corriechoille NN 255788
Distance	13km/8 miles
Ascent	900m/3000ft
Approx time	5.5hr
Max altitude	Cruach Innse 857m
Terrain	Rough hillsides

'Sgurr' is the generic name of only the finest mountains, such as the Cuillin. Among Corbetts south of the Great Glen, just two receive this top designation (and Sgor Mor on Deeside doesn't deserve it!). Sgurr Innse is an impressive cone of crag and heather; this route, while remaining on the heather, takes you right in among the crag.

Start by following Route 19 towards **Lairig Leacach bothy** (2hr). From the bothy itself, there's a good view of the ascent route. But 300 metres before it, turn off left on a rough track fording the stream. Head up grassy slopes with wheelmarks to the col south of **Sgurr Innse**.

Go up the steep spur northeast, on heather with some projecting rock, until a stonefield leads to the base

Sgurr Innse from Lairig Leacach bothy: Route 23 follows the shadow-edge spur

121

The Lairig

526
Cnoc nan
Ceann Mòra

Ruigh na
Gualainn

Cruach
857
Innse

Beinn
Bhàn

Stob Coire
958
Gaibhre

Coire na
Ceannain

Sgurr
809
Innse

Stob Coire
1123
na Ceannain

1121

Stob Choire
ire 1177
Claurigh

Bothy

of a final crag
(NN 2891 7458,
675m). Turn right,
along the crag base,
on a heathery shelf with
deer path, and more big
crags below. After 100
metres, with stonefield
ahead, turn up left to the

re Ràth

977
Stob Bàn

dismantled tramway

258

Parallel Road

258

261

593

18

23

19

20

21

24

45

Lairig Leacach

knolly summit plateau. Head uphill to pass a small pool to the summit of **Sgurr Innse.**

Direct descent northwest leads to crags, so head down north for 200 metres. As the slope gets steep, slant down left, northwest, with traces of path, into the broad **593m col** (589m on old maps). A small path winds up peat and outcrops to the plateau, where ground of compact quartzite, like the Grey Corries opposite, leads to the summit of **Cruach Innse**.

Descend gentle grassy slopes northwest, steepening towards a col. Before reaching this, turn down left, west, to reach the track of the outward walk.

24 Lairig Leacach:
Corrour to Spean Bridge

Length

Difficulty

Start	Corrour station NN 356664 (or Loch Ossian youth hostel)
Finish	Spean Bridge NN 221814
Distance	24.5km/15.5 miles
Ascent	200m/700ft
Approx time	1 short day (6.5hr going)
Max altitude	Lairig Leacach 510m
Terrain	Tracks and paths, quite rough by Allt na Lairige
Transport	Spean Bridge to Corrour, trains evening (for Loch Ossian overnight) or early morning
Sketch map	See overview map (page 13)

Shorter than the Glen Nevis trek (Route 5), this takes in the fine and historic Lairig Leacach pass. Alternatively, a night in Lairig Leacach bothy could prelude a romp along the Grey Corries.

Start along the tracks of Route 5 to the head of Loch Treig (6km, 1.5hr). Cross Abhainn Rath to the boarded-up

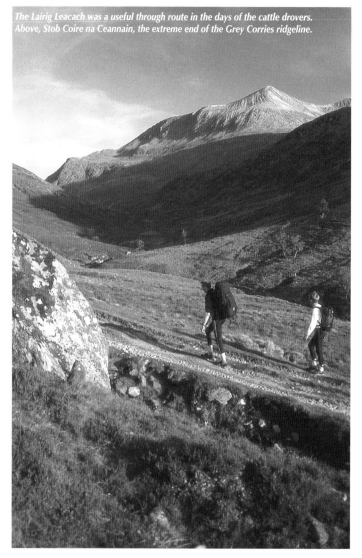

The Lairig Leacach was a useful through route in the days of the cattle drovers. Above, Stob Coire na Ceannain, the extreme end of the Grey Corries ridgeline.

The path east of the river is very narrow and vague but has great views of the waterfalls Easan Dubh. To reach it, drop right to a footbridge among the first trees.

Creaguaneach Lodge and follow the loch shore to the next river, **Allt na Lairige**, where the path rises through a gate into a small enclosure.

Of the paths up-valley, the one west of the river, which happens to be the right-of-way, is clearer. ◄ Ignore a footbridge down right, but climb slightly through a col behind a small knoll and then drop right, to the riverbank.

The path runs up-valley, mostly alongside the river. After 3.5km the valley levels and the path gets boggier, to a new footbridge over Allt a' Chuil Choirean near **Lairig Leacach bothy**.

A good track runs north through the Lairig Leacach pass and down through forest into cattle pastures.

- **Quick way** Continue past **Corriechoille** to the lane below, which runs pleasantly alongside **River Spean** to Spean Bridge.
- **Way of plantations and woodland** About 800 metres below the forest foot, turn left, signed 'Spean Bridge'; this forest route is signposted 'Spean Bridge' throughout. Follow the new track into plantation for 2km, then turn down right on a smaller grassier track. After 700 metres, as the track bends right, a path down left leads to a footbridge under birches. Turn right on a cycle path, which after 2km becomes a mossy old track.

  Ignore a side-track down right (leading to **Killiechonate**). After 1km the track ahead reverts to cycle path, which descends to cross a track (NN 228808). Take the path down ahead until it bends right, then on a track immediately below, turn left. After 200 metres, a path forks down right, signed 'station'. It slants through woods to emerge above **Spean Bridge station**.

PART FOUR

MAMORES

We ought to be be non-judgemental and pretend all hills are equal. But... Sgurr a' Mhaim, Stob Ban, Am Bodach: their shapes alone send a tingle into every limb. Link them along a ridge that's steep-sided and sometimes rocky, that swoops westward over 5 hours of walking and six Munros – and you have hillwalking perfection.

The gentler granite section at the western end of the Mamores; westbound walkers heading to Mullach nan Coirean

The two sides of the range represent two different sides of hillwalking. Glen Nevis is slightly gloomy, unless you follow it right up into the Nevis Gorge, when it's seriously gloomy, also grand and grim. All the way along above Glen Nevis the hill slope is steep. The steep paths lead up to the northward spurs of Sgurr a' Mhaim and An Gearanach, or the north ridge of Stob Ban. Each of these offers scrambling that's technically easy, but still serious and exposed. On the day I was taking the photos here, in a wind that swept clouds across the ridge of Stob Ban, a Royal Marine Commando fell to his death from An Garbhanach.

With most of this north side so steep, it's tempting to flop down the gentle grass into Coire a' Mhail, with its little river winding out towards Glen Nevis. A mistake: that little river drops over the famous waterfall at Steall. The circuit of the deceptive corrie links the ridges of An Gearanach with the Devil's Ridge to Sgurr a' Mhaim. It's the 'Ring of Steall', one of the classic hard hillwalks. I've lifted this out of the Summit Summary as the separate Route 39.

Walkers from Kinlochleven have the opposite approach, literally but also metaphorically. Instead of the concrete malls of Fort William they have a peaceful little village. Instead of spruce trees and gloom, they have birchwoods, and sunset all the way along Loch Leven. Instead of Steall Falls they have the green splashiness of the Grey Mare's Tail. When it's time to head uphill, instead of steepness they have well-graded stalkers' paths; and because of the geography, they don't get to walk those challenging northern spurs.

But once you're up, it doesn't matter which way you got there. Between Binnein Mor and Mullach nan Coirean, 12 wonderful kilometres await you.

You get all the variety of quartzite, schist and granite; but always the same narrow and shapely ridgelines, the same views of Ben Nevis hanging above you, and Bidean peering over the jagged wall-top of the Aonach Eagach. Ahead is the Atlantic, going golden under the sunset.

All this is pretty popular, and some paths are wide and eroded. So do the Mamores in winter, cramponning all day from peak to peak before leaping down some accommodating snowslope into the darkening glen.

SUMMIT SUMMARY

Mamores

Route 25 (at the start of the Summit Summary) is the entire main ridge, eastbound. Route 38 (at the end of the Summary) is the same main ridge in the westbound direction. The classic Ring of Steall is a separate stand-alone outside the Summit Summary, at Route 39. Route 40 visits the two eastern outliers, Sgurr Eilde Mor and Binnein Beag.

MAMORES ROUTES

25 Mamores Main Ridge Eastbound

Difficulty
■■■□□

Start	Mullach nan Coirean NN 122662
Finish	Binnein Mor NN 212663
Distance	11.5km/7.5 miles
Ascent	4300ft/1300m
Approx time end-to-end	6hr
Terrain	Paths, some quite steep and eroded

A fine varied ridge, over many peaks.

Route 27 joins

Route 28, the one comfy descent into Glen Nevis.

Route 29, and its bypass, 29A, also arrive here.

For the Bodach bypass (Route 25A), at the lowest point of the col look out for a grassy groove crossing the ridge, marking where that path starts on the left.

From **Mullach nan Coirean**, steep drops on the left guide eastwards over two minor tops. The path then skirts right of the small grass top above Stob Ban's north ridge and climbs stony slopes southeast to **Stob Ban** summit. ◄

Head south along crag tops for 30 metres, then down a ridge that curves left to display Stob Ban's eastern crags. Just before the ridge tip, the path drops off right (east). The slope eases, and a small hummock is crossed to the col with cairn at the top of **Coire Mhusgain.** ◄ The better path now contours along the northern (left) side, just below the crest, to the outflow of **Lochan Coire nam Miseach**. Cross the stream, and take a zigzag path up the steep slope to the col at the base of the Devil's Ridge. ◄ Turn right, up stony slopes, to the summit of **Sgurr an Iubhair**.

The pathed ridgeline runs down southeast to a long, level col. ◄ Keep ahead up the pleasant ridge onto **Am Bodach**.

Head down northeast, on steep rocky scree with various nasty paths. At the foot of the steep quartzite summit cap, keep to the right of the small crest outcrop, for the less uncomfortable path. The ridge continues over a narrow top, then rises to **Stob Coire a' Chairn**. Pathed ridge continues to the northern top of **Na Gruagaichean**, with

Mamores main ridge, steeper in the east; the east ridge of Na Gruagaichean

a drop into a spectacular notch before the southern and main summit.

Ignore the apparent ridge continuing ahead south, as the true ridgeline turns down left, east. An attractive sharp ridge leads to the next col, then a wider one runs up to the 1062m **south top** of Binnein Mor. Route 33 from Kinlochleven arrives here. Head north up the ridge to **Binnein Mor**'s main top. A rocky crest leads onwards for 100 metres to a lower sub-summit: anyone who likes scrambling will decide that must be the true ridge end and so require a visit, but it's not needed for Munro-bagging purposes.

25A Bodach Bypass: Eastbound

See Route 38A for the same route westbound. **Note** This path could be strayed off in mist, and dips into **Coire a' Mhail**, which runs down not to safety but to the top of Steall Falls – see Route 31.

At the lowest point of the ridge west of **Am Bodach** (NN 169652), a grassy notch crosses the ridgeline. Here look over the left-hand (northern) edge to see the path slanting

Difficulty

101

down across chunky scree. At the scree foot continue on the same line; the grass path is hard to see, as it passes below a strip of stonefield. The path becomes clear again, crossing a mossy stream, then contouring below a large stonefield with a prominent outcrop at its head.

At the end of this stonefield, with the path unclear again, slant up the grassy slope ahead (east) to reach the col east of **Am Bodach**.

26 Mullach nan Coirean North Ridge

Difficulty

Start	Achriabhach NN 145683
Distance up	4.5km/2.5 miles
Ascent	900m/2900ft
Approx time up	3.5hr
Terrain	Path, rough path under trees, pathed ridge

Nice once you're out of the forest, and makes a fairly comfortable descent.

Start from the car park by taking the road down-valley for 300 metres to the corner of plantations. Take a path under the trees just inside the forest, up to a bend in a forest road. Turn right on the higher, uphill, branch for 800 metres. A steep, rough path heads up left under the trees – the **Allt a' Choire Riabhaich** (stream) is heard nearby to the right. A ladder stile (NN 133681) leads out of the trees. A small path leads ahead, with a deer fence nearby on its left for 1km. By the time the fence turns away, the ridgeline ahead is well defined and clear all the way to **Mullach nan Coirean** summit.

Descent From the **summit**, start down north but bend to the right along the tops of crags dropping to the right, to find the ridgeline running down east. The ridge bends left, northeast, and soon has a deer fence along the crest. Follow the path and fence down to the ladder stile at NN 133681.

A path runs down between the trees to a forest road. Turn right to a hairpin bend, and then take a downhill path close to the forest edge and a stream.

27 Stob Ban North Ridge

Start	Achriabhach NN 145683
Distance up	3.5km/2 miles
Ascent	950m/3200ft
Approx time up	3.5hr
Terrain	Steep grass, ridge, a little scrambling (Grade 1)

Difficulty

A fine ridge with some easy scrambling.

Stob Ban in summer, its north ridge running down to the right

Stob Ban six months later (see p.103)

Start from the car park and head down-valley on road for 250 metres, then take a gate on the left just before the road bridge over **Allt a' Choire Dheirg**. Cross swampy ground near the river on your right (with forest beyond it). Level with a forest road bend within the forest, slant away left towards the first steep rise. A wooded rock band obstructs the slope above; near its right end is a grassy gap. Head into this to find a path starting. Above the rockband this path slants leftwards to a cairn at the ridge tip (**Sron Dearg**).

The ridge now runs almost level, with a path and remains of a fence. Where it steepens, the rocky crest can be avoided by a path just to right of the crest. The crest rocks are crampon-scratched and have good holds. However they are lichened, and being schist are slippery when wet.

A spectacular tower leads to the final crest, almost level but narrow, with a small path. It finishes at a triangular summit just northwest of **Stob Ban**.

28 Coire Mhusgain

Difficulty

Start	Achriabhach NN 145683
Distance up	4.5km/2.75 miles
Ascent	950m/3100ft
Approx time up	3.5hr
Terrain	Good path

A scenic and easy path with trees and waterfalls; good also in descent.

Start by turning right out of the parking area across one road bridge to the bridge over the Polldubh lower falls. Just before this bridge, take a stile on the right (not the gate beside it onto a riverside path). Follow a good path left of the stream up **Coire Mhusgain**. After 2km, at 400m, you're crossing a steep slope with waterfalls around. Here a small wrong path runs ahead, but the clearer main path zigzags up left before heading back right towards the stream. The path remains mostly good right up to the main ridge.

Descent At the lowest point of the ridge between Stob Ban and Sgurr an Iubhair, a cairn (NN 156653) marks the top of the clear path down **Coire Mhusgain**. This has one steep zigzag section but is mostly comfortable walking, with waterfalls below. It reaches the Glen Nevis road beside the Achriabhach car park.

29 Sgurr a' Mhaim
and Devil's Ridge

Difficulty
■ ■ ■ ■ ■

Start	Achriabhach NN 145683
Distance (to Sgurr an Iubhair)	4km/2.5 miles
Ascent	1100m/3700ft
Approx time up	4.5hr
Terrain	Steep climb, then narrow grass ridge with a scrambling moment (Grade 1)

A fine, narrow ridge with some easy scrambling.

Sgurr a' Mhaim (left) and its Devil's Ridge, seen from Route 27

Start by turning right out of the car park to cross **Allt Coire a' Mhusgain**. Just before the next bridge over the River Nevis (with the waterfalls underneath), take a stile on the right (not the gate beside it onto a riverside path). Follow a good path to left of the stream up **Coire Mhusgain** for 1km. As the main path starts to contour above the stream, fork off left, up a spur. The path is steep, relentless, and rather eroded, on grass to a slight flattening at 850m; then up quartzite stones to the summit of **Sgurr a' Mhaim**.

A good path heads quite steeply down south from Sgurr a' Mhaim, first on rocky stony ground, then on grass. ▸ The path bends a bit west of south to where the ridge levels and narrows into the Devil's Ridge. There is one rocky gap to scramble down into (slightly right of the crest) and then a spectacular grass knife-edge. After the drop to a final col, either climb steep stony ground ahead to **Sgurr an Iubhair** or else turn down right on zigzags to **Lochan Coire nam Miseach**.

Descent See Route 39 (Ring of Steall).

Devil's Bypass (Route 29A) turns off at the start of the grass.

29A Escaping the Devil

This route avoids the exposed, windswept ridge. It is indistinct in mist, and escape into Coire a' Mhail below is a bad idea (see Route 31).

From **Sgurr a' Mhaim,** the good path (towards Devil's Ridge) heads quite steeply down south over rocky stony ground. After about 5min the angle eases and the path is on grass. Here leave it to head left, pathless, across a grass dip and over a grass knoll (NN 1652 6656), then down southeast on a grass spur. An unused zigzag stalkers' path could soon be discovered underfoot. Follow it down to just above where the ridge angle eases, 930m (NN 1664 6638). Here the path turns right (south) to contour above a grassy hollow with the headwaters of a stream. It becomes indistinct, but is clear ahead and somewhat lower down, as it passes the toe of an outcrop (NN 1650 6599). It then slants gradually up below the **Devil's Ridge**, steepening in zigzags to reach the Devil's col.

Turn left up **Sgurr an Iubhair**, or directly ahead across the col is the path descending to **Lochan Coire nam Miseach**.

Difficulties

30 Gearanach and Garbhanach

Difficulty
■ ■ ■ ■ ■ ■

Start	End of Glen Nevis road
	NN 168692
Distance (to Stob	
Coire a' Chairn)	5km/3 miles
Ascent	1000m/3300ft
Approx time up	4.5hr
Terrain	Steep climb, then narrow stony
	and rocky ridge with a scrambling
	moment (Grade 1)

A steep climb onto a fine ridge with scrambling.

See Route 39 (Ring of Steall).

31 Escape from Coire a' Mhail

Descent If you have, by design or accident, descended into the trap of Coire a' Mhail, continuing downstream will lead onto crags on either side of Steall Falls. To escape, at the point where the valley narrows (NN 179675) head up northeast, to right of the hump **Cnoc Reamhar**, to reach the northwest ridge of An Gearanach at a levelling (NN 184677). Contour onwards to join the steep descending path of Route 30.

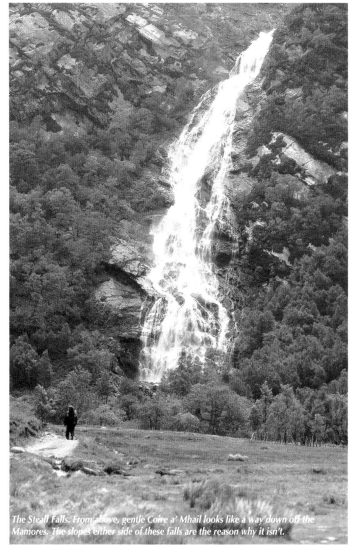

The Steall Falls. From above, gentle Coire a' Mhail looks like a way down off the Mamores. The slopes either side of these falls are the reason why it isn't.

32 Round the Back to Binnein Mor

Start	Grey Mare's car park, Kinlochleven NN 188623 or Mamore Lodge NN 185629
Distance up	8.5km/5.5 miles
Ascent	1300m/4300ft (from Mamore Lodge 1100m/3700ft)
Approx time up	5.5hr
Terrain	Paths and tracks, pathless stony and grassy ridge

Remote and romantic. To bag Sgurr Eilde Mor or Binnein Beag on the way, switch into Route 40.

Start as for Route 33, onto the steep southeast spur of **Sgor Eilde Beag**. At the first zigzag, ignore a peaty path ahead but zig back left and then zag right. At the second zig, keep ahead on a clear path that contours north, to pass left of a large lochan (**Lochan Coire an Lochain**). The path then drops steeply into the hollow of **Coire a' Bhinnein**. It follows a stream down for 30 metres, then crosses it and contours north around the base of Binnein Mor. It climbs slightly to reach the outflow of a narrow lochan on the plateau between the two Binneins. ◀

To bag Binnein Beag now, see Route 40.

The easy way up Binnein Mor from here is southwest up grass into the corrie with the two high lochans, then onto the north ridge. Also, immediately ahead is the northeast ridge, which starts steep, levels, then rises again in a rock arête that looks to offer some easy scrambling (I haven't yet been up this ridge).

The preferred route contours out to the left, south, to a little ravine. Go up to right of this into Binnein Mor's hidden little **northeast corrie**. Cross its floor to its bounding ridge, which is gently angled with quartzite outcrops. This ridge goes up, southwest then bending south, becoming fairly steep and sharp to reach **Binnein Mor** summit.

33 Sgurr Eilde Beag to Binnein Mor

		Difficulty
Start	Grey Mare's car park, Kinlochleven NN 188623 or Mamore Lodge NN 185629	
Distance up	7.5km/4.5 miles	
Ascent	1200m/4000ft (from Mamore Lodge, 1000m/3300ft)	
Approx time up	4.5hr	
Terrain	Paths, one steepish ascent	

Starting at Mamore Lodge saves 200m. It has inexpensive parking, which fills up at weekends. The Kinlochleven start is very beautiful.

- **Starting** in **Kinlochleven**, leave the car park on a wide, smooth path, turning left (multicoloured way-mark arrows). The path soon drops to a footbridge where you can turn left (blue arrow) for 100 metres to view the waterfall. Return and continue past the footbridge for 100 metres, where the path bends back left, steeply uphill. At the top of trees, with a low-voltage power line above, fork right (yellow, green arrows). The path follows a spur to a gate in a deer fence (NN 192628), then contours along the spur's left side under birches across three streams to a final path junction. Turn up right (yellow arrow).

- **Starting** from **Mamore Lodge**, head up to a contouring track just above. Turn right to the keepers' cottages, where a bypass path is on the right to rejoin the track beyond. In 150 metres, just before some gravel pull-offs, take a path down right. It descends

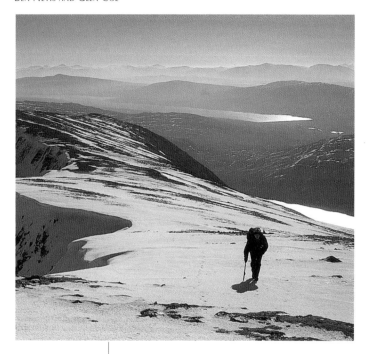

On Sgurr Eilde Beag, looking back across Loch Eilde Mor to the Blackwater Reservoir

briefly but erodedly, then runs level to a footbridge. In 150 metres is a path junction, where you follow a yellow arrow ahead.

The yellow-arrowed path rises between two streams to join the track above. Cross to pass a stone bench and rejoin the track. Follow the track for 1km, to just before its highest point, where a cairned path turns off left (in a few steps more, another path turns off right for Kinlochleven). The peaty well-used path crosses **Allt Coire nan Laogh** and turns uphill beyond it for 200 metres. Then it slants up the face of **Sgor Eilde Beag** in a climb that's been visible for most of the walk so far.

Once on the steep southeast spur of Sgor Eilde Beag, the path rises in steep zigzags to a cairn at its top. A gentle ridge runs up to Point 1062 (**Binnein Mor South Top**), then a fine sharp one rises north to **Binnein Mor**.

34 Coire na Ba to Stob Coire a' Chairn

Start	Grey Mare's car park, Kinlochleven NN 188623 or Mamore Lodge NN 185629
Distance up	6km/3.75 miles
Ascent	950m/3200ft (from Mamore Lodge 770m/2600ft)
Approx time up	4.5hr
Terrain	Good paths

A good, comfortable path with an attractive wood and waterfall to start.

- **Starting** from **Kinlochleven** Grey Mare's car park, you will follow green waymarks for the first part of the walk as far as the high track. Leave the car park on a wide, smooth path, turning left. The path soon drops to a footbridge where you can turn left (blue arrow) for 100 metres to view the waterfall. Return and continue past the footbridge for 100 metres, where the path bends back left, steeply uphill. At the top of trees, with a low-voltage power line above, fork right. The path follows a spur to a gate in a deer fence (NN 192628), then contours along the spur's left side under birches across three streams. At the next junction keep ahead (the final green arrow) to arrive at a track above. Turn left for 200 metres to a gate on the right just before a stream.

- **Starting** from **Mamore Lodge**, head up to a contouring track and turn right. Bypass the keepers' cottages by a path down on their right, then rejoin the track for 1km. Just after crossing **Allt Coire na Ba**, take a gate on the left.

Go up a rough track into **Coire na Ba**. This high valley is pleasingly wooded beside its stream, with a big cirque ahead around Am Bodach by the two tops of Stob Coire a' Chairn to Na Gruagaichean. The track degenerates to a path, which after 1km crosses a stream and 200 metres later turns uphill alongside a second stream. ◀ The path ahead goes up a wet slope where it may be lost. It reappears slanting right to pass a small pool. After 100 metres it turns sharp left, and contours across the steep slope of Na Gruagaichean, going gently downhill for a while. Finally it climbs in zigzags to the main ridge at the col southeast of Stob Coire a' Chairn (NN 1939 6559).

Here Route 35 turns off.

35 Am Bodach East Corrie

Difficulty
■■■■□

Start	Grey Mare's car park, Kinlochleven NN 188623
Distance (to Bodach summit)	5.5km/3.5 miles
Ascent	1000m/3300ft
Approx time up	4.5hr
Terrain	Steep pathless grass

A dramatic and little-used back way in to Am Bodach.

Again, save 200m by starting at Mamore Lodge – but miss the wonderful waterfall.

Follow Route 34 into the cirque between Am Bodach and Na Gruagaichean. ◀ Where the path turns uphill by a second stream, leave it and contour left, then slant up to join the ravine that emerges from the eastern corrie of Am Bodach.

At 540m altitude the ravine splits. Continue up to right of the right-hand branch to cross its head (with the stream steepening in further falls above), or else cross the right-hand branch above its lowest waterfall and go up the spur between the two branches, then switch into the left-hand ravine branch (bouldery but otherwise easy). At 600m the left-hand branch peters out. Here (NN 182650) bend up left, following the remaining stream southwest into a grassy hollow, with an imposing crag up left.

In the broken ground on the right is a gully with a weathered rockfall emerging from its foot. From under the rockfall, a grassy old path slants across the grassy hollow. Take this path up left, to reach grassy slopes immediately above the imposing crag. Head straight up south onto a narrow grass ridge. This bends to the right around the head of the grassy hollow to a small summit on Am Bodach's southeast ridge (NN 180645). Cross the small summit, to find the ridge path beyond, and turn right on this. Follow it to the summit levelling, with a preliminary cairn and 50 metres later the summit of **Am Bodach**.

36 Sgurr an Fhuarain: Descent

		Difficulty
Ends	Grey Mare's car park NN 188623	■ ■ ■ ■ ☐
Distance (from Am Bodach summit)	5.5km/3.5 miles	
Height loss	1000m/3300ft	
Approx time	4hr (up), 2hr (down)	
Terrain	Rough grass	

A grassy trudge up, but a comfortable descent, especially when holding snow.

Descend Am Bodach's south ridge, on a small path, to a slight rise at 900m, or else right down to **Sgurr an**

Fhuarain. Turn down right wherever good snow overlies the rough grass. Cross **Allt Coire na h-Eirghe** to join the path beyond and follow it down to the **West Highland Way** track. The track itself leads to Mamore Lodge: the WH Way forks down right to Kinlochleven (see Route 41 Mam na Gualainn).

37 Coire na h-Eirghe

Difficulty
■■■□□

Start	Grey Mare's car park NN 188623
Distance (to Sgurr an Iubhair)	5km/3 miles
Ascent	1000m/3300ft
Approx time	3.5hr
Terrain	Good paths

A comfortable ascent on path all the way.

Looking back from Na Gruagaichean towards Binnein Mor

Start by taking the **WH Way** out of Kinlochleven along the Fort William road, forking up right at village edge on a signposted path. The path crosses the Mamore Lodge access lane, to reach a high track. Turn left for

400 metres to cross **Allt Coire na h-Eirghe**, then continue for 100 metres to the highest point of the track. Here a path, inconspicuous at first, turns up right across bare slabs. It heads up to left of the stream, crosses it above a waterfall, then continues up to its right. In the upper corrie the path zigzags towards the summit of Am Bodach, thinks better of this, and swings left to the **Bodach/Iubhair col**.

38 Mamores Main Ridge Westbound

		Difficulty
Start	Binnein Mor NN 212663	
Finish	Mullach nan Coirean NN 122662	
Distance	11.5km/7.5 miles	
Ascent	1100m/3700ft	
Approx time		
end-to-end	6hr	
Terrain	Paths, some steep and eroded	

Eastbound is Route 25. This direction looks at the sea and the sunset.

The cairn of **Binnein Mor** lies just before a narrow rocky ridge running north; the further, lower, cairn does constitute the true start of the Mamores ridge.

From Binnein Mor, a shapely ridge descends south to Point 1062 (**Binnein Mor South Top**). This enjoyable ridge, not as narrow as it looks, continues southwest to **Na Gruagaichean**; the path, down left of the crest, misses out a little of the fun.

From Na Gruagaichean a sharp descent north into a spectacular little col leads to Gruagaichean's lower northwest top (between the two tops you pass over three different rocks: white quartzite, grey schist and pinkish granite). Easier ridge continues northwest to **Stob Coire a' Chairn** (981m, this Munro is among several unnamed on old Landranger maps).

Here a cairn (NN 178655) marks the start of the Bodach Bypass (Route 38A).

Head down southwest, across a sharp narrow hump, to the following col. ◄ Ahead, now, the climb to Am Bodach is rather steep, and the path zigzags up loose scree, seeking the firmest footing. In winter patches of hard snow are much nicer. Quite soon the ground eases to the stony top of **Am Bodach**.

The descent is on a gentle ridge westwards, with a short climb to **Sgurr an Iubhair** (1001m). This used to be the 11th Mamores Munro, but was downgraded in 1997. Its stony top doesn't show much path: there are two descent routes westwards, with the first option being steeper but more sheltered.

- **Lochan route down Iubhair** Make a short steep descent northwest into the col at the south end of the Devil's Ridge. Here turn down left, soon to find a zigzag path to the small **Lochan Coire nam Miseach**. Contour westwards for another 400 metres, to right of the ridge crest, to regain the crest at the cairn marking the top of the path down Coire Mhusgain (Route 28).

Hill-runner on the east ridge of Na Gruagaichean

- **Ridge route down Iubhair** Descend southwest, towards Stob Ban, to arrive at crag tops. Turn left along them. As they turn downhill, nearby on the left is a lightly used stalkers' path that zigzags off southwest before returning to the col above Lochan Coire nam Miseach. Continue ahead on a path just to left of the crest to the low point of the col, with the cairn at the top of Coire Mhusgain's path (Route 28).

Cross a small rise, then head up steeply onto a ridge curving left, with big drops on the right, onto **Stob Ban**. Head down northwest, passing left of a stony sub-summit, to a grassy col. Ahead is a triangular grass summit (the top of Route 27). The main path contours to left of this grass summit to regain the ridgeline, and follows drops on the right over two minor summits to **Mullach nan Coirean**.

38A Bodach Bypass: Westbound

Route 25A is the same route eastbound. **Note** This path could be strayed off in mist, and runs around the top of Coire a' Mhail, which runs down not to safety but to the Steall Falls – see Route 31.

From the col with cairn to east of Am Bodach (NN 178655) slant down roughly west. Ahead is a prominent little outcrop, and below it a stonefield: at the toe of the stonefield the good path will be found. It contours below the stonefield, crosses a mossy stream, then slants slightly uphill on grass with small strip of stonefield directly above. On the dry grass it becomes unclear but can be seen ahead, still on the same line, as it slants up chunky scree to the col west of Am Bodach.

Difficulty

39 Ring of Steall

Start/finish	End of Glen Nevis road NN 168692
Distance	14.5km/9 miles
Ascent	1600m/5300ft
Approx time	8hr
Max altitude	Sgurr a' Mhaim 1099m
Terrain	Long, steep ascent and descent, small ridge paths, easy scrambling

Length

■ ■ ■ ☐ ☐

Difficulty

■ ■ ■ ■ ■

Link the ridges of An Gearanach with the Devil's Ridge to Sgurr a' Mhaim, and you have the 'Ring of Steall'. With its narrow ridges, scrambling sections, and four Munro summits, this is one of the classic hard hillwalks. So I've lifted it out as a stand-alone from the Mamores Summit Summary where it belongs. Once up on Stob Coire a' Chairn, you can switch into previous routes for half a dozen different continuations, even if none will be quite as airily inspiring as the Devil's Ridge.

The name comes from the 'Ring of Steel', the Soviet tanks that surrounded General Paulus' Sixth Army at Stalingrad in the winter of 1942. The Stalingrad campaign left the German army shattered and destroyed. The Ring of Steall can have a similar effect on the walker of today. It's best done clockwise, starting up An Gearanach. The descent off Sgurr a' Mhaim is slightly less steep; more importantly, that direction allows an escape from the start of the Devil's Ridge down Route 28. There are *no earlier escapes*, as the route circles Coire a' Mhail with its waterfall exit (see Route 31).

See Route 2 for an exciting variant here.

Start from the end of the car park, along the wide, smooth path above Nevis Gorge. ◀ At the top of the gorge, the path emerges suddenly onto a flat riverside meadow. Cross it to the footbridge below the huge **Steall Falls**. As noted above and very visible here, there is no descent line alongside the waterfall: so don't descend into Coire a' Mhail above it.

The footbridge is three steel cables, giving a wobbly crossing. Make things easier by crossing one at a time,

The so-called footbridge at the Steall Falls is just the first challenging point in the route

An Garbhanach, 'the Rough One', seen from An Gearanach, 'the Steep One'

and by placing feet along the cable rather than sideways across it. Bear left past the Steall hut, to cross the stream below the Steall Falls.

Continue up the valley for 300 metres, then turn right up a steep path alongside a scoured-out earth gully. This erosion feature appeared during a single storm a few years ago. The path beside it is quite good, but the climb is steep. At the top of the steep valley (Coire Chadha Chaoruinn) the path contours right, onto the ridgeline alongside. (If you do later end up in Coire a' Mhail, you'll have to climb back out to this point.) Now the climb is less steep and the views wider. Follow the pathed ridge to the summit of **An Gearanach** (982m, unnamed on old maps).

From An Gearanach the sharp ridge runs south to the rocky summit of **An Garbhanach**. After the summit comes a moment of easy scrambling (Grade 1). There's a choice between an exposed downward step left of the crest, or a short groove descent right of the crest. Continue down an eroded path or rocks alongside, over a subsidiary hump, to a wide col, then easily up the walk's second Munro, **Stob Coire a' Chairn** (983m).

The ridge path runs down southwest, rises over a sharply defined bump, then drops to the col before Am Bodach. ▶ The climb ahead to Am Bodach is rather steep, and the path zigzags up loose scree, seeking the firmest footing. If you're not used to such ground look for rock handholds, and spend some time picking out the most comfortable line. But quite soon the ground eases to the stony top of **Am Bodach**.

The descent is on a gentle ridge westwards, with a short climb to **Sgurr an Iubhair** (1001m, unnamed on older maps). This used to be the walk's fourth Munro, but was downgraded in 1997. From its top, make a short steep descent northwest into a col. ▶

Ahead, a path leads up onto the start of the **Devil's Ridge**. ▶ This is grassy, but astonishingly sharp. At the end of the narrow crest is a notch, which requires a few steps of scrambling, just left of the crest. Less exposed ridge runs downhill to the steep cone of **Sgurr a' Mhaim**. The path leads straight up, north, onto stony ground and the summit.

Bear left to descend a worn scree path northwest, to a slight flattening at 850m at the foot of the screes. Crossing this flattening the path is briefly invisible, but reforms on a grassy spur below. At this steepens (NN 1587 6722) the main path turns down left, onto a spur descending northwest. (A smaller path north, down the apparent spurline ahead, soon turns left to rejoin the proper, main path.) Steep and rather eroded, the path descends the spur to **Allt Coire a' Mhusgain**, where an easier path leads downstream to the Glen Nevis road near **Polldubh**.

As your foot touches the road, turn back sharp right, through a gate, onto a fenced riverside path. Follow this, to right of the **Water of Nevis**, for 1.5km. After a down-hill section, look out for a footbridge down on the left. Cross it to rejoin the road, and turn right for 1km to the car park at the walk start.

From here you could take the Bodach bypass path, around its northern flank (Route 38A).

From here if time is short you could escape left down to Lochan Coire nam Miseach, to descend the good path of Route 28.

It'd be mere Munro-bagging to reach Sgurr a' Mhaim without the Devil's Ridge: Route 29A reversed.

40 The Back of the Binneins

Start/finish	Mamore Lodge NN 186629
Distance	18km/11 miles
Ascent	1300m/4400ft
Approx time	7.5hr
Max altitude	Sgurr Eilde Mor 1010m
Terrain	Paths, but rough up and down Eilde Mor

Length
■ ■ ■ □ □

Difficulty
■ ■ ■ ■ □

This walk takes you into some wonderfully remote country at the eastern end of the Mamores, to bag a pair of out-of-the-way Munros. The return is by the same route; however, if energy levels and clouds are high, then cross Binnein Mor (Route 32) for a fine ridgewalk over Na Gruagaichean and a descent to Coire na Ba (Route 34). That full day, the back *and* the front of the Binneins, gives 11.5 miles/5300ft of serious hill (18.5km/1600m of ascent).

Starting in Kinlochleven (as Route 33) adds 180m/600ft of ascent, but would let you end the day along the Pipeline Path (see Route 42).

Mamore Lodge has inexpensive parking, but fills up at weekends. ◀ From Mamore Lodge, **start** up the track to the contouring track just above. Turn right to the keepers' cottages, where a bypass path is on the right below the cottages to rejoin the track beyond. In 150 metres, just before some gravel pull-offs, take a path down right to a footbridge. After another 150 metres, at a path junction, follow a yellow arrow ahead. The path rises to rejoin the track above. Cross to pass a stone bench and rejoin the track.

Follow the track for 1km, to just before its highest point. A cairn on the left marks the start of a peaty well-used path, which crosses **Allt Coire nan Laogh** and turns uphill beyond it for 200 metres. Then it slants up the face of **Sgor Eilde Beag** in a climb that's been visible for most of the walk so far.

At the first zigzag, where the main path heads on up towards Sgor Eilde Beag, keep ahead on a small peaty path. It contours round to the flat wet plateau south of the lochan that's presumably called **Lochan Coire an Lochain**. Continue northeast across flat ground to cross the outflow of the lochan, onto the southeast spur of **Sgurr Eilde Mor**. Follow it up, with some loose blocky quartzite scrambling if wished, to the summit.

A clear path heads west down a well-defined spur. But before the spur end, the path heads down right, on eroded scree zigzags, then down northwest on steepish grass until below the steep ground on the left (800m altitude approx, NN 2280 6586). Here the path turns abruptly to contour left for 200 metres before descending between the small lochans north of Lochan Coire an Lochain to join the stalkers' path opposite. ▶

Turn right, as the new path zigzags down steep grass into the hollow of **Allt Coire a' Bhinnein**. After descending briefly beside the stream, the path crosses it and contours out north along the slope of Binnein Mor. It rises gradually to reach the plateau between the two Binneins. Turn off right, to cross the outflow of a long lochan and follow a low ridge containing it on its right. This flat ridge

Here you could turn left to contour the slope foot above Lochan Coire an Lochain and rejoin the outward route – leaving Binnein Beag inconveniently unbagged.

Sgurr Eilde Mor and the body of water presumably called Lochan Coire an Lochain, seen from Sgurr Eilde Beag

*Binnein Beag from the
Grey Corries ridge*

leads to the steep southern spur of **Binnein Beag**. Go up this on bits of path and block-field to the summit.

Descend the same way: or, from the summit, return for 50 metres to where the path starts to descend. Here turn off right down an eroded hollow leading to the top of a long scree slope, which can be descended fast by those who can fast descend scree. Either way, return to the long lochan's outflow.

Here you decide whether to continue onto Binnein Mor by Route 32. Otherwise, return along the path through **Coire a' Bhinnein**. Having climbed up the zig-zags from the stream, keep ahead on the main path. This takes you above, and to right of, **Lochan Coire an Lochain** along the slope of Sgor Eilde Beag, to rejoin the outward route.

PART FIVE

KINLOCHLEVEN

Kinlochleven and its loch glimpsed from the Pap of Glencoe (Route 51)

Kinlochleven is all that Fort William isn't. Where the Fort is big and busy, Kinlochleven, bypassed by the Ballachulish Bridge, is quiet. The Fort has great rail and coach links; Kinlochleven is reached by the occasional bus, or by the West Highland Way. Above all Kinlochleven, between the waterfalls and the sea, fringed by birchwoods, is a pretty place to be. And while it's a great jumping-up point for the Mamores, it also has – what's rare in this big-hill district – a network of attractive low-level walks.

Kinlochleven's independent hostel and campsite, pubs and late-opening shop make it a comfortable place to stay, and a welcome staging-point on various long-distance routes to north and east, as well as the West Highland Way. For wet days its unique feature is indoor ice-climbing in the former aluminium factory, the Ice Factor.

41 Mam na Gualainn

Start/finish	Grey Mare's car park, Kinlochleven NN 188623
Distance	19km/12 miles
Ascent	1000m/3300ft
Approx time	7hr
Max altitude	Mam na Gualainn 796m
Terrain	Tack and path, sometimes rough

Mam na Gualainn breaks my rule that small hills are tougher. It may not have the trampled paths of the main Mamores, but the West Highland Way and an old stalkers' path make for comfortable walking. A short day on the hill lets you choose among all the interesting ways down through the woods at day's end.

West Highland Way in Lairig Mor above Kinlochleven

Start out of **Kinlochleven** along the B863 towards the north side of Loch Leven and Fort William. At the village edge, fork up right on the signposted footpath of the **West Highland Way**. It slants uphill, crossing the tarred lane of Mamore Lodge, to reach a high track along the 250m contour.

Turn left on this wide, smooth track, still the West Highland Way. It contours above Loch Leven then turns up the valley of **Allt Nathrach** (serpent stream). ▶

Across the stream you may notice the steep descending path of the return route.

Follow the wide track through a pass and past the 'dangerous building' of **Tigh-na-sleubhaich**. After another 400 metres, cross a footbridge beside the track's ford. After another 1km, beside stone sheep-handling pens, turn off left onto a path with a wobbly signpost for Loch Leven Side. The path fords the stream (**Allt na Lairige Moire**) – or cross just upstream at a rocky narrows. The path slants uphill, southwest. Just below the top of the heather, at a small cairn (NN 108630), fork up left on a smaller path. Once out of the heather and on grass, you can head up anywhere to the ridge crest. Join the fence running uphill, east, along the crest, crossing it to reach the cylinder trig point on **Mam na Gualainn**.

Head down east, across a wide damp col, and then drop slightly right, on a small path, to a lower col and the narrow ridge up to **Beinn na Caillich**.

Direct descent ahead is very steep. So, from the final cairn, backtrack 20 metres or so, and head down steeply north for 60m to a small shelf with a pool. Here meet a good path that heads to the right and zigzags down steeply, to join Beinn na Caillich's east ridge below its steep section. At the 450m contour the ridge steepens again; here the path heads down onto the right (Loch Leven) side, then crosses the crest and heads down north-east. It is quite steep and eroded down to a footbridge over **Allt Nathrach**. It continues up to a kissing gate, and continues as a peaty trod to join the **West Highland Way** track above.

Turn right and retrace the outward route along this track. You can return along the WH Way path of the outward route. If the sun is setting along Loch Leven, you may prefer to stay high. So continue along the track, past a radio mast. At **Mamore Lodge** turn downhill. Just below the hotel a path forks down left, with a waymark pole. It crosses the **Allt Coire na Ba** at a footbridge, then rises gently for 150 metres to a waymarked junction. Turn downhill on a steep zigzag path to the **Grey Mare's Tail** waterfall, then return for 100 metres to cross a footbridge with the car park just beyond.

42 Kinlochleven's Pipeline Path

Start/finish	Grey Mare's car park, Kinlochleven NN 187622
Distance	11km/7 miles
Ascent	450m/1500ft
Approx time	4hr
Max altitude	High track 400m
Terrain	Paths, sometimes small and steep, and track

Length

Difficulty

With the closure of Kinlochleven's aluminium works, funding came for a network of waymarked walks by woodland and riverside and on the lower slopes of the mountains. Where those mountains are the Mamores, even the low slopes are rather high. This walk takes you to a waterfall that'll be just as good whether it's swollen with rain or a mass of winter icicles. Above, you'll wander the 300m contour with a view past the Pap of Glencoe along one of Scotland's loveliest sea lochs.

Pap of Glencoe, Loch Leven and Mamore Lodge, from the high track above Kinlochleven

131

Grey Mare's Tail
waterfall at the start
of most routes out
of Kinlochleven

Start along
the smooth
path at the back of
the car park, turning
up left at multicoloured
waymarks. It soon drops to
a footbridge. Cross this, and turn
left (blue waymark arrow) to reach
the foot of the **Grey Mare's Tail** waterfall.

Return past the footbridge, continuing left of the
stream for another 100 metres. Now the path turns up
left at a waymark post. It is rather loose and eroded as
it climbs steeply under birch trees. Emerging from the

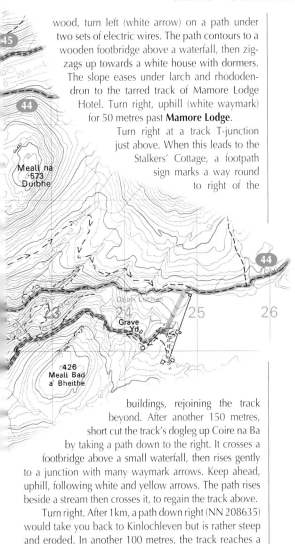

wood, turn left (white arrow) on a path under two sets of electric wires. The path contours to a wooden footbridge above a waterfall, then zig-zags up towards a white house with dormers. The slope eases under larch and rhododendron to the tarred track of Mamore Lodge Hotel. Turn right, uphill (white waymark) for 50 metres past **Mamore Lodge**.

Turn right at a track T-junction just above. When this leads to the Stalkers' Cottage, a footpath sign marks a way round to right of the buildings, rejoining the track beyond. After another 150 metres, short cut the track's dogleg up Coire na Ba by taking a path down to the right. It crosses a footbridge above a small waterfall, then rises gently to a junction with many waymark arrows. Keep ahead, uphill, following white and yellow arrows. The path rises beside a stream then crosses it, to regain the track above.

Turn right. After 1km, a path down right (NN 208635) would take you back to Kinlochleven but is rather steep and eroded. In another 100 metres, the track reaches a pass with a view ahead to **Loch Eilde Mor**.

Keep on down the track for another 400 metres, when a cairn marks a path on the right. It crosses stepping stones, then forks right (the smaller left fork just leads to the loch shore). The path bends round to right of a knoll, to the dam across the loch's outflow.

Cross the dam, and turn right on a narrow muddy track that runs above a concrete **waterpipe**. After 1.8km the track crosses the pipe to run below it; 200 metres later, look out for the cairn where the path turns steeply down to the right.

The path zigzags down into birchwood, becoming rather rough. At the slope foot, turn right on a much gentler path. This runs above the **River Leven**, with a long wooden footbridge across a side stream with a waterfall.

Just outside Kinlochleven bear left on the main path to a junction of tracks. Keep ahead following a West Highland Way marker along Wade's Road. ◄ In 50 metres bear left on a path under larches beside the river, soon to join the tarred path of the WH Way. Keep ahead under the road bridge of the B863, to a tarred path continuing along the right bank of River Leven.

The path bends right, past black garages, to an earth path that follows Kinlochleven's other river, **Allt Coire na Ba**, upstream. It runs under hazels to join a street. Turn left to cross the main B863 road into Wade's Road, which leads back to the car park.

Ahead now would lead back to the car park.

43 Blackwater Dam

Start/finish	Kinlochleven NN 189619
Distance	16.5km/10 miles
Ascent	400m/1300ft
Approx time	4.5hr
Max altitude	Blackwater Dam 340m
Terrain	Path and track

Length
■ ■ □ □ □

Difficulty
■ ■ □ □ □

In an area where low-level walks are rare, this is, quite simply, the good one. It leads through beautiful woodlands into rugged country, with an easy return along a high track.

The glen of River Leven on the path to Blackwater Dam

There's parking alongside River Leven past the Ice Factor (ice-climbing wall), or a formal car park behind the Visitor Centre library (NN 187618). **Start** along the track to right of River Leven, past the old aluminium works, to turn left across the river on a track bridge. Turn right onto a small path signed for Blackwater Dam and marked as Ciaran Path.

Keep ahead on this path. After 1.2km it crosses the footbridge of **Allt na h-Eilde**, then climbs. ▶ Keep ahead, following the river valley, with a waterfall high on the other side, whose flow depends on water being released at the top of the hydro pipe.

At its high point, a path from above left joins, the Pipeline Path (Route 42).

The path descends gently to a riverside meadow, passing concrete pillars and foundations of prisoner-of-war huts from World War II. The path continues in woods above the river, and is very beautiful. It dips into a little gorge, with a fallen bridge, but an easy crossing anyway unless in spate. Then it climbs onto moorland, where it passes above the two **Dubh Lochans** to join the high pipeline from Loch Eilde. After 500 metres, you arrive at the corner of **Blackwater Reservoir**.

The walkway across the dam has low but padlocked gates. Many walkers cross anyway (and the Scottish access law includes a presumption in favour of dam tops). One alternative is to head down concrete and bare rock along the dam foot; otherwise retreat 15 metres along the approach path and turn left onto a small path along the down-valley edge of scattered birch below the dam.

At the wide swathe of bare rock that's the valley's occasional waterway, the small path is lost. Cross into scattered birch on crushed rock. Below the centre of the dam is a fenced hut. From this a faint track runs to the right, soon joining a clearer one, which in turn joins the main track from the southern end of the dam.

Follow this track, and its culvert, down-valley. After a stream crossing, a knoll on the right has the low concrete gravestones of some of the navvies who built the dam. ◄

One is labelled as 'unknown'. The men were buried as they died in their mud-stained work clothing, their cheeks unshaven.

The track follows the conduit; you can walk on either. At the hydro pipe top, the **West Highland Way**'s broad path joins from up on the left. The track ahead winds downhill through woods, with some short-cut paths at zigzags. It passes below a small, high dam, then rejoins the pipeline, and crosses it just above the old aluminium works. Keep ahead on the track to River Leven and the Ice Factor.

44 The Back of the Blackwater

Start/finish	Kinlochleven NN 189619
Distance	26.5km/16.5 miles
Ascent	1150m/3800ft
Approx time	9.5hr
Max altitude	Glas Bheinn 792m
Terrain	Paths, rough grassy hillsides

Route 44
Back of the Blackwater

Beinn na Cloiche

45

Glas Bheinn

Loch Eilde Mor

46

Loch Chiarain bothy

44

← to Kinlochleven

42

River Leven

43

Blackwater Reservoir

N

0   1   2
km

Away from the main mountain areas, this is a taste of the wild moorland. The ground is pathless, the solitude complete. You'll grab a Corbett, 2597ft Glas Bheinn, and even one from the next lower category of hill heights, a Graham, 2120ft Beinn na Cloiche. This long ramble into the back country can be made into an easy two-dayer using the bothy at Loch Chiarain.

Start by following Route 43 to the north end of **Blackwater Dam**.

Cross the culvert arriving from the left, and follow sketchy paths above the shore of **Blackwater Reservoir**. A better path soon forms, about 200 metres in from the reservoir. It bends left alongside the small river Allt an Inbhir. After 500 metres there's a Celtic cross monument visible on the opposite side. As the river turns north, the path crosses it and keeps its previous direction, northeast,

The bothy has working fireplaces, so it's worth carrying in some fuel.

over a spur. Still northeast it drops slightly to join a new stream, follow it briefly, then contour to the bothy at the foot of **Loch Chiarain** (13km; 4.5hr). ◄

Go straight up the grassy slope behind the bothy, northwest at first, with the uphill direction bending imperceptibly right (north) to the summit of **Beinn na Cloiche**. This has outcrops, pools, and a small cairn.

Head down southwest for 400 metres/5min, then turn down right, west, to cross the valley floor 500 metres to right of **Lochan Tom Ailein**. This lets you take the slope opposite to right of its steepest part. After a stiff climb, reach the smoothly rounded northern ridge of **Glas Bheinn** and proceed pleasantly and gently up it to the well-built summit cairn.

For a longer but beautiful continuation, divert now to Route 42 the Pipeline Path.

Descend gentle slopes southwest. These get rough and heathery below 550m, so aim to join the stalkers' path at its closest point. Turn right along it; the path is washed out in places. After crossing the southern slopes of Point 558, it drops to contour pleasantly above **Loch Eilde Mor** to its southwest corner. ◄

Cross the dam at the beginning of the pipeline to Blackwater. The path bends round right and back left to join a track. Turn up left for 600 metres through a broad col, then turn off left on clear well-built path that climbs slightly onto a ridgeline. The path then descends rather steeply and eroded, eventually in woods.

After a gate through a deer fence, a path to the right with waymark arrows leads to the **Grey Mare's Tail** waterfall. Otherwise keep ahead, to join a wide path that in a few steps reaches the Grey Mare's car park in **Kinlochleven**. Turn left along Wade's Road to a track bridge over River Leven, with the walk start just downstream.

45 Loch Eilde Mor to Lairig Leacach

Start	Grey Mare's car park, Kinlochleven NN 188623
Finish	Spean Bridge NN 222817
Distance	30km/18.5 miles
Ascent	650m/2200ft
Approx time	2 short days (9hr going)
Max altitude	Meall Mor col 600m
Terrain	Tracks and path
Transport back	Citylink coach Spean Bridge to Ballachulish, then local bus to Kinlochleven
Sketch map	See overview map (page 13)

Length
■ ■ ■ ■ □

Difficulty
■ ■ □ □ □

The one problem with this route is the river crossing at Luibeilt, difficult after rain and impossible after heavy rain. Otherwise it's the easiest through route in the area, nearly all on smooth tracks. While it passes through seriously remote country, it does have two bothies for shelter. A good choice for a first-ever backpack trip – just so long as the river isn't in spate.

A worthy pre-amble would be to cross from Kings House to Kinlochleven by the Devil's Staircase of the West Highland Way. This is equal to the main walk in easiness and scenery, and gives a short first day to shops and shelter. It's also convenient, as Kings House and Spean Bridge are served by one Citylink coach.

Start from Kinlochleven's Grey Mare's car park, and follow green waymarks. Don't be discouraged by the steep climb to start – there won't be more like that, so just enjoy the birch trees. The green arrows lead to the high track below Na Gruagaichean (see Route 33). Turn right, after 2km passing through a col. The track then passes to left of **Loch Eilde Mor** and **Loch Eilde Beag**, before ending at the ruined house at **Luibeilt** (11.5km, 4hr).

Just upstream from the house is the crossing point of the Abhainn Rath, on jagged red boulders. If the river is

For more detail of this first section see Route 33.

Meanach bothy, at the intersection of many long paths

too full, the first option is to head 6km downstream past Staoineag bothy to the bridge at **Creaguaineach Lodge**; then take either Route 5 to **Corrour station** or Route 24 to **Spean Bridge**. The second option is to head upstream, crossing further up or switching into Route 5 out to **Glen Nevis** (22km, 5.5hr, Luibeilt to Fort William). All of these are fine walks.

Having successfully crossed Abhainn Rath, the bothy at **Meanach** is over on the right. But the path of this route turns left upstream briefly, then heads up, north, beside **Allt nam Fang**. The path is old but still fairly firm and dry, and the stream alongside has waterfalls. As the stream dwindles and then turns away north, the path keeps ahead, northeast, through a wide flat col. It crosses Allt Feith nan Sac and other streams, as it slants down around the flank of Stob Ban to reach **Lairig Leacach bothy** (17.5km, 6hr).

A track runs north through the steep-sided **Lairig Leacach** pass, and down through a plantation. Back in the open, it descends grassland to **Corriechoille** and the end of a tarred lane below. Thus runs alongside River Spean for 3km to **Spean Bridge**. ◄

For a slightly longer finish through woodland see Route 24.

46 Gleann Iolairean or Leum Uilleim to Corrour

Start	Kinlochleven NN 189619
Finish	Corrour station NN 355664
Distance	24km/15 miles (Treig); 22.5km/ 14 miles (Uilleim)
Ascent	600m/2000ft (Treig); 1050m/3500ft (Uilleim)
Approx time	1 day or 2 short ones (7.5hr Treig/8.5hr Uilleim)
Max altitude	Leum Uilleim 902m
Terrain	Rough paths and grassy hillsides
Sketch map	See overview map (page 13)

Length

Difficulty

This is rougher backpacking than Route 45 (Loch Eilde Mor), with a path that vanishes here and there. After a green beginning to the Blackwater Dam, it passes through bleak and unpeopled country and a bothy that really is at the back of beyond. Consult the overview map on page 12 to see how this can also be a trail to Glen Nevis or Spean Bridge.

Leum Uilleim is a grassy hump with great views. With the cloud down, you'd probably prefer the dramatic little valley to Loch Treig.

Start by following Route 43 to the north end of **Blackwater Dam**.

Cross the end of the culvert arriving from the left, and turn right on sketchy paths along or just above the shore of **Blackwater Reservoir**. A better path soon forms – a lapsed stalkers' path – about 200 metres away from the reservoir. It bends left alongside the small river **Allt an Inbhir**. As the river turns north, the path crosses it and keeps its previous direction, northeast, over a spur. Still northeast it drops slightly to join a new stream, follows it briefly, then contours to the bothy at the foot of **Loch Chiarain** (13km, 4.5hr). ▶

The bothy has a fireplace, so it's worth carrying in fuel.

141

Creaguainich Lodge at the head of Loch Treig

- **To Corrour by Gleann Iolairean**

  In bad weather, or if your destination is not Corrour but Fort William or Spean Bridge, then continue above the bothy on a path that at once drops to the side of Loch Chiarain. Along the valley that follows, the path sometimes disappears as it crosses the firm stony grass of a stream run-off. Keep along the foot of the left-hand slope and the path should reappear.

  As the slope on the left steepens across the foot of **Meall a' Bhainne**, the path rises about 10–20m above the valley floor. It is mostly firm and quite comfortable. Once through the pass, the path (now boggy) runs down to left of a new stream, and joins the track by **Loch Treig** at a SRWS green signpost towards you saying 'Kinlochleven' (19km from Kinlochleven; 6hr going).

  Here you would turn left for **Fort William** (Route 5, 28.5km, 7.5hr to Fort William) or for Spean Bridge (Route 24, 19.5km 5.5hr). For **Corrour** turn right across a bridge. After a second bridge the track turns uphill away from the reservoir. After 2km it turns left, passing under the railway by a bridge which also has a stream passing under it.

For Corrour station don't pass under the railway, but keep ahead over the stream, and take a green track that keeps to right of the railway. The track can get very wet for the last 1km to Corrour station.

For Loch Ossian youth hostel stay on the track as it passes under the railway alongside the stream, then reappears across the stream running southeast around the flank of Beinn na Lap. After 2km you can fork right onto a rough old track, or keep ahead on the smooth new one. Either way, you join a big track at the head of **Loch Ossian**, with the youth hostel just ahead and Corrour station 1km up to the right.

- **To Corrour by Leum Uilleim**
  From **Loch Chiarain** it's almost as easy to get to Corrour over the Corbett Leum Uilleim (less

Leum Uilleim stands at the edge of Rannoch Moor

distance, more climb). If you're overnighting in the bothy, you can make an afternoon up-and-down of this undemanding hill.

Cross stepping-stones below the bothy at the foot of Loch Chiarain. Even if the stones are underwater, this wide sandy bit of river is the best wading point. Above the stepping-stones there's a small path, which is most welcome as it gets you up into the zone of shorter grass. Moderate grassy slops lead up to the preliminary top **Beinn a' Bhric**. Its final ridge has small outcrops of orange rock.

From the small cairn on Beinn a' Bhric you may need to take a compass bearing to avoid being carried down slopes southwards. Make a way east down a short but steep slope to reach a wide col. Head east up the slope opposite to summit **Leum Uilleim** with its fair-sized cairn with small shelter arms.

Retrace your steps westwards into the wide col. Contour round right, eventually north, below the northeast ridge of Beinn a' Bhric, finding quad-bike wheelmarks. The quad-bike trail climbs very slightly, to reach the crest of the northeast ridge, and goes straight down it. The faint track over short grass and moss is a very pleasant stroll. At the levelling at 580m, wheelmarks go down right towards **Corrour station**, but keep ahead northeast off the ridge end, as this gives you just a few hundred metres of rough tussocks to the **Allt a' Chamabhreac**. Before the railway turn right on the rough track to Corrour station.

PART SIX

GLEN COE

The A82 runs eastwards into Glen Coe, between dark walls of Aonach Eagach (left) and Bidean nam Bian

Glen Coe, Glen Coe – it's the place to go. Nowhere else in Britain has such a concentration of absolutely top mountains. Having been up Bidean nam Bian for this book four more times, I'll say there's no other hill with such richness of interest. Its Summit Summary is in Part 7.

But then there's Beinn a' Bheithir, the Thunderbolt, a classic high ridge-line. There's Buachaille Etive Mor, the mountain for climbers of rock and ice, but still supplying another lovely ridgeline behind its classic pointed pyramid. There's Buachaille Beag, with the same atmosphere but on a smaller and more approachable scale. And looking at them all from across the glen is the thrilling ridge of the Aonach Eagach, the hillwalkers' moun-taineering bit.

What the glen doesn't have is attractive low-level walks. Routes 49 and 50 (Signal Rock and the Hospital Loch) are short and rather tame. Route 58 (Lost Valley) is short, but is at least adventurous. Route 56 (the Two Passes) is, if you catch it in the week when the bogs dry out, a long and satisfying plod. All these are ways of resting the legs before the next fierce, fantastic, big hill.

145

47 The Thunderbolt:
Beinn a' Bheithir

Start/finish	Ballachulish NN 083585
Distance	15.5km/9.5 miles
Ascent	1300m/4400ft
Approx time	7–7.5hr
Max altitude	Sgorr Dhearg 1024m
Terrain	Ridge paths, but a rough descent
Map	Harveys Glen Coe doesn't cover the descent

Beinn a' Bheithir means Hill of the Thunderbolt – and it's certainly a cracker. This is classic ridgewalking, pleasantly narrow in parts, but without scrambling. (If you want scrambling, Sgorr Bhan's northeast ridge is Grade 1.) There's an easy descent from between the two Munro summits, but this route completes the horseshoe beyond Sgorr Dhonuill, with a steep descent into Coire Dearg.

Start at the information centre and car park at the east end of Ballachulish village (East Laroch) below a slate quarry face.

Leave the car park by its entrance, and take the village street opposite (southwest) past a useful Co-op shop. After 500 metres the street crosses **River Laroch**, with a footbridge alongside. Turn left, following an SRWS signpost with its writing on the back, to pass a primary school. Just after it, a gate on the right leads onto open hill.

Go straight up quite steep grass, to a low fence crossing at 250m. Not far above (depending on where you crossed the fence) a small path runs across to the right, onto the northern spur of Sgorr Bhan. The path turns left up this. It is fairly eroded, often down to bare rock (grey schist).

Beinn a' Bheithir, the Hill of the Thunderbolt. The Munros are Sgorr Dheirg (back left) and Sgorr Dhonuill (right).

Sgorr Dhonuill from the slopes of Sgorr Dheirg

After the levelling of **Beinn Bhan**, the ridge steepens, with one path taking to the right flank – but following the crest is good. The rock changes to quartzite, whence 'Sgorr Bhan' (white peak). A sharp elegant ridge leads to **Sgorr Bhan**, and then to the first Munro, **Sgorr Dhearg**.

In mist you might be tempted onto a sharp, pathed, ridge running north – but the correct path turns left, southwest, down a broader slope to the **757m col**. ◄ The ridge path continues ahead, quite steeply at first. After a knoll at 950m, where the side ridge to Point 782m (the Dragon's Tooth) branches off, a narrower and slightly rocky ridge leads up to **Sgorr Dhonuill**.

Here a popular descent route runs down north into the forest.

Descend a wide ridge west, with drops on the right and views of islands ahead (Lismore, Mull, Jura). At the ridge base (NN 031554), a gully down right has a cairn at its head. Easier is to continue 100 metres over the next slight rise to the next dip. Turn right to confront the drop into **Coire Dearg** (NN 030555), then slant down left, passing along the base of a small crag, to the top of a wide scree slope. Directly below is a gully cleft. Pass straight down the scree to just above the cleft (NN 0310 5573 – a lone Sitka spruce grows in the scree). Now slant down left, still on scree, for 100 metres to a clump of

Sitka spruce. Descend directly to the grassy corrie floor. Keep directly downhill, through fence remains, and pick up a rebuilt path that starts at a boulder (NN 0327 5609). It runs into forest to left of a stream, and follows it to the corner of a forest road.

Turn right (blue marker arrow), and follow the main track gently downhill. Above South Ballachulish keep ahead with a waymark for St John's Church. From **St John's Church**, follow the pavement of the A82 to the edge of Ballachulish village. Move right, onto the old main road running parallel. Before the junction on the outward route (near the Co-op), turn left into a street that bends right then offers a short path between trees into the car park.

48 Meall Lighiche and Sgor na h-Ulaidh

Start/finish	Parking 200 metres east of Gleann Leac na Muidhe track end NN 120564
Distance	14.5km/9 miles
Ascent	1100m/3700ft
Approx time	6.5hr
Max altitude	Sgor na h-Ulaidh 994m
Terrain	Grassy ridges, a steep, broken hillside, path and track

Length

Difficulty

Gleann Leac na Muidhe is green and fertile, as the name 'Slab of the Milk-churn' suggests. Here was the home of the MacDonalds' chieftain in the days before the Massacre. At its head lies Sgor na h-Ulaidh, one of the less-visited Munros. Its 'standard' route, a straight up-and-down from the upper glen, is used here for the descent – the little path beside the stream is a delight. Fiercer is the first half of the day, with extra effort added by the Corbett Meall Lighiche, followed by a steep ascent to the main mountain.

Route 48
**Meall Lighiche and
Sgurr na h-Ulaidh**

P P

GLEN COE

Gleann Leac na Muidhe

48

Bidean nam Bian

Meall Lighiche

△

Sgor na
h-Ulaidh

N

0 1 2
━━━━━ km

Start up the smooth track into **Gleann Leac na Muidhe**
(private road, no parking). The track crosses a bridge to
houses. Keep on the track, past a farm, to its end at a gate
below a plantation corner (NN 106545; the route can be
cycled to this point).

A rough path continues ahead. Where it approaches
the stream after 200 metres, cross at an island – the footbridge on old maps has been swept away. Head up onto
the spur of **Creag Bhan**. Turn left along the crest, with
the first knoll offering scrambling (bypassed down right
if necessary). Grassy wide ridgeline leads up to the top
of Creag Bhan, where the ridge levels and bends right
(west). Now a small path and old metal fence stakes lead
over a preliminary knoll to the small cairn at the summit
of **Meall Lighiche**.

Return along the old fence to the end of the level section, then follow the fence down right, quite steeply, to a

broad col. Here the fence has a metal gate still standing (NN 104524). Above, the fence runs up to crags, so stop following it and head away slightly to the right, south. Slant up steep ground, to right of a small stream to start with. At 750m head straight uphill, southeast, on steep grass. As a slight re-entrant forms, keep to its right-hand side (west) to reach the ridge-end knoll **Corr na Beinne** (NN 1056 5157). Follow the easy ridge eastwards, level at first, soon joined from below by the fence remnant, to the summit of **Sgor na h-Ulaidh**.

Head east for 100 metres, then turn northeast down a fairly well defined ridgeline. As it steepens, take a path down the left flank (northeast, not east-northeast down the crest) to reach the col below. The ridgeline opposite leads up onto **Stob an Fhuarain**.

Head down north, on ridgeline not clearly defined but with path traces, to the col at the start of **Aonach Dubh a' Ghlinne**. Here turn left (west) to head straight down grassy slopes and join the stream below. A charming small path follows the right bank of the stream back to the gate at the plantation corner.

In reverse When descending northwest from Ulaidh people have got into difficulties among crags. If attempting this, follow the west ridge right out to Corr na Beinne; even from there, it's tricky.

Sgor na h-Ulaidh (back left) and slopes of Meall Lighiche, from the stream-crossing point on Route 48

49 Signal Rock

Length
■ □ □ □ □

Difficulty
■ □ □ □ □

Start/finish	Former Visitor Centre NN 126564
Distance	2.5km/1.5 miles
Ascent	100m/300ft
Approx time	1hr
Max altitude	Signal Rock 70m
Terrain	Paths

The Signal Rock was used to gather Clan MacDonald in the centuries before the massacre. It is an atmospheric spot, even if the views would benefit from some clear-felling. So short a walk scarcely needs the pub break after the first mile – but it could be a summer evening stroll after a Clachaig pub meal.

Start at the unsigned tarmac car park where the Glencoe Visitor Centre once stood – considered intrusive, it has been resited 2km down the valley.

A tarred path runs to a footbridge over the **River Coe**. Across it, turn back up left, to a gate in a deer fence marked 'An Torr'. The wide path runs into woods, after

150 metres forking, with ahead signed 'Signal Rock' and right signed 'Clachaig Inn and An Torr' (which you'll follow on the way back).

Take the Signal Rock path ahead, over a ridge and down to a path junction. The wide main path to the right is signed 'Signal Rock'. It passes out through a gate in a deer fence, across a faint track, and up to **Signal Rock**. Scramble the front, or take a path around the knoll to steps at the back.

Return to the junction with the path signed for Clachaig, and now turn left onto that path. It runs above and to left of the Clachaig Inn, passing a small path sharp back left. ▶ The main path ahead drops through a gate in a deer fence, to reach the road through a kissing gate.

Turn right past **Clachaig Inn**, to a road sign (clearway) just after its car park. Here turn off right on a path (entangled in places with a stream) to the riverside. Bear right along the riverside, to the footbridge across River Coe.

This runs for 200 metres through forest to the minimal viewpoint An Torr, a rock knoll surrounded by trees.

50 Hospital Lochan

Start/finish	Hospital Forest car park NN 105593
Distance	2.5km/1.5 miles
Ascent	100m/300ft
Approx time	1hr
Max altitude	110m
Terrain	Smooth paths

Length

Difficulty

A short walk on pre-laid paths through a plantation – but it involves a wooded lochan, and great views of Loch Leven and Beinn a' Bheithir.

At the east edge of Glencoe village, the main street crosses the River Coe. At once, a tarred driveway on the left leads towards Glencoe Hospital and is marked with a forest walks signboard. Drive up it, and where it bends left to

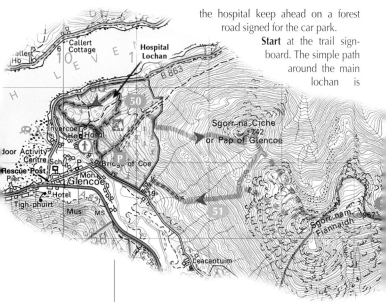

the hospital keep ahead on a forest road signed for the car park.

Start at the trail signboard. The simple path around the main lochan is waymarked with 'Red Indian' feathers, because of a story (which you can read on the signboard) about Lord Strathcona and his quarter-Indian homesick wife. But head out of the car park uphill, following the blue-top posts of the mountain trail, immediately

*Hospital Lochan at
Glencoe village*

154

turning right and climbing. After quite a stiff ascent the path contours left to a viewpoint with a picnic table. Past this it drops to the side of the **Hospital Lochan**.

Turn right around the lochan, following the red-feathered waymarks. Pass across the end of the lochan and down its northwest side to its west corner. The car park is ahead around the lochan, but turn right, now following yellow-top posts. The path wanders through woods, gradually bending left. On the right a short side-path branches off to a bench; then another leads to a viewpoint with a railing – the view is to Beinn a' Bheithir. The path bends left away from the sea view, through woods, clear and waymarked. Ignore a smaller side-path on the right. The path descends to a cross-track (left to the lochan, right to Glencoe Hospital). Cross it to pass a rhododendron pool, and regain the car park.

51 Pap of Glencoe

Start/finish	Hospital Forest car park
	NN 105593
Distance	6.5km/4 miles
Ascent	750m/2500ft
Approx time	3.5hr
Max altitude	Pap of Glencoe 742m
Terrain	Steep rough hillsides and paths

Length

Difficulty

It's not just the name that's provocative; this is the area's outstanding small hill, with rocks at the top making some scrambling likely. You could include Sgorr nam Fiannaidh for a walk of 9km with 1100m climb (5.5 miles, 3600ft, 5hr), then get the second of Aonach Eagach's Munros, with hardly any Aonach Eagach scrambling, by Route 53.

The Pap of Glencoe from Ballachulish Bridge

Start back towards the public road for 300 metres. Just before the bend right to the public road, a clear small path heads up left, to right of a stream, through a narrow gateway in old fencing. At a forest road a log-and-earth ramp marks the continuing path, now to left of the stream. It climbs steeply, then runs along a clearing under low-voltage power lines. At the high point of the wires (NN 111596) the path turns up right, under trees. It reaches the forest top at a fence bend without a stile (NN 1126 5951).

Turn right on a small path above the trees, then head uphill to a levelling. A dry stream on the right has paths alongside. At the stream top the path contours southwest towards the Pap-back col, but head left up the rough hillside. At the foot of the final outcrops, you may find the old path (NN 1242 5933) giving one easy way through to the rocky summit of **Pap of Glencoe**.

A slightly trodden direct **descent** southeast involves some easy scrambling. Easier is to descend northeast towards Loch Leven for 50 metres, when the path turns back right along the foot of the outcrops. (The two routes rejoin at NN 1255 5932.) Various paths zigzag stonily down to the wide Pap-back col. ▶

Arriving on the slabby summit of the Pap of Glencoe

To bag Sgorr nam Fiannaidh now, head straight up the pathless ridge opposite, then east along gentle ridge. Descend using Route 52.

A path of stones and peat runs down to the right, crossing a small stream then slanting down and left (south). At the 430m contour it turns back right and improves, to run down to left of a ravine. At the ravine foot, take the path contouring right to a smooth track, and descend this to the road near a plantation edge.

Turn right, and after 400 metres fork left onto a riverside path to the car park turn-off.

52 Aonach Eagach

Length
■ ■ ■ ☐ ☐

Difficulty
■ ■ ■ ■ ■
(scramble Grade 2)

Start	Allt-na-reigh NN 173568
Finish	Old road near Glencoe village NN 112586
Distance	8.5km/5.5 miles (plus 7km/4.5 miles valley floor back to start)
Ascent	1200m/4000ft
Approx time	6–7hr (+ 1.5hr valley floor)
Max altitude	Sgorr nam Fiannaidh 967m
Terrain	Exposed scrambling (Grade 2) on good rock

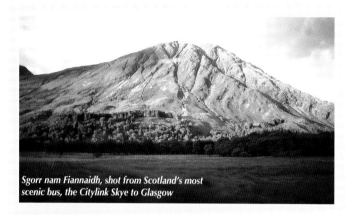

Sgorr nam Fiannaidh, shot from Scotland's most scenic bus, the Citylink Skye to Glasgow

The Aonach Eagach, or Notched Ridge, links the two Munro hills on the north side of Glen Coe – so much so that the names of the actual hills, Sgorr nam Fiannaidh and Meall Dearg, are almost unknown.

Glen Coe's many excellent scrambling routes are well described in Cicerone's *Scrambles in Lochaber* (see Appendix 3) and so are not covered here. However, as one of the most popular and best ridges in Scotland, the Aonach Eagach has to be included.

While it is not technically difficult, the hardest section has truly terrifying drops on both sides. *Scrambles in Lochaber* gives it a Grade 2 – implying that a rope would not normally be used in dry summer conditions – and I agree. Other authors have given it Grade 3, considering its exposure rather than actual difficulty. One even attaches Grade 3S, equivalent to a rock-climbing grade of Mod or Diff and certainly requiring the protection of a rope; that author must have taken the difficult option at the end of the Crazy Pinnacles.

While many hundreds of people cross the ridge every year, one or two do come to grief. Most rescues involve walkers cragfast and unable to continue or retreat, or else benighted on the final descent from the ridge. In the three years 2003–06 just two walkers fell from the ridge, one of them losing his life.

If the party includes the inexperienced or nervous, a short length of rope could be carried by a member who understands its use – 10m is enough to protect the end of the Crazy Pinnacles and the chimney pitch.

That rope could be kept concealed in the rucksack so as not to cause premature alarm.

There is *no safe descent* off the ridge between Am Bodach and Stob Coire Leith, apart from the ridge of Meall Dearg running unhelpfully north towards Loch Leven. More helpfully, though: on a westbound crossing, up as far as the Crazy Pinnacles, the difficulties are all in descent. So if you do turn back, retreat eastwards from the Crazy Pinnacles will be considerably easier than it was getting there.

Scramblers enjoying the rock moves on Aonach Eagach ridge

The car park is on the north (uphill) side of the road, 200 metres down from Allt-na-reigh. **Start** up the rough path slanting right. After 20 metres is the start of path repairs (not from the car park itself, as that might encourage casual walkers). The path is rebuilt or on bare rock to 450m altitude.

Alternatively a Grade 2 scramble, from the Study straight up onto A' Chailleach, is described in *Scrambles in Lochaber*. Good when dry, but its mossy central section is slimy when wet.

Now the ridge steepens, with an outcrop just above. Here the path bends back left (a small path ahead is a variant by Allt Ruigh's green valley). It zigzags northwest up the steep spur, with short sections over bare rock giving easy scrambling, finally becoming grassier and less steep to the first cairn on **Am Bodach**. Continue for 100 metres to a second cairn, at the true summit.

The ridge bends left (northwest) and narrows. Soon it steepens. Easy scrambling down the crest leads to a levelling. Here the well-trodden path descends on the right, by short rock steps and exposed ledges, then a gangway slants down left to a notch in the crest above a steep tower. Go through this notch, and down two moves of blocky scrambling, onto slabs to left (south) of the crest. Take a ledge slanting down left to the slab's edge, then another ledge back right, to an old fence post at the base of the steep tower.

The path runs on along level ridge for a few steps, then descends bare rock on the left. There are various well-worn lines here, but the easiest one descends towards Glen Coe (south) straight down the ridge side, to a path running to the right. Descend a short slab step to regain the ridge crest at another fence post below the difficulties.

The path crosses a col northwest, and rises gently to a preliminary top (approx 920m, cairn). Here turn right, and descend a steep eroded slope to a col. Climb steep grass paths on the north flank, onto a grass ridge where old fence posts lead to the summit of **Meall Dearg**.

From here to Stob Coire Leith the ridge is narrow and almost continuously interesting. The way is well used and clear. Significant features are a narrow gully/chimney rising from a col; a gully descending to the right, with big holds on the rocks to its left; and a rock tower climbed on the left over a worn slab (look for a high handhold on the right for the awkward step onto the slab). A narrow arête leads to a sudden drop: just before this scramble down left, steep but with many handholds. Another narrow arête across a col is balanced along or avoided just down on the left.

After all this, the ridge narrows spectacularly to the so-called **Crazy Pinnacles**. A well-worn route passes to right of each of the pinnacles, to the col before a final 5m wall. The well-used direct ascent of this is a rock-climbing move of at least Moderate standard in an exposed situation. However, passing to the right will reveal an easier way on the north side, where some dampness of the rock is offset by largeness of handholds. ◄

> There is an exposed path on loose dirt descending on the right (north) side, avoiding the Crazy Pinnacles; this looks less safe, and possibly more difficult, than the rocky way described.

While the Crazy Pinnacles form the hardest section, three challenging moments remain along the ridge. A squarish rock tower is climbed by a shallow, open chimney on the left; as this steepens at its top, a fine final handhold is directly overhead. There's a long, slabby descent on outward-sloping ledges. At the lowest point of the ridge, a narrow col leads to a steep groove; after the first step, this becomes easy, and the dirty and exposed path avoiding it on the right again looks nastier.

The ridge path leads over quartzite rock of **Stob Coire Leith** (2–3hr from Am Bodach). It continues onto **Sgorr nam Fiannaidh**, where a stone trig pillar stands within a large shelter cairn.

The **descent** is where late or slow parties can get into difficulties. Continue west for 600 metres to a cairned col (NN 135583). Now the direct descent southwest, to right of Clachaig Gully to Clachaig Inn, is not recommended due to its steepness and looseness, and the risk of injuring oneself or others by falling stones. A way can be made down very steep slopes, southeast across the head of Alltan t-Sidhein and to the northern corner of Loch Achtriochtan.

The least uncomfortable descent, though, is by a rough path roughly west (marked on Harveys map). From the cairned col 600 metres west of the summit, edge round to right of the final slight rise, to head directly towards Glencoe village, with the path gradually forming down stony quartzite slopes. At 480m (NN 124586) turn left on a path descending from the Pap of Glencoe. This turns back right to descend beside a small gorge. Below the gorge, a path continuing downstream peters out in rough pastures, so take the path contouring right to join a track. This runs down to join the **Old Glencoe Road** at the end of plantations recently clear-felled.

There remains the 7km walk back to Allt-na-reigh. Two cars provide one solution, as does a strategically placed bicycle. However, the least disreputable-looking member of the party should be able to hitch-hike carrying the car keys, as most of the passing traffic is fellow walkers. Otherwise, the paths in **Route 69** make fairly pleasant walking that avoids the busy A82.

Looking east along Aonach Eagach from the slopes of Sgurr nam Fiannaidh

53 Am Bodach and the End of the Aonach Eagach

Length

■ ■ □ □ □ □

Difficulty

■ ■ ■ □ □ *or*

■ ■ ■ ■ ■

Start/finish	Altnafeadh NN 221563
Distance	14km/8.5 miles
Ascent	1050m/3400ft
Approx time	6hr
Max altitude	Am Bodach 943m
Terrain	Gentle ridgewalking, with a steep descent. Excursion to Meall Dearg is scrambling Grade 2, fairly exposed

Glen Coe abounds in high, demanding ridgewalks amidst spectacular surroundings. By contrast, A' Chailleach offers a ridgewalk over short, gentle vegetation and gravel, gently rising for 5km from the top of the Devil's Staircase. The surroundings, however, remain superb.

After Am Bodach, Meall Dearg could be reached by a first taster of the Aonach Eagach's scrambling.

It belongs to the obscure hill class called 'Metros', those that would be Munros if Munros started at 900m rather than 914.4m. Pinky-orange rhyolite boulders decorate its summit.

Start up the broad, smooth path of **Devil's Staircase**, usually companionable with WH Way walkers. It zigzags to a col. At the first of two cairns, turn left on a small rough path up gently onto **Stob Mhic Mhartuin**. Pleasant walking on smooth short grass and gravel, with occasional peat, leads to **Sron a' Choire Odhair-bhig**.

Rocky drops on the right add character to the still pleasant ridgeline onto **A' Chailleach** (903m, unnamed on most maps). ◄

Grassy ridge continues to the col before **Sron Gharbh**. This summit could be bypassed left without difficulty. In the col beyond, a large cairn marks the possible descent path left to Allt Ruigh. For now take the well-used path, over stones or easy-angled bare rock, up to the main top of **Am Bodach**.

It is now possible to use **Route 52** for an excursion to the Munro **Meall Dearg**. The descent from Am Bodach is exposed, but with big holds and at a lower level of terror – and because it's downwards, retreat will always be less difficult than it was to get there. Allow 1.5–2hr for the excursion and return to Am Bodach. Meall Dearg can also be reached without any scrambling but over rough ground, by its north ridge from the West Highland Way above Kinlochleven.

There are two **descent** routes from Am Bodach to the valley floor at Allt-na-reigh.

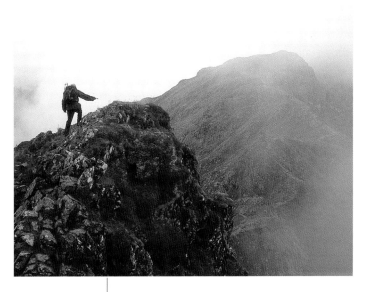

- **Allt Ruigh** Easier but less exciting. Return to the col before Sron Gharbh (NN 171581). A cairn marks the top of a path down to the right.

    This path is eroded for the first steep descent, then joins **Allt Ruigh** stream down grassy slopes. Paths now are on both sides of stream. Keep near the stream as the valley narrows, closed on the right by a small steep crag. At 500m altitude, the path contours out to the right across a steep slope towards this crag, zigzags down scree, then again contours to the right, along the crag's foot. Here it rises slightly, to join the spur path descending from the right.

- **Spur path** More rugged, this reverses Route 52. From **Am Bodach** summit, head south for 100 metres to a lower cairn. Now a clear path heads down the steep rocky spur, southeast. The path is well marked, weaving among outcrops and occasionally crossing bare rock. Below the lowest outcrop, at 500m altitude, bend right as the alternate path rejoins from the left.

The path on down is rebuilt with occasional stone steps, to the car park 200 metres west of Allt-na-reigh.

It is fairly easy for folk dressed for the hill to hitchhike up the A82. However, it is also a reasonable walk of 5km back along the valley floor. Take a small path above the road to the cottage **Allt-na-reigh**, and cross below it on the road bridge. Take another small path on the left, to where the Old Glencoe Road (NN 180563) forks up left. Follow this track past the viewpoint called **the Study**, rejoining the A82 about 1km later. Cross diagonally onto a path for 250 metres, then re-cross onto a wet grassy track that remains near the A82 for 2km, to a car park. The Old Road track continues to left of the road for another 200 metres. Use the road verge for the last 400 metres to **Altnafeadh**.

On Am Bodach, looking along the Aonach Eagach

54 Buachaille Etive Beag

Start/finish	Near the Study NN 188562
Distance	11km/7 miles
Ascent	1100m/3700ft
Approx time	6hr
Max altitude	Stob Dubh 958m
Terrain	Valley and ridge paths, and moderate grassy slopes

Routes 54 + 55
Buachaille Etive Mor
Buachaille Etive Beag

Buachaille Etive Beag means the 'Small Shepherd of Etive', but it's only small because of the company it keeps. Wedged between two of Glen Coe's giants, Bidean and Buachaille Mor, it can easily be passed over.

Better, however, to pass over it with your feet. It's a classic little ridge, technically undemanding but attractively sharp. In the original *Tables*, Buachaille Beag (being a single freestanding hill) was counted as a single Munro. But the second summit, Stob Coire Raineach, has 600ft (177m) of clear drop round it: considerably more than any other non-Munro. To the pedantic 20th century this seemed increasingly unsatisfactory, and from 1997 Buachaille Beag has been two Munros.

The standard way to get them is by a path out of Lairig Eilde to the Mam Buidhe col between; up left for Stob Coire Raineach; up right for Stob Dubh; and back down the path. But the proper way to do a ridgewalk is all the way along, so this route heads up the long pass of Lairig Eilde, to complete the classic ridge end-to-end. This gives a very scenic ascent, with views along the fjord of Loch Etive. The northwestern facet holds long streaks of snow right through the winter, which can offer a fast and exhilarating descent. Indeed, the 'Wee Buachaille' is an excellent choice for a first winter Munro.

Looking along Glen Etive from Stob Dubh of Buachaille Etive Beag

The cairn doesn't commemorate the Massacre, nor the acquisition of Glen Coe by the National Trust for Scotland, but marks the start of the coffin road through Lairig Eilde.

From this point I have watched a herd of about 100 red deer cross the ridgeline below.

From here, a rough path down left is the normal approach to the mountain; your escape line if avalanches are forecast on northwest-facing slopes (such as this route's descent line off Stob Coire Raineach).

Start from the new car park at the large domed cairn, just east of where the A82 enters a ravine at the Meeting of Three Waters. ◄

A well-made signposted path climbs gently southwest. After 600 metres it dips right, towards the river 100 metres away. At this point the 'standard route' continues ahead on a small side-path, after 400 metres turning up left between two streams to the Mam Buidhe col southwest of Stob Coire Raineach.

The main path drops slightly to cross **Allt Lairig Eilde** on monster stepping-stones. After 1.5km it recrosses, and climbs gently to its high-point, which is 200 metres east of the actual **Lairig Eilde** col. The path descends south, to cross the new stream (also called **Allt Lairig Eilde**) and go down to right of it. At 300m (NN 1717 5239) cross the stream above its small gorge, onto a small path slanting down across the grassy face above the stream, and contour round onto the grassy nose running up northwards.

A small but clear path runs straight up the ridge, which becomes a narrow grass crest. Its steepness demands pauses to look southwards along the gleaming length of Loch Etive. At the 600m contour a boulder has retained a small platform of level ground, ideal for a brief rest or longer lunchstop. ◄

Above this, the spur runs up into scree – tiresome in summer, better if snow-covered. A short section of stony ridge leads to **Stob Dubh** (Black Spike) which at 958m is the main summit of Buachaille Etive Beag.

The ridge runs down northeast, and after 200 metres it steepens. This north-facing slope gets less sun than the ground you've been on, and any snow may suddenly become harder at this point. This narrower ridge can carry a cornice, more commonly on the right-hand side. After this first descent, the ridge undulates gently. A long, gently angled, descent leads to the low col of **Mam Buidhe** ('mam bui', the yellow pass, unnamed on some maps at NN 187544). ◄

From Mam Buidhe a steeper climb leads to the summit of **Stob Coire Raineach**. Descend gently northeast onto a rocky plateau at 800m altitude. From here the descent will be northwest: but first wander out to **Stob nan Cabar**, a rocky viewpoint.

From Stob nan Cabar return across the rocky plateau to the foot of Stob Coire Raineach (NN 195552). From here descend northwest. If there is snow, simply seek out the longest streaks for a bit of fun downhill. Otherwise a comfortable way down is to follow the small spur immediately to right of the stream (Allt Coire Raineach). Once below the steep rocky ground, slant left to the path of the outward route, or head straight downhill to the closest point of the A82 road.

Stob nan Cabar, the impressive northern end of Buachaille Beag, stands above the start of the Lairig Gartain

55 The Big Buachaille

Start/finish	Altnafeadh NN 221563
Distance	13.5km/8.5 miles
Ascent	1200m/4000ft
Approx time	6.5hr
Max altitude	Stob Dearg 1022m
Terrain	Easy scrambling (Grade 1) or rough grass; hill paths

Length

Difficulty

Seen from Kings House, Buachaille Etive Mor is an iconic hill; a cone of bare rock composed of exciting rock climbs divided by gullies filled with last winter's ice. But at the back, like the tail on a tadpole, is a fine 4km ridge for walkers. In 1996 that ridge was unpathed, and I had to find my own way down the steep, steep slope of Stob Coire Altruim. The following year, Stob na Broige at the far end was elevated to Munro status; consequently, by 2006 the path down was so eroded that it was ready to receive its first helicopter loads of repair stones.

The hill is very steep on all sides, making the ridgewalk along the top very fine. By the same token, getting on and off the ridge is not such fun. The new-built path is the only pleasant way off (a descent southeast into Etive from the western knoll, NN 179518, is possible but not nice). The standard way up, by Coire na Tulaich, is an atmospheric trudge with a nasty steep scree (often snow-covered) to finish. The alternative here, a ridge just to the west, offers rough grass or an easy scramble.

You may occasionally see the hill and its neighbour named as 'Buachaille Eite'. This is correct Gaelic, but the English name for over a century has been, like the glen it guards, Etive. 'Buachaille' is a cattle herdsman.

Start at Altnafeadh, where a track leads down to a footbridge over the River Coupall. Continue on well-made path, past **Lagangarbh** cottage and up towards **Coire na Tulaich**, the corrie that's the standard walkers' route onto the Buachaille. To right of the corrie is a broad spur. Over the bottom half of this, the left side (next to Coire

The Crowberry Tower above Rannoch Wall, Buachaille Etive Mor

na Tulaich) is a ridge of rocky humps that form a Grade 3 scramble (the northeast ridge of Creag na Tulaich). To right of this is a band of steepish grass, and to right again a line of broken rocks. These rocks will be the line of ascent: they form the top edge of Creag a' Bhancair, a steep crag forming the right edge of the spur behind. ▶

Creag a' Bhancair, out of sight from here, is noted for its extremely difficult rock climbs.

The good path from Lagangarbh crosses the Allt Coire na Tulaich. After another 50 metres, strike off to the right, contouring below the foot of the Grade 3 scramble and across the grassy band onto the broken rocks. Go up gentle slabs, and then rocks above. At one point, a short drop on the left prevents escape and lends a smidgeon of commitment to the scramble; the steepish tower here is scrambled most easily from bottom left to top centre.

At 600m, opposite the top of the Grade 3 scramble, ease left onto the grassy centre of the spur to avoid a fairly steep slab. Above this, the grass band runs up to the base of a rock tower blocking the spur line. Pass up to right of this for 50 metres, then up left into a grassy bay. Directly above is a short but very steep rock wall; however, up and to the right is a rake with a stream, easily ascended, before slanting up left to the level ground at the top of the tower (720m, a couple of tiny pools here). Continue up the ridge, on stones and small outcrops of clean rock, with drops on the left into Coire na Tulaich (where you can see walkers toiling up the steep scree of the standard route). At **Point 902m**, bend round left to the cairn (NN 2162 5413) at the top of Coire na Tulaich.

> To **descend** Coire na Tulaich go down steep scree zigzags until you can contour left into a small subsidiary corrie. Here is the top of the built path.

On this section take care with loose stones, as there are climbers below.

Scree paths lead up the stony outcroppy slope above to the first top of Stob Dearg. Our altimeter gave this 1021.5m, which is good as it enforces the continuation for 150 metres along a narrow, stony ridge. ◄ This true 1022m summit of **Stob Dearg** is a splendid perch overlooking Rannoch Moor.

Calculations of drop and distance suggest that this may one day become the Buachaille's third Munro summit.

Return past the top of Coire na Tulaich. Skirt left of the minor rise **Point 902** to find a ridge path ascending to **Stob na Doire**. ◄ A misleading path runs down the narrow ridge ahead, but this is actually the east spur running to crag tops. Instead turn sharp right at the summit on a pathed ridge that descends west, bending left to southwest. The path crosses a col, then rises to a slightly higher col: here the clear path down on the right will be the descent route. Keep ahead up the gentle short slope to **Stob Coire Altruim**, then along almost-level ridge to the final rise to **Stob na Broige**.

Return over **Stob Coire Altruim** to the first and slightly higher of the paired cols beyond (NN 2008 5291). The rebuilt path heads down, north, to left of the stream, to a crossing (currently without stepping-stones)

Stob Dearg of Buachaille Mor, from the Black Mount

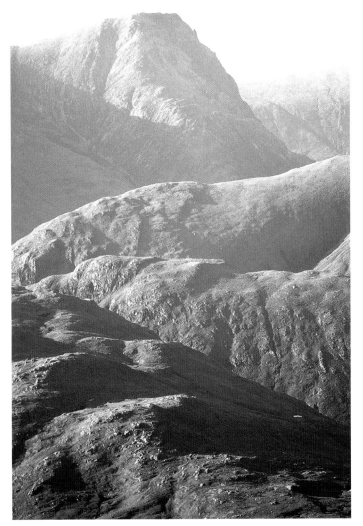

of River Coupall (NN 198541). Turn right on the well-used and somewhat boggy path down **Lairig Gartain** to a car park on the A82.

Cross and immediately turn right on the overgrown Old Glencoe Road. After 300 metres it rejoins the A82, whose verge you must follow for the final 500 metres to the walk start.

56 Round Buachaille Beag: the Two Passes

Length

■■□□□

Difficulty

■■□□□

Start/finish	A82 at Lairig Gartain end NN 213559
Distance	13km/8 miles
Ascent	400m/1300ft
Approx time	4hr
Max altitude	Both pass tops are 490m
Terrain	Paths rough or boggy in parts

This route links two passes that were used by cattle drovers, and so are long-established rights of way. It used to demonstrate the principle: 'In the Western Highlands, you walk high or you walk in a bog.' But with increasing use, the Munro approach paths are getting done over by the National Trust so that, after a dry spell at least, this can be enjoyed as walking as well as for the massive mountains all around.

Anyway, it's the only serious low-level walk in Glen Coe.

A parking area is on the south side of the road, below the cone of Buachaille Beag. (Alternatively, the north end of Lairig Eilde NN 188563.) A SRWS signpost indicates the path **start**. The well-worn path runs southwest to join the **River Coupall**, and goes up the long valley keeping to right of it.

After 2km, you pass the end of a path that turns back left to cross the river, heading for Stob na Broige, the southern Munro of Buachaille Mor. Keep to the main path to the right of the river; this path is through wet peat. Approaching the head of the pass, now on stony grassland, the path passes cairns, with a final big one at the pass top **Lairig Gartain**. Ben Starav fills the slot, with Glen Etive unrolling in front of it.

Heading down towards Glen Etive, the path is at first unclear over wet grass, but as the new stream forms, the path becomes eroded to its right. At about 400m altitude, the path starts to slant out onto the right-hand hill face; the path is gently downhill but gradually getting higher above the stream. ▸ At 300m the path reaches the nose of **Stob Dubh**, with

A fading path follows the line of the right of way down beside the stream, to Dalness in Glen Etive.

a regeneration fence (with a gate in it) 20 metres below (NN 174521). Here leave the main path, which continues down through the gate.

The route around Buachaille Beag is unclear over the next stage, though a path is likely to form over the next few years. Contour forward, to cross the **Allt Lairig Eilde** just above the fenceline (NN 172521 – above this point the stream runs in a small gorge). Ahead, a grassy path heads up to the right: a few metres further on, a better path runs parallel, this one having just come up through a gate in the regeneration fence.

The path runs uphill to left of the Allt Lairig Eilde stream. As ground eases towards the pass top, the path crosses the now small stream (NN 170530) and heads north alongside an even smaller stream. The path crosses the **Lairig Eilde Pass** some 200 metres to right of its lowest point.

The path is clear, down north to join the new stream, also called **Allt Lairig Eilde**. The path runs to right of it for 800 metres, then crosses. The path here has been reinforced over wet bits. After 1.5km it recrosses the Allt Lairig Eilde at huge stepping-stones, then rises up the

Looking back along Glen Etive from the top of Lairig Gartain

moor for 200 metres, before running down to a recently built car park (NN 188563).

Cross A82, then a stream, to the **Old Glencoe Road** on its stone embankment. Turn right along the pleasant track. In 500 metres it rejoins the A82; cross diagonally onto a firm path through heather, soon rejoining the road. Cross to the continuing path to left of the main road; it is soggy in places, and leads to the start car park.

Lairig Eilde from the north

57 Beinn a' Chrulaiste

Start/finish	Kings House NN 260547
Distance	12.5km/8 miles
Ascent	700m/2300ft
Approx time	5hr
Max altitude	Beinn a' Chrulaiste 857m
Terrain	Moderately rough slopes and gentle plateau

Length
■ ■ □ □ □

Difficulty
■ ■ ■ □ □ *or*
■ ■ ■ ■ ■

This one is for the views of Buachaille Mor, or else climbed just as a Corbett. After the mildly challenging start, it's possibly the book's least exciting hill – so take a friend for conversation.

A quick descent
takes steep slopes
southeast to Allt a'
Bhalaich, and follows
it downstream to
Kings House.

Start west along the Old Glencoe Road. After 1.2km fork right onto the broad stony track of the **West Highland Way**. After 800 metres uphill, it runs slightly downhill for 400 metres to ford a stream with a small gorge above. Turn up to left of the gorge. As the slope steepens at 400m altitude, the stream above is in a small ravine.

Head up the fairly steep spur to left of the ravine on a small deer path. (Alternative in ravine: see below.) On plateau above, turn right up gentle slopes to **Beinn a' Chrulaiste**'s cairn of rhyolite boulders. ◄

Head away west of north, a direction that's unexpected in mist, down a wide outcroppy spur bending right (northeast) to a wide col. Cross this eastwards, with a small path somewhere among the peat, then up to the small cairn on **Meall Bhalach**. Head southeast across plateau, past some glacier-dumped granite lumps, to the even smaller Meall Bhalach Southeast Top.

Descend southeast, on soggy grass, which becomes heather at the slope foot. Join the small gorge of **Allt Chailleach**, with a track just below. Follow it to the right to the walk start, with Allt Chailleach forming foreground for photos of Buachaille Etive Mor ahead.

Alternative is in the **ravine**, which is shallow and not too steep, with scrambling (Grade 1) mostly on vegetation. It will be awkward or impossible if the stream is full.

At half-height, the ravine has stream on left, stone-field on right, and a midway spur of rocks and heather rising to a triangular buttress. From the foot of the buttress, you can escape left out of the ravine; otherwise follow heather to right of the buttress top. Above, the ravine narrows, with a few very short rocky moves.

Beinn a' Chrulaiste, a hill that's mostly for looking at other hills from

58 The Lost Valley Visit

Start/finish	A82 car park opposite Coire nan Lochan, NN 168569
Distance	4.5km/2.75 miles
Ascent	250m/750ft
Approx time	2hr
Max altitude	Lost Valley 380m
Terrain	Rough path

Length

Difficulty

181

This walk is short but very rugged, with an exposed passage above a water-fall gorge, boulder-clambering, and an awkward stream crossing. For hill-walkers it makes an excellent pre-amble to a day on Bidean's ridges (see Routes 63 and 64). For others it's a challenging and spectacular little outing in its own right. I start it at a car park that's not the closest, to make it a little less short and add some River Coe and Old Road.

The suggested car park is, if coming from Glencoe village, the first on the right after Loch Achtriochan, 2km after the loch. Coming down Glen Coe it's the second car park on the left after the passage between the little crags of Meeting of the Three Waters.

Start downhill to the gravel track of the Old Glencoe Road. At a cairn, a path continues ahead across the track, heading for Coire nan Lochan (the gap between No 2 and No 3 of the Three

River Coe gorge below the Lost Valley

Sisters). Before a footbridge over **River Coe**, turn left, upstream, on a small path. This passes some pools full of clear water and bottomed with pinky-grey and grey-blue boulders.

On the opposite bank, a fence to the riverbank is the start of a regeneration area, where the exclusion of deer has let heather and birch flourish. As you pass opposite this fence end, don't stray onto a sheep path that runs on a ledge along the gorge side. Keep a little higher on the left, along the gorge rim.

The path joins a much larger clearer one. Turn right for 20 metres to the ravine edge. The path descends a ladder, to a footbridge, then up out of the **River Coe** gorge on easy rock steps. It runs up through the birch and heather of the regeneration area to a gate. In another 80 metres the main path turns left, with a boulder perched on the path.

- **Easier** The path ahead is about to run along the side of a gorge, rather exposed. If you don't fancy this (there have been accidents, particularly when it's wet), then look for a path continuing uphill on the right, not obvious for its first few metres. This upper path runs along the top edge of the gorge, to pass a monster 15m boulder with a tiny rowan in it. Just after this it turns sharp left, down into the gorge, and heads downstream for 50 metres or so to the crossing place.

• **More exciting** The main path runs along the gorge side, above a waterfall, soon getting less exposed. The river rises to join the path, which clambers over big boulders to reach the crossing point.

On either path, the crossing point of the stream is a gravel beach below a hut-sized boulder. The stream here is wide and fairly shallow, so can be paddled if the stepping stones are under water or wobbly. On the opposite (east) side, the path continues to left of the stream as refurbished stone steps. There's a section up a rock groove, harder in descent and when wet. The path then crosses the boulderpile that blocks off the **Lost Valley** and descends onto the gravel plain. It arrives beside a notable boulder, with a much larger one back on the right.

From here you can wander up the gravel valley between its high walls of steep grass, little streams and big crags. Return the same way. If you came by the gorge wall, you could return by the upper path. After the stream crossing, that upper path turns left, upstream, for 50 metres before clambering up right, out of the gorge.

PART SEVEN

BIDEAN NAM BIAN

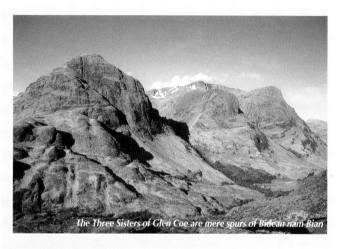

The Three Sisters of Glen Coe are mere spurs of Bidean nam Bian

The name has been interpreted as Bidean nam Beann – the hill of the hills – and that would be entirely right. Take four normal mountains and squash them together; this will also make for some unusually steep slopes all around.

The three rocky pillars you see from Glen Coe, known as the Three Sisters, are mere foothills. Three interestingly different ravines lead up between. Coire nam Beitheach is a steep 'V' between rock faces; Coire nan Lochan opens to the sky with its three little pools; and Coire Gabhail, the Lost Valley, is a gravel-floored sanctuary among the crags.

Above the ravines, high and misted and bearing the snows of previous winter, are the preliminary summits: Stob Coire nan Lochan, Stob Coire nam Beith, Stob Coire Sgreamhach. There are several miles of sharp ridges to link the various tops together; and round the other side a remote and shaggy back country.

It takes at least four visits before you begin to discern the big themes, and feel how it all hangs together. These 10 routes are just a start! Be on

Bidean in winter, when the ridges are crisp white edges, and the black crags drop into corries filled with golden afternoon light, and a hundred mountains surround you except in the west, where the sea reaches its bronze finger in under the Ballachulish Bridge – and ignore it all as you worry about your crampon technique, and how easy it's going to be getting down that headwall into the Lost Valley.

In summer too there's plenty to get anxious about. Noel Williams' *Scrambles in Lochaber* offers 10 more scrambling routes alongside the Zigzags described here. (Ben Nevis itself only gets nine.) For real rock-climbers there's enough up Bidean to wear out several sets of fingertips; and all of it on rough, chunky volcanics allied to the Lake District and Snowdonia, but nearly twice as high.

The Wordsworths, Dorothy and William – probably the most observant observers ever of British hills – came up the glen in 1803. Dorothy was overwhelmed. 'I cannot attempt to describe the mountains. Those on our right were the grandest I have ever seen… more majestic in their own nakedness than our imaginations could have conceived them to be, had they been half hidden by clouds yet showing some of their highest pinnacles. They were such forms as Milton might be supposed to have had in his mind when he applied to Satan that sublime expression – His stature reached the sky.'

Whether Bidean with its satanic slopes is actually the UK's most majestic hill is arguable. Maybe it is; maybe it isn't quite so fine as An Teallach, or Sgurr nan Gillean, or Coire Mhic Fhearchair of Beinn Eighe. Undoubtedly, Bidean is the finest hill that could be seen from a wheeled vehicle in 1803.

Pretty it isn't. Pretty amazing it is.

SUMMARY SUMMARY

Bidean nam Bian

Routes 59–66 are from Glen Coe; the headwalls to the main ridge on this northern side carry steep snow into early summer. Routes 67 and 68 on the southern side are wild and untrodden. Route 67, around the mountain's base, allows you to link any of the others.

BIDEAN NAM BIAN ROUTES

59 Coire nam Beitheach to Stob Coire nam Beith
60 East Coire nam Beithach
61 Aonach Dubh to Stob Coire nan Lochan
62 Stob Coire nan Lochan Northeast Ridge
63 Gearr Aonach by the Zigzags
64 The Lost Valley
65 Beinn Fhada
66 Stob Coire Sgreamhach from Lairig Eilde
67 Dalness Waterfall Way
68 Beinn Maol Chaluim

59 Coire nam Beitheach to Stob Coire nam Beith

Difficulty

Start	Loch Achtriochtan NN 147572
Distance	4.5km/3 miles
Ascent	1100m/3700ft
Approx time up	4hr
Terrain	Rebuilt path, stony ridge

Despite its steepness and uncompromising surroundings, the well-built path makes this the least difficult route up Bidean. The corrie headwall can hold snow late into spring. The turn-off from the ridge is fairly easy to find, making this the least tricky route for coming down.

Start from a lay-by on the north side of the A82, 400 metres up from Loch Achtriochtan. (There are also spaces at the track end of Achnambeithach house.) A path below the road runs alongside Loch Achtriochtan to the Achnambeithach track end. Rejoin the A82 and cross its bridge over the **River Coe**. Immediately after the bridge a well-made path sets off uphill. It soon climbs steeply, with a rocky passage next to a small stream, straightforward unless the stream has playfully coated the rocks with ice. The path zigzags, then enters the slot valley **Coire nam Beitheach**.

The path joins the stream bed, with scrambling above the water if the stream is full. Cross the stream just below a small waterfall with a rock block just above. The path continues to left of the stream for 50 metres, to where it divides at 500m altitude. ◄

Route 60 forks left here.

The main path crosses the left-hand branch and goes up between the two streams. Above is Stob Coire nam Beith's crag face. Below the bottom outcrop the rebuilt path turns to the right, then heads up into the upper corrie to right (northwest) of **Stob Coire nam Beith**. It passes up the left side of the corrie and up the steep headwall to a slight col (NN 1347 5468). This col **Bealach an t-Sron** is just south of a small summit with cairn that could be considered the summit of An t-Sron.

Turn left along a fairly narrow ridge, which bends left and steepens. The zigzag scree path ascends the edge of a stony slope, with crags dropping on the left into Coire nam Beitheach. At the slope top, the cairn of **Stob Coire nam Beith** stands on a promontory overlooking the corrie.

Turn right, as the gently undulating ridge continues southeast. After a couple of minor bumps, the ridge narrows pleasingly (path to right of the crest) to arrive at **Bidean's summit**.

Descent The first essential is to find the correct ridge – the one running west from the summit of Bidean. After a narrow bit (with the path to left of the crest) it levels, descends again, and turns northeast over a hump to the summit of **Stob Coire nam Beith**, whose cairn is poised over the northern abyss.

Turn left, on scree zigzags down the edge of a stony slope, with the abyss to your right. The ridge narrows again, descending northwest to a col before the slight rise to a cairned minor summit. The col **Bealach an t-Sron** has a small cairn (NN 1347 5468) marking the top of the clear path running down to the right.

Bidean nam Bian, seen from a ridge of Stob Ghabhar, looms above lesser ridges

The path descends the right (east) side of the upper **Coire nam Beitheach**, then keeps to right of the stream to the stream junction at 500m altitude. Descend into the stream ravine, and go down it to left of the stream. The path reappears, and leads down into Glen Coe.

60 East Coire nam Beitheach

Difficulty

Start	Loch Achtriochtan NN 147572
Distance	4.5km/3 miles
Ascent	1050m/3500ft
Approx time up	4hr
Terrain	Path, steep stony slope to col

The upper corrie under Bidean summit is crag-rimmed and romantic. The ascent out of it is good in crampons, but arduous and uncomfortable in summer.

Start by following the previous route through the ravine of Coire nam Beitheach to the stream junction just above (NN 139553).

The left-hand stream has a long waterslide. Head up to right of this, southeast, on a rough path. Above the waterslide the ground eases into the upper corrie. The small path stays to right of the stream, wandering over grass to a band of clean rock bounded by a waterfall. Cross this band to rejoin the stream and cross the right-hand branch of it. Scree zigzags lead up ahead to a hollow with a tiny pool (NN 1440 5465). Ahead is steep scree with outcrops, where snow can linger into early summer. Go straight up this, on a loose steep eroded path, to reach the col south of **Stob Coire nan Lochan**.

Turn right on a path just below the col crest, continuing up the ridge to Bidean summit as on Route 61 following.

61 Aonach Dubh to
Stob Coire nan Lochan

Start	A82 opposite Coire nan Lochan (NN 168569)	
Distance	4.5km/3 miles	
Ascent	1150m/3900ft	
Approx time up	4hr	
Terrain	Paths and stony ridges	

A beautiful route of ravine and ridge, and one that cleverly avoids steep climbs and late snowfields.

The car park is on the downhill side of A82 (there's a twin car park 300 metres up-valley). **Start** by heading downhill to cross the track of the Old Glencoe Road at a cairn, where a built path ahead runs down to a footbridge over **River Coe**.

The northwest ridge to Stob Coire nan Lochan

191

A well-made path heads uphill, then contours to the right across a stream. It turns uphill again before slanting up to the right, eventually to join the stream in lower **Coire nan Lochan**. The path, currently being repaired, runs up to left of the stream to where it bends left at a slight easing of slope (630m) below a small crag with a scooped front (NN 155553). ◄

Route 62 now bears left up the stream.

Bear right across the stream. Head up west, on a small path to left of two small streams. Small outcrops for scrambling are available. Above the streams is a gentler slope of grass and rock. Keep straight up northwest to the bare rock summit of **Aonach Dubh**. Visit its north edge for the view down into Glen Coe.

Descend bare rock south, to pass a small pool in a col. Head up the ridgeline opposite, along the pinnacled and turreted top edge of crags. The ridge of stones and rocks leads to the summit of **Stob Coire nan Lochan**.

Descend south, on a fairly wide stony ridge, with the path to right of the crest. After the col, the path leads up the steeper ridge; the crampon-scratched boulders of its crest can be taken direct, especially if the path on the left flank has old snow. **Bidean's summit** has an elegant conjunction of three ridges.

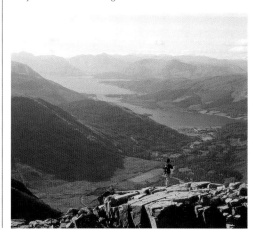

On the northwest ridge of Stob Coire nan Lochan

62 Stob Coire nan Lochan Northeast Ridge

Start	A82 opposite Coire nan Lochan (NN 168569)
Distance	4.5km/3 miles
Ascent	1150m/3800ft
Approx time up	4hr
Terrain	Paths, stony ridge, a little avoidable scrambling (Grade 1)

A fine ridge with a little easy scrambling.

Follow the previous **Route 61** to the stream bend at 630m below the small crag with scooped front (NN 155553). Here the path bends left, keeping to left of the stream, which is now a narrow ravine topped with a waterfall. As the path divides and becomes unclear, make a way up the slopes to left of the waterfall, and over the rim into the shallow **upper Coire nan Lochan** (the bit that actually has the lochans in it).

Head left (east) along the corrie rim and up the gentle slope onto the foot of Stob Coire nan Lochan's east ridge. Go up the grassy, rocky crest on a small path. At half-height is a rock tower with a little easy scrambling, or a scree path down left. Then comes a steeper scree ridge with a zigzag loose path. At the top take the final rocky steepening up its crest, on ledges, or contour out left on scree onto the south ridge.

From the summit of **Stob Coire nan Lochan** continue on Route 61.

Descent From **Bidean summit** take the well-defined pathed ridge down northwards. At 1080m the ridge crest appears to bend left, but this arrives at a buttress top. So at this bend either slant down the right flank on a path, or keep ahead northeast down the crampon-scratched boulders. From the col below, ascend onto **Stob Coire nan Lochan**.

The top of the northeast ridge is not obvious. Head down east, keeping to the crest of the first rocky step to find good ledges and footholds – or divert around to the right, north, on loose scree. Follow the ridge crest (over, or down right of, a rocky section) until it levels off at the beginning of the Gearr Aonach. Here head down left, without path, into the shallow **Coire an Lochan**.

When the rebuilt path from below finally reaches the corrie, it will be at a definite point – possibly at NN 1540 5515, 50 metres to right (east) of where the stream plunges out of the corrie into the waterfalls. Or just drop over the corrie edge anywhere to right (east) of the stream, and slant down left to join the stream below the waterfall as the various possible paths converge. Stay to right of the stream to find the clear path that leads down the lower corrie to Glen Coe.

63 Gearr Aonach by the Zigzags

Difficulty

■ ■ ■ ■ ■

(scramble Grade 1)

Start	500 metres down-valley from Allt-na-reigh cottage (NN 173568)
Distance	4.5km/3 miles
Ascent	1050m/3800ft
Approx time up	4hr
Terrain	Pathed ledges, scrambling Grade 1

The Zigzags are a genuine scramble, so don't really belong in this book. But the scrambling is short, and the situations are spectacular, so in it goes anyway.

From the car park on the north side of the road, cross and follow a wide path downhill to the **River Coe** (see Route 58). Cross a footbridge hidden in the gorge, and take the path up to the gate at the top of the regeneration

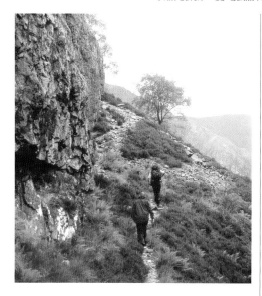

On the first zigzag to Gearr Aonach

area. After 80 metres the path bends left into the gorge: here fork up right onto the upper path and follow it along above the gorge. The heather ledges of the Zigzags are visible from here on the towering face of **Gearr Aonach**, above on the right.

The path reaches a monster boulder with a tiny rowan in it. Turn uphill, trending right then back left to avoid black damp outcrops, to the base of the crag above. Turn up left along the crag base to the start of the ledge heading back right (NN 1674 5588). This is the most obvious of the ledges, with marks of path, and small overhangs immediately above.

Follow the broad ledge on grass and some bare rock to just before the nose of Gearr Aonach (trees on skyline). Here another rocky ramp heads back up left; but first, continue ahead round the corner on a small path along grass for 40 metres, for the view of the north face.

Return along the grass path, and head up the rocky ramp. This develops into a damp slab; avoid this by

195

> About 10 metres along this grass path a Grade 3 scramble heads straight up the face, the 'Easy Route' – its rock is good but steep and exposed, holds plentiful but not positive. The climbing gets less steep to a grassy terrace, then steepens again immediately above.

scrambling a metre or two up to its right, on big holds. The scrambling is soon over, but the situation remains spectacular. Continue on a small path between trees; after about 100 metres the ground above becomes broken, with paths heading up right. Take one of these, slanting around onto the nose of Gearr Aonach at its crag top. Turn left, up the nose, with more scrambling on small outcrops, to reach the almost level ridge above.

Follow the ridge southwest, on small path with big views, until the steeper northeast ridge of **Stob Coire nan Lochan** rises directly ahead. Go up it, now on **Route 62**, following the crest for a little more scrambling.

In descent the top of the Zigzags is not clear to find. The best way may be to descend the nose of **Gearr Aonach** to the top of the north face crags, then contour right on sketchy paths to find the top of upper zigzag slanting back left below (NN 1663 5598).

64 The Lost Valley

Difficulty
■ ■ ■ ■ □

Start	500 metres down-valley from Allt-na-reigh cottage (NN 173568)
Distance	5.5km/3.5 miles (including Stob Coire Sgreamhach)
Ascent	1150m/3800ft
Approx time up	4.5hr
Terrain	Paths, steep scree to col, stony ridge

The Lost Valley must be visited at some point in your Bidean career.
Note The headwall is steep and nasty, and can hold snow right into May.

For a detailed version of the route **start** see Route 58 (Lost Valley Visit). Cross the road and follow a path downhill towards the towering face of Gearr Aonach, to cross the footbridge hidden in the **River Coe**'s gorge. Take the path up to a gate at the top of the regeneration area. After another 80 metres, the path bends left into the gorge, where it contours above a waterfall then reaches the stream. Head up the stream among boulders, to cross it at a gravel beach below a hut-sized boulder, with the remade path continuing opposite.

The path crosses the hill of rockfall debris and drops to the gravel floor of the **Lost Valley** (Coire Gabhail). Head up-valley; as the slope rises again at the end of the gravel area, a well-made path forms immediately to right (west) of the stream. It rises gradually across the steep slope above the stream's ravine. Finally it crosses the very top of the stream, to leave you at the foot of the final steep scree.

The apparent pathline up the scree centre is OK for descending by the sure-footed. Going up it's better to choose the chunkier, more stable scree or zigzag up rough ground on the left. Finally, a steep path leads up left towards the pass in a horrid, loose groove; it's better to take the un-eroded grass and sound rock forming the outer rim of this groove (to its left). Emerge at the pass (**Bealach Dearg**) just west of Stob Coire Sgreamhach (small cairn, NN 1510 5366).

If you want to bag **Stob Coire Sgreamhach**, the up and down on stony ridge path is soon accomplished. Then head west–northwest, on an undulating ridge with path. Drops on the right are steep crag, those on the left are gentler, and where a mild rock obstacle is met, it may be avoided on the left although the clearer path stays on the crest. Two small subsummits precede **Bidean's summit**, which has a large cairn and is the convergence of ridges from east, west and north.

If you find snow and lack the skills or the ice axe, then switch into the descent of Route 66 over Stob Coire Sgreamhach to Lairig Eilde.

Descent From Bidean summit take the ridge eastward, which dips and rises over a slightly lower summit. There are a couple more rises on the way down, with a slightly rocky section. The **Bealach Dearg** (NN 1510 5366) has a small cairn, and an obvious steep ascent on the ridge ahead. The path down to the left is also clear – unless it's under snow. ◄

Descend the right-hand rim, not the bottom, of the initial loose groove. Below, the steep scree path quite soon gets less steep. Head down to left of the ravine to the flat floor of the **Lost Valley**. A low boulder at its far right-hand corner marks the start of the continuing path down to **Glen Coe**.

65 Beinn Fhada

Difficulty
■ ■ ■ ■ ■

Start	Lairig Eilde car park NN 188562
Distance	6 km/3.5 miles
Ascent	1200m/4000ft
Approx time up	4.5hr
Terrain	Steep grass, stony ridge, a short scramble (Grade 1)

Third Sister of Glen Coe is Beinn Fhada, pronounced 'Attow' and meaning long. Long it is but also rewarding, little trodden in its entirety because of the trouble getting onto its end. However, there is a way on steep pathless grass. In descent that gap between the crags would be hard to find, unless possibly with GPS.

Start by taking the Lairig Eilde path (signed for Glen Etive) for 1km until it dips and crosses the **Allt Lairig Eilde** on big stepping-stones. Leave the path and head west, gently uphill, for 300 metres, crossing a slight spur with a rocky knoll below, to reach a shallow grassy valley. Keep slanting up to the lowest point of the steep rocks (NN 1789 5578).

Heading south along Beinn Fhada

Now a grass rake slants southwest up the left flank, along the foot of broken crag. Head up this rake, using rock slabs sticking out of the grass for easier going, to a slight shoulder spur at its top (NN 1769 5560). The rake line continues gently rising along the left (east) flank of Beinn Fhada, now with only a low rock wall above. You could head up through this at various points, but the simplest line is to follow it until it levels off, then strike to the right up a little runnel of stones at 600m altitude (NN 1760 5542). Slant up to the right (north) to gain the ridge crest at exactly the point where it becomes gently angled (NN 1755 5553, 670m).

Enjoy the ridge of grass and outcrops, over a minor top to a col with a cairn. Here most descending walkers strike off down the east flank or, with difficulty, down to the Lost Valley. Accordingly the ridgeline onwards has a clear path. Continue over 931m Beinn Fhada (Harvey map) or Beinn Fhada NE Top (*Munro's Tables*). After a col, climb to the rather rockier 952m summit of **Beinn Fhada**.

In the following col the ridge narrows, to the base of a rock buttress that looks from below to be a formidable

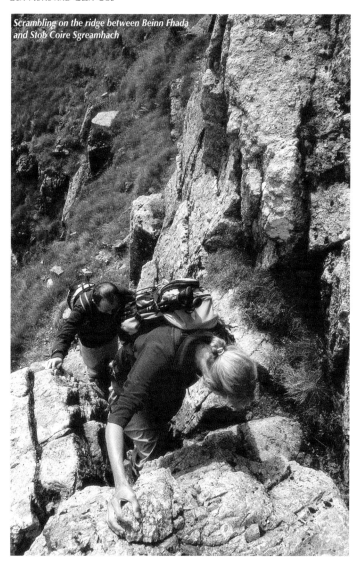

Scrambling on the ridge between Beinn Fhada
and Stob Coire Sgreamhach

small overhang. Pass to left of this along a ledge for 30 metres, then turn back up right in a well-trodden rocky groove with good holds – a moment of Grade 1 scrambling. A gangway continues up to the right onto the ridge crest above the steep crag. Turn up the crest, scrambling easily by ledges and low walls, until the ridge eases. Take the rocky crest or the path to its left to the summit of **Stob Coire Sgreamhach**.

Head west to find the top of pathed, stony ridgeline leading down to **Bealach Dearg** at the head of the Lost Valley. Continue up pathed stony ridge, **Route 64**, to **Bidean summit**.

66 Stob Coire Sgreamhach from Lairig Eilde

Start	Lairig Eilde car park NN 188562
Distance	6.5km/4 miles
Ascent	1050m/3800ft
Approx time up	4hr
Terrain	Path, steep pathless to col, stony ridge

A roundabout route that avoids the difficulties of Bidean, and may be safe when the northern corries are carrying hard or avalanche-prone snow.

A signpost for Glen Etive indicates the path up the **Lairig Eilde**. Follow the path for 3.5km to the cairn at its high-point, and fork off right, dropping slightly to cross the high-point of the pass. Ahead is a fairly steep hillside that you will ascend to the col to right (northwest) of **Point 778m**. ▶

Low down on the face below Point 778m is a rocky boss; to its right is an impressive little ravine. Go up to right of the ravine until the slope eases at the stream top.

To the right of the ascent slope, a buttress rises to a higher high-point: the Sron na Lairig, a Grade 2 scramble and winter climb that leads to a short but very airy crestline.

Route 67 joins here.

Ahead is a further steepening to the col; go up to right of screes. ◄

At the col (NN 164528) below Point 778m turn up right, and follow a gentler stony slope, eventually with crags dropping on the right, to arrive at the top of **Sron na Lairig** (unnamed, NN 161532). Turn left, and follow drops on the right around the rim of Coir' Eilde to the top of **Stob Coire Sgreamhach**.

Head west down the pathed, stony ridge to the col **Bealach Dearg** at the head of the Lost Valley, and follow the ridgeline (Route 64) up west–northwest to Bidean's summit.

Descent From **Bidean summit**, descend as **Route 64** to Bealach Dearg, and ascend the stony ridge ahead to **Stob Coire Sgreamhach**. Descend south for about 50 metres to clear the top rocks, then work round left to find the tops of crags. Turn down to the right (southeast) along the tops of these drops, until a slight rise leads to the top of **Sron na Lairig**. Turn right to avoid falling over crags ahead, and descend with crags dropping on your left, then down open slopes, to the wide col (NN 164528) before **Point 778m**.

Turn down left (northeast), and descend to left of screes to a grassy hollow. Descend from this to left of its stream, to the saddle at the head of **Lairig Eilde**. Cross the saddle point to find the clear path just beyond. Turn down left for **Glen Coe**, or down right for **Glen Etive**.

67 Dalness Waterfall Way

Difficulty
■■■■□

Start	Glen Etive, at Allt nan Easan NN 165509
Distance	5.5km/3.5 miles
Ascent	1200m/4100ft
Approx time up	4.5hr
Terrain	Steep grass, then gentler slopes and stony ridges

The back of Bidean lacks its craggy character, but has some fine waterfalls. This route starts up steep grass, then eases.

Start at a parking area at the start of plantations, 300 metres down-valley from **Dalness**; or at another one, 100 metres further down, beside **Allt nan Easan**. Head up the left-hand bank of this stream to a deer fence, which is crossed by a primitive stile 10 metres in among the trees. Continue on grass beside the stream to the foot of the lowest waterfall. Here easy rock to left of the water is an alternative to the grass slope further left.

Above the waterfall's top is a small steep crag with an overhanging top. The straightforward way is to pass up to left of this, next to the trees, to a derelict fence. The interesting way is to pass up to right of the crag – one awkward step – to find a mini-ridge of grass and rocky knobs rising across the front of the middle waterfall, to reach the same derelict fence.

Pass through a fallen section of the fence, and go straight up, steeply, to a flat-topped boulder perch with

The upper waterfall above Dalness, from the flat-topped boulder

a face-on view of the **upper waterfall**. Directly above the boulder perch, a steep grassy bay leads up between small crags – slightly easier slopes are further left. Above the crags, you arrive on the small ridge that encloses the half-hidden upper valley above the waterfalls.

Head left up the small ridge for 50 metres, then contour right on a sheep path to cross the stream at its bend (NN 159519). Go up steep grass, soon becoming gentler, to the small but scenery-surrounded **Point 778m**. Drop northwest into a wide col, where you join the previous route.

68 Beinn Maol Chaluim

Difficulty
■ ■ ■ ■ ■

Start	Glen Etive, bridge over Allt Fhaolain NN 158509
Distance	6km/3.5 miles
Ascent	1300m/4400ft
Approx time up	5hr
Terrain	Pathless, with a very steep ascent

Bidean the back way is a different experience: less cragged, but more wild and remote. It also bags you a Corbett on the way. The slope onto Bidean is formidably steep; this is not advised as a descent route.

A forest ride runs up west with a small path in it. At the top of the ride, the path ducks in under trees. Head uphill, on a faint path to left of a dry watercourse; dead lower branches have been cleared to ease passage. Then slant up left away from the watercourse, and into wet ground with low scrubby spruce and a fence just above. Turn left along the fence for 25 metres to a break in it at the high-point of forest (NN 1525 5092).

Directly above is broken ground with low wide outcrops. A way could probably be made straight up through. Easier is to slant up left, along the foot of the

Bidean nam Bian from the south

broken ground, to gain gentler slopes running up north-west. The grassy ridge undulates to the summit of **Beinn Maol Chaluim**. It has two cairns, the larger standing on white quartzite and made of it, with a smaller but higher-up cairn on schist.

Descend north, down quite steep quartzite stones, then along a grassy ridge with some iron fence posts. An iron gateway, lacking gate, marks the col. Fence posts continue uphill, bending northeast to the foot of a steep boulderfield. Slant up left for 200 metres, to a pair of seasonal streams. Go up beside (or between) these, very steeply, to pass through a band of broken ground. Above are boulders and grass, still steep but more comfortable as the boulders are rough and blocky.

The ground relents, and a stony slope leads up east to the Bidean ridgeline. Here is the small ridge path across, and sudden drops ahead. Turn right, up the ridge. As it narrows, the path keeps to right of the crest, to the **summit of Bidean**.

69 Old Glencoe Road

Length
■ ■ □ □ □

Difficulty
■ □ □ □ □

Start	Kings House NN 259547
Finish	Glencoe village NN 098587
Distance	20.5km/13 miles
Ascent	75m/250ft
Approx time	5hr
Max altitude	Military Road 320m
Terrain	Paths, minor road

This must have been a most magnificent walk 77 years go. Today it is ruined by the road – and what of the hideous proposal from Fort William Chamber of Commerce to render the A82 dual carriageway, thus letting us arrive 20min earlier at what would no longer be worth visiting?

If we can't escape the noise of the A82, we can at least escape its traffic. This route links the various start-points of Bidean, or the two ends of Aonach Eagach, without more than 800 metres of smelly and dangerous verge.

Start at the Kings House, and cross a bridge behind the hotel onto a tarred section of the Old Glencoe Road. After 1km fork off right on the waymarked **West Highland Way**. The wide path wanders up the northern slope of the valley, then down again to the roadside at **Altnafeadh**.

Now you must walk the verge of the unpleasant A82 for 800 metres. Then look out for the old road forking off right, heather covered and hard to see. If you get to a large car park on the left, you've already passed the start of the old road, but will find it a few steps off the A82 opposite the car park.

The old road is a clear path, mostly grassy and in some places rather wet – what has happened to the firm surface my Grandpa drove along? After 2km, the path runs into the A82, but continues ahead on the opposite side. After 250 metres it again crosses to the north side, and is now a clear, firm track. In 500 metres it passes the large domed cairn at the foot of **Lairig Eilde**.

Continue along the old road for 500 metres to a cairn at the sudden and stunning viewpoint **the Study** (Stiddy, anvil, Gaelic An t-Innean). The old road track wiggles downhill to run into the new road. Continue on a small path just to right of the main road. It joins the road again just above the first (dated 1930 in a 1930s typeface) of two bridges at **Allt-na-reigh**. Walk the verge past the cottage to cross a bigger bridge made of pink stone.

Step over the crash barrier on the left, onto a small path beside the road through gorse. After 50 metres fork off left, directly towards **Gearr Aonach**, down a small path to arrive at a larger one.

- **Scenic way** Turn left towards the Lost Valley. Just before a birch/willow clump, and 20 metres before the gorge, turn right on a small path that follows the gorge edge. After 600 metres it approaches the footbridge below Coire an Lochan. Turn right, away from the river, and then turn left on the clear wide path of the old road.

Looking up the Lost Valley to Stob Coire Sgreamhach from the Old Glencoe Road. (Note snow cover on the exit to Bealach Dearg (Route 64) at the corrie top.)

- **Smooth way** Turn right, on wide built path that merges into the track of the old road. It passes below two large roadside car parks, often equipped with bagpipers.

The old road crosses a small bridge, then goes through a gate. Approaching **Achtriochtan** house, take a stile beside a second gate. The track ahead joins the road, so fork left on a made path below the road to join the access track of Achtriochtan house. As this in turn joins the road, again take a made path below the road. After 300 metres, just after a culvert marked 1929, cross the main road onto a grass path opposite (the old road again).

It slants away from the A82, passes above a tree clump, and slants back to rejoin the main road at a car park lay-by. Cross to a path below the road (the same path that you left earlier). It runs between road and loch, to join the access track end of Achnambeithach. Cross the main road (but not its bridge) into a tarred side road to **Clachaig Inn** (where you could divert around Route 49 to Signal Rock.)

The road continues past the campsite and hostels. Finally you can take a riverside path on the left to the edge of **Glencoe village**.

PART EIGHT

GLEN ETIVE

Looking up Loch Etive from the pier at Taynuilt (Route 77)

On a first visit you may miss out Glen Etive. To get there you have to drive down between Buachaille Etive and the Black Mount – and it's rather hard to drive right past such fine mountain guardians.

But on a second or subsequent visit, make sure you do turn left at Kings House, and follow the green gorge of the Etive river down its long, long glen to the sea. This is granite country – but granite rainwashed, to give long grassy valleys with waterfalls, and above them great slabs of bare rock, and ridges all lumpy with granite boulder. How much of it you do at once depends on day length and your legs: use the sketch maps, and permute Routes 73 to 76 accordingly. Across the loch is Beinn Trilleachan, whose granite slabs are celebrated by rock-climbers; but the bare granite across its top deserves the appreciation of walkers as well.

70 Beinn Sgulaird

Start/finish	Druimavuic NN 008451
Distance	17.5km/11 miles
Ascent	1200m/4000ft
Approx time	7.5hr
Max altitude	Beinn Sgulaird 937m
Terrain	Tracks and open hill

Most folk visit the Appin Munros once each and never come back. A shame, as this one in particular is rugged and lovely, with great sea views. It's the only one of the three that's conveniently approached from the west, and was going to be the high-point of Part 11 of this book: Oban, Lismore, Glen Crean... but there wasn't space for Part 11.

There is a small parking pull-in at the north end of the floodable section of road, where the private road bypass rejoins.

Start along the road north for 800 metres, then a farm track passes **Taraphocain** to join a larger one arriving over a wooden bridge from the left. Continue past large Loch Baile Mhic Chailein and a small artificial lochan on the right. The track continues across open hill, then through a plantation, to pass near **Glenure** farm.

The track runs along the floor of **Glen Ure** then climbs, covering up the previous path marked on maps. Follow it all the way up: the valley is dramatic, despite this newly bulldozed scar. At the top the track runs towards a bridge (NN 077471) with Airigh nan Lochan ahead; but before this bridge, turn right up rough grassland with outcrops. Keep to left of the ridge crest at first

Beinn Sgulaird's high northeastern corrie

to avoid craggy ground, then work up to the right onto the crest. It ascends in small undulations to the hummock of **Stob Gaibhre**. Above this is a small shallow corrie; go up the spur that forms its right (northern) wall. This spur is fairly steep with granite boulders and small outcrops. At the top, pass to right of a minor top and make a final short ascent to **Beinn Sgulaird** summit.

The ridge down southwards looks narrow on the map, but is mainly grass, with a small path. Descend into a col, cross the hummock of **Meall Garbh**, and drop to a second col. A final climb leads up to **Point 863m**. ◄

For a longer and even more rugged outing, continue over the Corbett, Creach Bheinn.

A grassy broad ridge runs down west, steepening to the gap before the hummock **Point 488m**. After a stiff little climb to the hummock, descend just south of west towards **Allt Buidhe**. A track, marked on the new Explorer 377, runs just north of the stream, to enter woodland at a gate (NN 011447). It runs down through woods above **Druimavuic**, to the start-point.

71 Beinn Fhionnlaidh

Start/finish	River Charnan NN 143484
Distance	13.5km/8.5 miles
Ascent	1100m/3600ft
Approx time	6hr
Max altitude	Beinn Fhionnlaidh 959m
Terrain	Rough path, steep hillside, outcroppy ridge

Length

Difficulty

Solitary and steep among forests and bogs, Fhionnlaidh is most comfortably climbed by its 'standard' route, a straightforward up-and-down out of Glen Etive.

Parking is just up-valley from the bridge over Allt Charnan near Invercharnan. **Start** across the bridge and down the road another 200 metres, and turn through the

212

Beinn Fhionnlaidh

71

start/finish

GLEN ETIVE

start/finish

Coileitir

Routes 71–74
Ben Starav

N

P

Stob Coire
nan Albannaich

Beinn
Trilleachan

73

75

**Ben
Starav**

Glas Bheinn
Mhor

72

Stob an
Duine Ruaidh

74

Beinn nan
Aighenan

Loch Etive

77

GLEN KINGLASS

88

0   1   2
km

gates towards **Invercharnan**. Pass the house onto a forest road with rhododendron for 3km. At a sharp bend right, keep ahead on rough track for 300 metres to the forest edge.

Ignore quad-bike wheelmarks ahead (a boggy back way to Sgor na h-Ulaidh!) but turn left beside the trees on a boggy path slightly downhill to a stream. This is crossed by a loose footbridge.

The path, boggy at first then firmer, runs up to left of the stream. As the spur of **Meall nan Gobhar** steepens, the path crosses the stream, which above this point becomes a fine little gorge. The path crosses slopes to right of the gorge to the col behind Meall nan Gobhar. ◀ The small path turns right, and zigzags up a steep slope, generally west of north, to a slight levelling at 680m, with a strip of quartzite stonefield above. Here the path peters out. Slant up and left, past occasional small cairns, to reach the main ridge.

Turn left along a fence, with a path continuing as the fence turns down left. The final rise to the summit has two short, easy, scrambling steps that could be bypassed to the left. A short plateau leads to the **summit** with its concrete pillar trig.

In **descent**, from the fence corner follow the fence for 250 metres then slant down on a compass bearing (170° magnetic) for the col behind **Meall nan Gobhar**.

If it's misty, note landmarks between here and the main ridge to help your way back down.

72 Beinn Trilleachan

Start/finish	Loch Etive head NN 108449
Distance	8km/5 miles
Ascent	850m/2800ft
Approx time	5hr
Max altitude	Beinn Trilleachan 839m
Terrain	Steep grass, bare rock, and a path with some rock steps

Length
■ ■ □ □ □

Difficulty
■ ■ ■ ■ ■

This 'Hill of the Sandpipers' is interesting in quite a different way from the big ones all around. Instead of sharp ridges here are smooth, rounded slopes of bare granite. The normal route is an up-and-down of its northeast ridge. Here instead are the Etive lochside, the brink of a fine chasm, a grassy gully to descend, and a visit to the bottoms of the rock-climbs.

At the end of the Glen Etive road is a turning place (no parking) and some pull-ins. **Start** following a signpost for Bonawe, along **Loch Etive** shore path. There are boggy bits before the path enters a deer-fenced enclosure by a collapsed trap-door gate, and runs into woods with spring primroses. The path exits by a similar but still-hinged gate.

In further woods, the path is joined from above by a small bulldozed track. Ahead through the wood it's a green track, in spring adrip with bluebells. The path reverts to bulldozed track on moorland, and passes above a small fenced enclosure, to the start of another wood. Above now is the ravine of **Eas Doire Dhonncha**.

*On the western shore
of Loch Etive*

The track enters the wood and starts to descend, but now leave it and strike up through the wood (less heather than the open hill but more bracken). At the top of the wood, cross the stream Eas Doire Dhonncha, and then a fence by a supported strainer post.

*On Beinn Trilleachan,
looking across Loch
Etive to Ben Starav*

The ravine ahead is nicknamed the Chasm of Beinn Trilleachan. Go up rather steep grass with rocks in, to left of the ravine, with views into its wooded depths. As the slope eases continue uphill along the ravine brim.

Eventually the ravine terminates at a cave pitch. Above this, easily cross its stream, and head uphill over ground with much bare granite, to the neatly cairned summit of **Beinn Trilleachan**.

Head down northeast over grass and granite, with a small path forming at the first col. It runs slightly uphill to cross bare rock along the ridge of Point 729. Ahead rises the granitty **Point 767**. The standard route crosses that, and continues down the northeast ridge to the forest edge. Instead, from the col before Point 767, a grassy gully strikes down right, towards the loch. It is steep, but has a tiny path. Go down it.

As the rock walls either side get low again, an eroded stream runnel forms in the gully middle. Go down the last grass to left of this, then cross it onto heather slopes on its right. Keep downhill, with the edge of **Trilleachan Slabs** coming into sight on the left. With woods not far below, re-cross the gully runnel, now rock-floored, to the foot of the slabs.

A small path forms as you pass the feet of the climbs. The path contours on, still above all trees, then turns downhill. It is now clear, but rugged, sometimes on bare rock, with a couple of scrambling moves – one quite exposed move across a little stream, and then a steep step down alongside a larger stream. The path slants down towards the road end, becoming swampy, then arrives at the signpost at the walk start.

73 Ben Starav

Start/finish	Track end Coileitir NN 137468
Distance	12km/7.5 miles
Ascent	1100m/3700ft
Approx time	6hr
Max altitude	Ben Starav 1078m
Terrain	Pathed ridges, short rocky arête (avoidable)

Length

Difficulty

The grandest of the Etive hills, Starav would be much more popular if not for the 15km drive down the glen. Its north ridge is a classic, reasonably gentle but with drops on the left and views along Loch Etive on the right. The descent offers a sharp granite arête, sadly short and also avoidable.

One Etive Munro may not be enough; the bagging continues by switching into the following Routes 75 and 76 for up to three more.

A parking pull-off (four cars) is just north of the Coileitir track end. **Start** across the road to a bracken path down onto the track. It crosses a bridge over a deep pool of **River Etive** then bends right. Ignore a track off left, and pass the boarded-up **Coileitir** house. The track ends here but a path continues. At a side-path on the left keep ahead, signed 'hill path'. Sleepers reinforce the path across boggy ground near River Etive. At the side-stream **Allt nam Meirleach** it turns left for 200 metres to a pair of footbridges.

Cross and turn upstream on a rough path. Attractive waterslide falls are on the left. The path steepens for 30 metres; then fork off it to the right, on a path that's unclear to start with, up the north-northeast ridge of Ben Starav. This path is rough and quite steep until the ridge

The east ridge of Ben Starav, towards Glas Bheinn Mhor

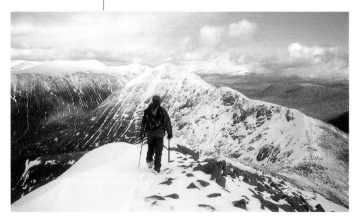

itself gets less steep at 400m. Follow the ridge, with well-marked drops on the left, to the summit of **Ben Starav**. Just before the cairn, the base of a concrete cylinder trig point is still visible.

The summit area is a curved plateau with drops to a northern corrie. Follow the corrie rim round to a minor top with a cairn, the **former Stob Coire Dheirg** (NN 1285 4246).

• **Escape** If the sharp ridge ahead discourages you can avoid it altogether by now descending the south ridge to 930m, then turning sharp left down a vague spur-line. Slant leftwards and gently downhill, to cross a small stream above its ravine at about NN 133423. Slant onwards, northeast, with a sketchy path contouring into the 766m col, **Bealachan Lochain Ghaineamhaich**.

• **Arête** A steep and eroded little spur runs down northeast, soon becoming a narrow rocky arête. The scrambling here is avoidable down right. The ridge runs level, then up the stony pyramid of the **current Stob Coire Dheirg** (1068m). Here a tempting spur heads away north – ignore. Take the eroded path southeast, next to the brink. It runs down the stony ridge, then in grassy zigzags southeast to the major 766m col **Bealachan Lochain Ghaineamhaich**.

At the far end of bealach, at the foot of the quite steep rise towards Meall nan Tri Tighearnan, a cairn stands in the final dip (NN 1394 4235). Here paths join, with the one we want slanting downhill back left, northwards.

At this same point another, smaller, path bears right, contouring southwards, for Beinn nan Aighenan, the path continuing through a lower col and up to **Beinn nan Aighenan**. Meanwhile the path ahead is for **Glas Bheinn Mhor** (Route 75).

The path down north reaches, then keeps to left of, the gorges of **Allt nam Meirleach**. It divides, with one branch staying close to the gorge. The path is fairly rough but scenic. At the valley foot it becomes the path of the outward route.

74 The Back of Starav

Length

Difficulty

Start/finish	Road end Coileitir NN 137468
Distance	22km/13.5 miles
Ascent	1300m/4300ft
Approx time	9hr
Max altitude	Ben Starav 1078m
Terrain	Rough paths and pathless hill, stony ridges

Route 73 is the Starav standard, and very good at that. For something wilder and less visited, here is Ben Starav's back way. It offers Loch Etive's shoreline, a little granite slabwork, and a couple of untrodden tops.

A parking pull-off (four cars) is just north of the Coileitir track end. **Start** along the track to **Coileitir** house. The track ends here but a path continues, bearing right to River Etive. At the side-stream Allt nam Meirleach it turns left for 200 metres to a pair of footbridges.

Cross and turn back right to continue along **River Etive** for 600 metres. As the river bends right, the path continues along the foot of the left-hand slope, past Kinlochetive hut (locked up), to reach the shore of **Loch Etive**.

The small path follows the shoreline. The first large stream, **Allt Coire na Larach**, has spate boulders indicating there could be problems after much rain. ◀ In 6.5km from Kinlochetive hut, don't cross the second large stream, **Allt Ghiusachan**. Head up sheep paths to left of the stream, through ruined shieling enclosures, until

The ridge to Ben Starav above this point has much stonefield, and does not tempt.

On Stob an Duine Ruaidh, Ben Starav

the ground cover eases. Then head straight up a steepish grass spur with some bare slab near its right edge. Near the top, at 760m, a low crag crosses – bypass this on its left or scramble its good granite direct.

Above this crag the spur eases, with more bare granite slab to cross. Then it narrows to the slightly pathed ridge of rocks and grass to **Stob an Duine Ruaidh**, which was promoted to Munro Top in 1997. From its 918m summit, a stony ridge leads over a second Munro top **Meall Cruidh**, and then through the col Stoineag. The stony spur above has a grass streak up its left flank, with a small path, giving the easiest way to the Starav plateau. Level ground is reached at a small shallow pool. At the crag edge beyond, turn left on the path along the brink to **Ben Starav**'s elegantly poised summit cairn.

From here you could continue ahead down Starav's north ridge, reversing **Route 73** – a small path, and drops on the left, guide down the ridge. The distances and times at the top of this route are for joining Route 73 in its forward direction, retracing steps around the rim for the rocky arete to **Stob Coire Dheirg**, to descend from Bealach an Lochain Ghaineamhaich northwards along **Allt nam Meirleach**.

75 Glas Bheinn Mhor

Length
■■□□□

Difficulty
■■□□□

Start/finish	Road end Coileitir NN 137468
Distance	13.5km/8.5 miles
Ascent	1050m/3500ft
Approx time	6hr
Max altitude	Glas Bheinn Mhor 997m
Terrain	Hill paths

Combination routes
Ben Starav with Glas Bheinn Mhor:
    15km/9.5 miles with 1400m/4600ft; 7.5hr
Glas Bheinn Mhor to Meall nan Eun:
    20km/12.5 miles with 1600m/5400ft; 9hr
Ben Starav to Meall nan Eun complete:
    21.5km/13.5miles with 2000m/6600ft; 10.5hr

Glas Bheinn Mhor is a simple east–west ridge, which taken on its own makes a pleasant and not demanding day. However, it's the Munro in the middle, and as the complicated combinations above suggest, it really comes into its own as the easier peak in a walk starting over Ben Starav (Routes 73, 74) – or continuing over Albannaich (Route 76) – or both.

A parking pull-off (four cars) is just north of the Coileitir track end. **Start** across the road to a bracken path down onto the track. It crosses a bridge over a deep pool of **River Etive** then bends right. Ignore a track off left, to pass the boarded-up Coileitir house. The track ends here but a path continues. At a side-path on the left, keep ahead signed 'hill path'. Sleepers reinforce the path across boggy ground near River Etive. At the side-stream **Allt nam Meirleach** it turns left for 200 metres to a pair of footbridges.

Cross and turn upstream on a rough path. Attractive waterslide falls are on the left. The path steepens for 30 metres, then eases left across the flank of the spur and rejoins Allt nam Meirleach.

- From here you could reverse Route 73 to continue up the well-used path, to the 762m pass Bealach an Lochain Ghaineamhaich; there turning left, up a path. After a steepish rise, the ridgeline levels, before rising gently to **Meall nan Tri Tighearnan**.

- For an equally scenic, but tougher, ascent, where the path reaches Allt nam Meirleach (NN 138450) cross the stream onto a smaller path that zigzags onto the end of the long narrow ridge **Glas Bheinn Chaol**. Easy walking follows the crest of this to level ground at its end. Now ascend a steep stony slope, with no path, southeast onto **Meall nan Tri Tighearnan**.

Meall nan Tri Tighearnan is the Hump of Three Houses. The ridgeline continues east, dipping then rising gently to the summit of **Glas Bheinn Mhor**.

Turn right (south of east) for the descent ridge. At first it is gentle and grassy. It levels, then drops more

The east ridge of Glas Bheinn Mhor

If continuing to Albannaich, you would now keep straight ahead up the opposing slope (Route 76).

steeply towards a **738m col**. Just before reaching the col the path turns left, to cross the top of **Allt Mheuran** stream (NN 1630 4333). ◄

The path descends alongside and to right of the stream. As the descent gets less steep at 200m, the path eases away above the stream; the waterfall Eas nam Meirleach is at the foot of a sidestream opposite. The path continues 50 metres to right of the stream, with a small soggy path down at the streamside for viewing waterslide falls. The main path joins the stream side, and eventually reaches the footbridge of the outward route (NN 136460).

76 Stob Coir' an Albannaich and Meall nan Eun

Length

Difficulty

Start/finish	Road end Coileitir NN 137468
Distance	17km/10.5 miles
Ascent	1300m/4300ft
Approx time	7.5hr
Max altitude	Stob Coir' an Albannaich 1044m
Terrain	Hill paths and a rough descent
Map	Due to bad overlaps, Meall nan Eun is particularly difficult to navigate on Explorer maps; Harvey 'Glen Coe' or Landranger 50 suggested

'Albannaich' is the Scotsman – the Englishman finds the drive down Glen Etive just too much. Or maybe what's too much is the way this ridge just keeps offering extra summits. The vigorous Scotsman can be reached over Ben Starav and Glas Bheinn (Routes 73–76); but then again, the ridge continues every bit as good over Stob Ghabhar and along to Creise and the Kings House – so see the Black Mount Summit Summary as well.

Route 76
Stob Coir' an Albannaich

0   1   2
km

Stob Coir' an Albannaich, from Meall Tarsuinn

Near Coileitir track end are three roadside pull-offs. Don't block passing places. **Start** along the track (marked 'hill path') around its locked gate and down to a beautiful bridge over **River Etive** under trees. The track bends right. Soon, a track forking off left is marked 'dogs on leads' but ignore it, as it's the return route from up-valley (all this is Route 75 reversed).

After **Coileitir** house, the track becomes a wide path. A forking path on the left is signed with a request not to use: it is boggy. The preferred path keeps right, to the riverside, follows it, then turns upstream beside **Allt nam Meirleach** to a footbridge. Do not cross the bridge but keep ahead up a small path to left of the stream, passing some fine falls. As the slope steepens, the main path is 50 metres up left above the river slope, while small boggy paths for river-viewing are nearer the water.

The path continues to left of **Allt Mheuran**, passing the fine Robbers' Fall at the foot of a sidestream opposite. It runs up between parallel streams, becoming less distinct, but staying to left of the main Allt Mheuran to cross it at its top (NN 1630 4333), just 50 metres below the **738m col** at the valley's head.

Just before this stream crossing turn off left and ascend steeply, finding a small zigzag path. At the top of the first steep rise (NN 164435) head north crossing stream tops, then up a long, sloping lawn to **Albannaich** summit. The small contemporary cairn stands on the flat top of a wide, circular, ancient one.

Descend east, along the top of drops on the left, down a ridge that's bare rock to start with. Soon it steepens, with a deeply worn path. After 350 metres (5min or so) just before a very small rise, a sandy patch occupies a tiny col (NN 1731 4424). Here turn down sharp left, down a grassy gully with a small path in it. Overshoot this turn-off and in 200 metres, after descending some bare granite, another little grassy gully leads down left: this is the line of the boundary on OS maps and, while unpathed, is a comfortable way down.

The small, pathed gully reaches a wide flat col below (NN 1725 4462). Cross the col northeast, and head up **Meall Tarsuinn** (I like Meall Tarsuinn a lot) over grass, bare rock slabs and boulders. Cross the summit and follow an ill-defined rounded ridgeline down east: the descent briefly steepens at the tip. Across the following col the ground becomes simple grassland. Slant up right, east, to the summit of **Meall nan Eun**.

Looking north from the granite slabs of Meall Tarsuinn

Descend northwest, along the top of drops on the right, to the ridge end with a small knoll. Here ignore the natural ridgeline bending down north, but keep the previous direction, north–northwest, down to the 750m contour; then turn north. Even on this line there are outcrops to be avoided by zigzags left and right. On the 'natural' line, further to the right, on coming to any crag top bypass it to the left (west).

And so, probably after a little entanglement in some crag, reach the wide, slabby **633m col**. Cross it, and turn left down the right-hand side of the main stream.

The **descent** is pathless, through longish grass. The easiest line is to right of the stream, moving away from it to a knoll at 375m (NN 177464). Pass down to right of this, then slant right, along a line of low drumlins with slightly less vigorous plant life. At the foot of the drumlins, across an old fence, slant down to the right, over ground with a little bare rock showing, to join a stream. Go down to left of this, cross it, and head down to the stream junction below. Now a rough path runs to right of the main **Allt Ceitlein** stream over cowpoked grassy meadows. After a gateway in a dead deer fence, a track forms. Follow it down to the valley's end, bending left to cross Allt Ceitlein. In another 1km the track rejoins the outward route.

> **In reverse** The rough grass to Lairig Dhochard (633m col) will be very arduous uphill. A well-commended way up Meall Tarsuinn (which I plan to do when next in Glen Ceitlein) walks up gentle granite slabs to east of Coire Leacach ravine (from NN 171463), with 450m of height gained on bare rock.

77 Loch Etive Linear

Length

Difficulty

Start	Dalmally station NN 160273 or Taynuilt NN 004312
Finish	Kings House NN 259546 or Kinlochleven NN 187620

Distance, ascent, time

Taynuilt to Kings House	42.5km/26.5 miles with 650m/2200ft: 1.5 days (12.5hr going)
Taynuilt to Kinlochleven	49km/30.5 miles with 900m/3000ft: 2 short days (14.5hr going)
Dalmally to Kings House	50km/31.5 miles with 1100m/3700ft: 2 days (15.5hr going)

Dalmally to	
Kinlochleven	56km/35 miles with
	1350m/4400ft: 2 long days
	(17.5hr going)
Max altitude	Lairig Dhoireann 612m
	(Dalmally start);
	Lairig Gartain 465m
Terrain	Tracks, rough paths, and 3km of
	rough hillside (Dalmally only)
Sketch map	See overview map (page 15)

This is a long and varied through route – especially from the Dalmally start – with high passes, an empty valley, and the side of salt-water Loch Etive. The Taynuilt start is easier, but could give you more Etive lochside (20km) than you actually want. The 7km of tarmac up Glen Etive is a necessary evil, before the impressive and well-trodden Lairig Gartain brings you through to Glen Coe.

- The **Taynuilt start** is described under Route 89 (Glen Kinglass) to **Glennoe** over the euphonious River Liver, and down to cross the fine track bridge near **Ardmaddy** (12.5km/8 miles and 200m/700ft so far).

- **Loch Awe start** If arriving by train, start from Dalmally (as Lochawe involves an unpleasant verge walk). If by bus, alight at Stronmilchan road end (NN 132283). ▸

  Route 98 (Eunuch and Cockle) gives extra detail of the first part of this walk.

  Follow B8077 to a bridge over **River Strae**. Immediately north of this, turn right onto a track. In 600 metres fork left past a long pool, then keep ahead on a wider track for 1km. Just before a bridge, turn left on quad-bike marks following the map's old stalking path, to left of the stream, up to the **Lairig Dhoireann** pass.

  An old and almost vanished zigzag path leads down the first steep descent into the upper valley of Allt Dhoireann. Follow the stream down to the

An adventurous short cut here turns upstream for 1km to a footbridge, and follows descents of Routes 88 and 73 to reach Glen Etive by the high pass east of Ben Starav.

300m contour. Now the path descending west on the Landranger doesn't exist on the ground, although regeneration fences that cross it are equipped with gates where it would pass if it still existed. Newer maps show a largely fictitious path down the Allt Dhoireann to **River Kinglass**. ◄ Head downstream on traces of path to a sturdy footbridge near **Acharn** (NN 123356).

Turn left along the track, keeping to the older track alongside the river for the first mile to **Narrachan**. The hut has in the past been available for unofficial bothy use. After another 3.5km the valley emerges to the side of Loch Etive (20km/12.5 miles and 600m/2000ft so far).

Take the northward track past **Ardmaddy,** where a smaller track leads to a ruined pier. The track continues, then becomes a small path along the high-tide mark keeping to left of a fenced enclosure. This path is hard to find at first, then clearer. It has some boggy bits but is mostly pretty good, if always small.

Loch Etive track near Glennoe farm

Cross **Allt Ghiusachan** – awkward in spate, judging by the wide swathe of spate-carried boulders. Opposite, Beinn Trilleachan displays its sweep of granite slabs. After another 6km of rough but beautiful walking, the path arrives at the head of Loch Etive. It continues along the foot of the right-hand slope to the hut at **Kinlochetive**, which was a bothy at one time but is now locked.

Beyond the hut a wider path continues along the right-hand edge of the valley floor, then beside **River Etive**. It turns upstream alongside Allt Mheuran to a foot-bridge, then returns downstream to the River Etive. In 800 metres it reaches **Coileitir**, where it becomes a track. This turns down left to cross the River Etive at a deep pool, and reach the Glen Etive road. ▸

However, there is no shop, hostel or bus stop. A very rough path does lead west from the loch head into Glen Ure; or one could turn down the west shore of Loch Etive on a path that starts nicely but becomes a wide timber track and eventually, at Bonawe, a road. However, the comfortable continuation is to continue northwards through Lairig Gartain to Kings House or Kinlochleven.

So turn up the valley road, which is very quiet and often has deer grazing the verges. After 6.5km, at the bridge just after **Dalness**, you reach the SRWS signpost at the foot of the Lairigs Eilde and Gartain. ▸

Turn left up the signed path, through a gate in a deer fence. The path heads straight up the grassy spur that's the southern end of Buachaille Etive Beag. Keep to the main path, straight up the regeneration area between streams of Eilde and Gartain, towards a deer fence gate high above. The path is good at first then faint, wet and peaty. Above the deer fence gate the path slants up right, climbing gradually across the steep hill face to join the **Allt Gartain**. After a short but rather nasty steep section, you reach **Lairig Gartain** pass top. A good path to left of the **River Coupall** runs out through the pass to a car park on the A82.

Cross and turn right along a heathery section of old road, then follow the A82 verge to **Altnafeadh** (from the foot of Glen Etive, 13.5km/8.5 miles and 450m/1600ft).

From Taynuilt: 25.5km/16 miles and 200m/600ft; from Dalmally 33km/20.5 miles and 600m/2000ft.

Take the Lairig Eilde here, joining Route 56, and the visually splendid but aurally noisy Old Glencoe Road will take you to Glencoe village (Route 69).

On the West Highland Way near Kings House, with Meall a' Bhuiridh behind

The wide, waymarked path of the **West Highland Way** now heads straight up the hillside on the left for **Kinlochleven** – a tempting continuation (10km/6 miles, 250m/800ft). For Kings House, follow the West Highland Way the other way, beside and to left of the road, then slanting left up the hillside for 2km. It then descends to join the Old Glencoe Road to **Kings House** (3.5km/ 2 miles).

PART NINE

BLACK MOUNT

Clach Leathad and Meall a' Bhuiridh from the southeast

The rock is Buachaille Etive Mor: the soft place is peaty Rannoch Moor. Between the rock and the soft place – where you look at both the Mor, and the moor – is the Black Mount.

The Black Mount ridge between Kings House and the Inveroran is the best pub-to-pub in all Scotland. It's gentle grass, and stony plateau, and at the plateau's edge a great rocky corrie half-full of cloud. The morning sun gleams on the hundred lochans of Rannoch, and early light turns the peatlands a delicious chocolate brown. At noon the hollows of the hill are warm as a Spanish beach but considerably more private. Just the summit of Ben Nevis peers in disapprovingly over the jagged wall of the Buachaille.

Stroll a few more miles, while behind Ben Cruachan the evening sun gleams on the sea, and suddenly you're at ridge's end. Beneath your toes they've just switched on the lights in the Climbers' Bar at the Kings House. You could almost spring energetically off Sron na Creise and splash down into your first glass of beer.

Better not believe it. There's scrambling on the slope below, and heathery scree, and you'll be wading through the Etive by torchlight and into the bar just after the last bar meal. So stay up instead, and pitch a tent in Bealach Fuar-chathaidh. Chathaidh is cats and Fuar is cold – it is indeed a place for cool cats as the darkness gathers in the long glens between the ridge and the River Etive.

Once you've bagged the four Munros, and walked the long ridge between, those long glens are the next place. Down there are dark slits of river between bushy banks, bright waterfalls, deer, and fine old stalkers' paths with dangling footbridges. There too, are a couple of Corbetts: 2500-footers to tick off as an extra excuse for coming to the Black Mount the back way. Beinn Ceitlein wouldn't fit on the map, so is a separate Route 87.

And when you've done all that, come again in winter for some crampon work in the Northeast Corrie of Stob Ghabhar, or the ancient ice-climb in the Upper Couloir. The Black Mount – or perhaps the 'you'll-be-backmount'.

SUMMIT SUMMARY

Black Mount

Routes 71–81 are from Inveroran, Routes 82–84 from Kings House or White Corries. Routes 85 and 86 are the main ridgeline taken northwards and southwards; note how the West Highland Way lets you get back to your starting point (or there's the Citylink coach from Kings House to Bridge of Orchy, followed by 4km/3 miles northwards along the WH Way). A route to Stob Ghabhar from lower Glen Etive wouldn't fit in, and is the separate Route 87.

BLACK MOUNT ROUTES

78 Stob Ghabhar by Mam nan Sac
79 Stob Ghabhar South Ridge
80 Coirein Lochain of Stob Ghabhar
81 Stob a' Choire Odhair to Stob Ghabhar
82 Meall a' Bhuiridh to Creise
83 Sron na Creise
84 Beinn Mhic Chasgaig
85 The Black Mount Traverse: Northbound
86 The Black Mount Traverse: Southbound
87 Beinn Ceitlein to Black Mount

summit summary
The Black Mount

Kings House

A82

West Highland Way

GLEN ETIVE

Buachaille Etive Mor

83

82

84

Creise

Beinn Mhic Chasgaig

Meall a' Bhuiridh

Clach Leathad

Coire Ba

87

Bealach Fuar-chathaidh

85

87

80

Stob a' Choire Odhar

81

Beinn Toaig

Stob Ghabhar

78

79

N

0 1 2 km

Clashgour

hut

Loch Tulla

88 89

Abhainn Shira

P

Inveroran

78 Stob Ghabhar by Mam nan Sac

Difficulty
■■■□□

Start	Victoria Bridge car park
	NN 271417
Distance (to	
Ghabhar)	10.5km/6.5 miles
Ascent	950m/3200ft
Approx time up	5hr
Terrain	Path, moderate slope, gentle ridge

A way to savour some of Stob Ghabhar's western ridge, and a safe descent.

Black Mount rises above Inveroran Inn

Take the road over **Victoria Bridge**, and turn left on the track signed for Loch Etive. It runs beside **Abhainn Shira** to the green Clashgour Hut. After another 200 metres, the track bears right into trees, but it's nicer to fork left outside the deer fence on the riverside path. A vague path reaches a big grand footbridge over Allt Ghabhar. Don't cross this, but head right, on a track that leads up to left of **Clashgour**. Turn left, just below the buildings, on a good path.

236

This old stalkers' path leads up into the wide col of **Mam nan Sac**. It can be followed further northwest until it peters out, then head up grassy slopes to **Bealach Coire Laoghan** (NN 214457). Follow the main ridge gently up eastwards over Sron a' Ghearrain. Old fence posts guide along narrower ridge and up the stony summit knoll of **Stob Ghabhar**.

In descent From **Ghabhar** summit head down northwest, following the iron posts of the old fence. The ridge curves to the west and levels. After 400 metres of narrow, level ridge, the fencing posts swing down to the left, and it's tempting to follow them down the western rim of **Coire Ghabhar**; however, this runs down to crags. So it's best to keep following the wide gentle ridge northwest across **Sron a' Ghearrain** for 300 metres until it bends north. Here turn down left, southwest, apparently off the ridgeline but in fact down gentle slopes to the **Bealach Coire Laoghan** (NN 214457). From here head down south to the wide **Mam nan Sac**.

From the col head down left, to left of the stream, to find the descent path.

79 Stob Ghabhar South Ridge

Start	Victoria Bridge car park	
	NN 271417	
Distance	6.5km/4 miles	
Ascent	900m/3000ft	
Approx time up	4hr	
Terrain	Path	

Difficulty
■ ■ ■ □ □

The standard baggers' route is a trudge with a fine finish; also the most straightforward descent route.

Take the road over **Victoria Bridge**, and take the track on the left as far as the green Clashgour Hut. Just beyond it

This isn't the famous and fearsome Aonach Eagach of Glen Coe, (Route 52).

a good path heads uphill to the right of the **Allt Toaig**. At a stream junction at 300m, fork off left, on a sketchy path to the right of the sidestream and its waterfalls; then bear up west to a shoulder at 920m. Head up steeper slopes to the level top section of **Aonach Eagach** ridge. ◄ Turn left, and follow the corrie rim to the summit.

Descent Follow old iron fence posts down southeast, with the huge drop into Coirein Lochain on your left, to the narrow col that's the top end of the **Aonach Eagach**. Now the fencing slants away southeast – in mist, follow it down. Otherwise continue along the crest for 100 metres, past a small cairn but before the narrow and more awkward section of the Aonach Eagach ridge, then turn down to the right, to rejoin the old fence posts and reach the 920m shoulder.

Head down southeast to join **Allt Toaig** and its path.

80 Coirein Lochain of Stob Ghabhar

Difficulty

Start	Victoria Bridge car park
	NN 271417
Distance	
(to Ghabhar)	7.5km/5 miles
Ascent	900m/3000ft
Approx time up	4hr
Terrain	Path, steep broken hillside and stony ridge

A winter route that can offer steep crampon snow; not recommended for summer unless you switch into Route 81.

Coirein Lochain harbours a classic winter climb, the Upper Couloir. This route admires the icy crags from a snowslope on the left. Check snow and avalanche conditions, pack the crampons, and start as Route 79, to continue up the path beside **Allt Toaig** to the col at the

Stob Ghabhar summit from Aonach Eagach

valley head. Turn left up the ridgeline for 400 metres, then contour out right into **Coirein Lochain**. ▶

From the southernmost point of its lochan, head up southwest on a steepening snowslope without interrupting crag. It deposits you at the tiny col at the top end of the **Aonach Eagach** ridge. Turn right, up the rim of the corrie, to the **summit** of Stob Ghabhar.

Route 81 keeps on up this ridge.

81 Stob a' Choire Odhair to Stob Ghabhar

Start	Victoria Bridge car park NN 271417
Distance	9.5km/6 miles
Ascent	1200m/4000ft
Approx time up	5.5hr
Terrain	Path, then rough steep slope and stony ridge

Difficulty

The standard baggers' route for the Munro pair, but a demanding way onto Stob Ghabhar.

Follow **Route 79** to the green hut and up the path alongside **Allt Toaig**. At 450m fork off right on a stalkers' path, not marked on the Landranger map, that zigzags up the steep southwest spur of **Stob a' Choire Odhair**.

From the summit, follow the ridgeline down west to the col at the head of Allt Toaig. The continuing ridgeline rises gently and bends left, to run into the steep northern wall of Aonach Eagach. An eroded path zigzags straight up this to the crest. Turn right, along the **Aonach Eagach**, which offers a little very easy scrambling. At the ridge's end, follow the rim of Coirein Lochain up to the **summit**.

In descent after the scrambly bit of the Aonach Eagach ridge, note where it kinks from just north of east to just south of east (cairn, NN 2369 4540). Here you must turn off left down the steep northern slope. Then head out right, east, to the col at the head of Allt Toaig and climb **Stob a' Choire Odhair**. From there, you can descend south then southeast to take in Beinn Toaig. Just before the first col, watch out for a small crag; it can be bypassed on the left. After the short climb to **Beinn Toaig**, the heathery south-west ridge is fun to descend, but less amusing uphill.

82 Meall a' Bhuiridh to Creise

Difficulty
⬛⬛⬛⬜⬜

Start	White Corries car park
	NN 266525
Distance	
(to Creise)	5km/3 miles
Ascent	950m/3100ft
Approx time up	4hr
Terrain	Pathed stony ridges

You may detest the ski paraphernalia, or quite like the way it lifts you (in winter only) to the 650m contour. Either way, the following ridgewalk is a fine one.

Head up a fairly nasty path under the ski lift – there is a waterfall which drowns the sound of the clattering cables. From the top station a mud track leads to the 'Plateau Chateau' café. Head up to right of all the ski runs, following the black-and-yellow 'edge of ski area' poles. Quite suddenly the ski zone drops out of sight behind and the summit cairn of **Meall a' Bhuiridh** appears 50 metres ahead.

Head down west, on a sharp stony ridge. Once across the narrow col, there's a steep climb through rocks. You'll use a handhold here and there, but the way is well trodden and clear. At the plateau, turn right along the cliff rim. There's a slight drop, and then a short, gentle climb to a cairn at 1100m (NN 238506). This, unmarked on older maps, is the summit of **Creise**.

In descent the drop-off for the east ridge is crucial, and not obvious in mist. Keep to the brink of the drop on the left, watching out for where it curves slightly to the left. A well-placed cairn (NN 2390 4999) marks the top of the descent spur.

On the west ridge of Meall a' Bhuiridh, looking to Clach Leathad and Creise

83 Sron na Creise

Difficulty
■ ■ ■ ■ ■

Start	Glen Etive NN 238536 or White Corries car park NN 266525
Distance (to Creise)	6km/4 miles
Ascent	800m/2600ft
Approx time up	4hr
Terrain	Very steep, weaving among crags, with at least a little scrambling Grade 1

This is a serious route, up steep ground with big crags: spectacular, with scrambling possibilities. It follows the line of an excellent (Grade 3) scramble, but avoids the scrambling (apart from a little easy Grade 1). The route is on grass among small crags. If a path should be starting to form, encourage it into zigzags to reduce erosion.

The line is best inspected from Glen Etive. The key is a gully of pink boulders, rising to the skyline on the right (northwest) flank of the nose. The gentle rock ridge to left (north) of this gully is the key to the ascent.

The **start** is from Glen Etive, or White Corries (convenient for a finish down Route 82).

• **From Glen Etive road** In normal water conditions the River Etive has wide, shallow sections between its small gorges, and you can cross it on stones at NN 236534, opposite the culvert where a stream off Buachaille passes under the road. Head straight towards the north-pointing steep spur. A low but wide outcrop crosses low down, with a grassy gap to right of centre. Go up to the base of this gap (NN 2393 5272), ascend for a couple of metres then slant up left, on rock holds projecting from grass, to the top of this first small rise (NN 240527).

- **From White Corries** Return down the access road to **Blackrock Cottage** and turn off past the cottages. A path is forming from here, and may be followed under some power lines, and then tending further to the left to look for drier ground around the base of Creag Dhubh.

  Work round to cross the foot of **Cam Ghleann** (the Crooked Glen), then contour on around the base of Stob a' Ghlais Choire's northeast ridge. You can now slant off up steep grass, to join the steep northern spur above its first small rise (NN 240527).

Head directly uphill (south) on a vague ridgeline of grass with some rock, to the foot of the first scrambling crag (NN 2400 5254). Pass up to right of it, on grass, to the foot of a tiny waterfall (NN 2400 5250). Scramble up to left of this on gentle rock with many holds for 15 metres to the top of the crag.

Creise from Kings House, with the Sron na Creise forming the right skyline. The photograph excludes Buachaille Mor, just to the right, which normally distracts the viewer from appreciating Creise.

Slant up left, on grass, to some shed-sized boulders visible on the skyline from below (NN 2409 5242). Directly above them swells the upper scramble crag. Pass up to right of it, on grass, then on loose stones to the foot of the gully of pink rocks (NN 2403 5226). This is the gully mentioned in the preamble, and has a small pinnacle above on the right. Contour left onto the crest of a ridge of gentle, easy, rock. Go up this ridge, or broken ground to its left, to the top of the pink-rock gully.

Head uphill across the top of the gully, to the foot of a final scrambling wall (NN 2401 5216). After 3m of genuine Grade 1 this eases for another 10m of scrambling: or avoid it by grass on the left. Head on up a well-defined ridge; those who avoided the scramble pitch can regain the ridge by a steep little grassy groove, or stay on grass to join the ridgeline further up. It leads by rocks and grass to the levelling **Sron na Creise** at 900m.

Go up stony ground, south, to **Stob a' Ghlais Choire**. After a short descent, a narrow ridge with a small path leads south to a preliminary cairn, and then after 400 metres almost level, to **Creise summit**.

DESCENT OF SRON NA CREISE

Given care – and spare energy for returning uphill where necessary – this intimidating line goes surprisingly well in descent. Crucial, but fairly straightforward, is to find the way through the upper crags. Below that it's possible to improvise.

From **Creise** follow the ridge northwards on a small path, to the rocky rise of **Stob a' Ghlais Choire**. Descend stony ground north, on undefined ridge becoming clearer, and then becoming a well-marked and somewhat rocky edge.

Keep to the crest, on a small path, descending more steeply to the top of a 20m scrambling pitch (the top is NN 2399 5214). If you scramble this (Grade 1), you'll find it steepest at the bottom; a groove slightly right (east) of the crest is easiest. Or avoid it by a steep little grass groove down to right; or else backtrack up the ridge for easier access to the grass on the right.

From the foot of the scramble continue south down the ridgeline, to pass across the top of the pink-stone gully falling to the left. Go down the gently angled rock ridge to right (east) of the gully, or the easy groove to right of the rock ridge. Return to the ridge crest opposite the foot of the pink-stone gully and contour into it (NN 2403 5226).

An alternative way down that's simpler to describe: descend northwest, avoiding crags as you come to them, to the valley floor. For a more precisely described route: go down the gully's right edge until you can slant down to the right on grass, still following the base of the rocks. From the crag toe descend grass to a clump of shed-sized boulders (NN 2409 5242). Slant down and leftwards to the top of the next scrambling crag. Head down the left edge of this, on grass with rock handholds, for 10m, to the foot of a tiny waterfall (NN 2400 5250). Head down between the stream (left) and the scrambling crag (right), and below the crag's foot reach an easing of the slope.

Here you can slant down right on steepish grass for the moorland trudge to the **White Corries**, or head down the ridgeline, north, on grass with occasional bare rock, to arrive above a wide, low rock band. Slant left on easy-angled rock, hands hardly needed, to reach the foot of a heathery gap in the crag (NN 2393 5272).

Head straight across the moor, to cross the River Etive at NN 236534, opposite where a stream off Buachaille passes under the road.

84 Beinn Mhic Chasgaig

		Difficulty
Start	White Corries car park NN 266525	
Distance		
(to Creise)	9.5km/6 miles	
Ascent	950m/3200ft	
Approx time up	5hr	
Terrain	Pathless ridges and open grassy slopes	

A Corbett on the way to Creise gives one of the wild ways up.

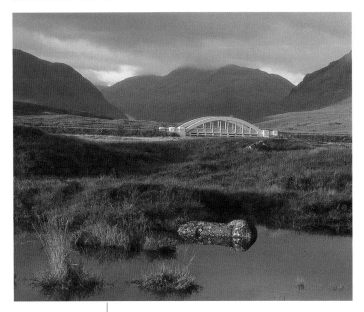

Beinn Mhic Chasgaig and the Etive bridge at Kings House

Again, this route could be started by crossing the **River Etive** at NN 224523 if water levels permit. Follow Route 83, and contour on around the base of **Sron na Creise**. **Allt Fionn Ghlinne** has slabby waterfalls. Cross it at around 330m, to gain the toe of **Beinn Mhic Chasgaig**'s northeast ridge. This is steep to start, but soon eases into a gentle uphill stroll.

From the summit, descend southeast across a col, and take the well-defined west ridge of Creise. It deposits you on the plateau close to **Point 1068**. Turn left, with drops on the right, on a small path, slightly downhill at first, and then up to the summit of **Creise**.

In descent In really bad conditions, with white-out and cornices on the east-facing crag top, it may be impossible to locate the spur to the west ridge; this is the safest descent route. Count paces carefully to Point 1068 (NN 238501), then descend southeast to the col at the head of the **Fionn Ghleann**.

85 The Black Mount Traverse: Northbound

Start	Lairig Dhochard NN 187460
Finish	Creise summit NN 238506
Distance	10.5km/6.5 miles
Ascent	950m/3200ft
Approx time	
end-to-end	5hr
Terrain	Wide ridgelines, steep grass slopes, mostly pathless

Difficulty

For Scotland's best high-level pub-to-pub this is the more difficult direction; but the intimidating descent of Sron na Creise will dry the mouth nicely in preparation for the Kings House beer. It is described from the Lairig Dhochard, north of Meall nan Eun, so as to link into Routes 73–76. That full ridge, from Ben Starav, is an over-the-top experience in both senses. For a more moderate exercise in high-timing it, start from Stob Ghabhar (Routes 78–81).

Reverse the descent of **Route 76** (Albannaich) to gain the slabby 633m col **Lairig Dhochard**. Turn left, northwest. A broken wall crosses the col to end against the foot of the intimidating upslope (NN 1883 4608). From there, go straight up a knoll of grass and rock to a slight easing of the slope. Directly above is broken outcroppy ground. Slant up to the left along the foot of this, and follow a small stream up through a grassy gap. ▶ Now the slope is slightly less steep; slant up slightly right to reach the slope top (NN 1900 4633) and **Meall Odhar**.

A broad grassy ridge runs east, down into Bealach Odhar, then gently over **Stob a' Bruaich Leith**. From its 990m summit old fence posts lead east along the ridge. This narrows enjoyably, then rises to the stony pyramid of **Stob Ghabhar** summit.

The top of the stream gap is NN 1888 4622.

Head down north-northwest, ignoring a small spur running north to crag tops, but then following the top edge of **Coirein Lochain** (the Northeast Corrie) on the right. As the broad ridgeline levels, the small path switches to its left-hand side, to follow drops on the left (Coire a' Chaolain) side. The path runs northwards, skirting to left of the 976m **Sron nan Giubhas** top.

The **Aonach Mor** ridge requires care or GPS in mist. Follow the spur down north, to a col with tiny pool, then uphill for 100 metres to a toplet with an even smaller pool. The ridge continues down northwest for 100 metres to another col, then up to another slight rise. After 200 metres of level ridge comes a gradual dip to a notch crossing the ridge (829m). Head up to the next flat-topped rock knoll, currently with a cairn on it (NN 2240 4748). ◄

Find this cairn in mist, without GPS, and be rightly pleased with yourself.

Now head northeast down steepish grass, to reach either the beginning of the continuing ridge (NN 2255 4773) or else the marked flattening at 730m which lies just northwest of the ridgeline (a cosy campsite). Follow the ridgeline northeast, over the rocky hummock **Creag a' Bhealaich**. The defined ridge is followed north to a slight

Looking across Aonach Mor ridge to Creise

drop, then northeast along grass ridge to the base of the slope out of **Bealach Fuar-chathaidh** (NN 2296 4849).

Head uphill, slanting slightly right to the grass-topped ridgeline above. Turn right, up the broad ridge that becomes stony with drops on the left. It bends left to the cairn at the summit **Clach Leathad** (Clachlet). The large cairn, perhaps reflecting Clachlet's former Munro status, has a big drop immediately behind it.

With drops on your right, descend initially northwest, but after 100 metres find the clear ridgeline with path heading north. After a shallow col, the path rises alongside drops on the right, to a plateau with a cairn at its corner (NN 2390 4999), marking the top of the spur to Meall a' Bhuiridh. The plateau edge bends slightly left, then back right, dips a little, then rises to the summit cairn of **Creise**.

86 The Black Mount Traverse: Southbound

Start	Creise summit NN 238506	
Finish	Stob Ghabhar summit NN 230455	
Distance	6km/4 miles	
Ascent	450m/1500ft	
Approx time end-to-end	2.5hr	
Terrain	Gentle ridges and one steep drop, mostly pathless	

Difficulty

The classic pub-to-pub ridgewalk in the easier direction.

Southward from **Creise** the ridge dips then rises very slightly to Point 1068. It dips again, then has a 60m ascent to **Clach Leathad** – pronounced (and sometimes spelled) 'Clachlet'. ▸

Until 1974 Clach Leathad was marked as higher than Creise and so was the Munro.

The descent to the next col – **Bealach Fuar-chathaidh** – needs care, as a direct compass bearing leads onto steep ground with outcrops. Go down the ridge to the 1000m contour, where it turns right, and continue down the ridge in its new, westward, direction for 400 metres (about 5min). Here the ridge bends slightly right, eases its angle, and changes from stones and moss to grass (NN 2339 4895). Now steep grassy slopes on the left lead down southwest to the col (NN 2296 4849).

Cross the **Bealach Fuar-chathaidh** col, and ascend steeply onto **Aonach Mor** (the Great Ridge). The crest of this is a green ridge-wander, with small pools, and deep corries running out on either side. At the ridge's end the ground rises and becomes stony. In mist, simplest is to keep uphill onto the top of **Sron nan Giubhas**; then follow the drops on the left round to the summit of **Stob Ghabhar**.

87 Beinn Ceitlein to Black Mount

Start/finish	Alltchaorunn, Glen Etive
	NN 197514
Distance	22km/13.5 miles
Ascent	1700m/5700ft
Approx time	10hr
Max altitude	Stob Ghabhar 1090m
Terrain	Grassy slopes and ridges,
	mostly pathless

Length

Difficulty

251

This is Black Mount from the back. Behind the River Etive are long, little-visited valleys with waterfalls and old stalkers' paths. The Corbett Stob Dubh gives motivation to the morning; 600m of drop into one of the little-visited valleys will occupy the noontide; arrive at Stob Ghabhar after the Munro-baggers have gone away. Through the long walk out, waters roar in black gorges, froth down slabs of pink rock, and gather in pools that reflect the orange sunset slopes.

Before the Access Law the gate was sometimes obstructed; there is a possible crossing of the Etive 200 metres upstream.

There's a small pull-off opposite the road end of Alltchaorunn. ◀

Start across the farm gate. Take the track towards **Alltchaorunn**. Where it bends away from the river through a gate, keep along the riverbank. Cross the Allt a' Chaorainn where it flows into the River Etive. If this is impossible there is a footbridge just above Alltchaorunn farm, but it leaves you inside a deer-fenced enclosure.

Cross a wet field diagonally, and go uphill alongside a broken wall and deer fence to the top of the fence. Cross the broken wall and slant uphill on quite steep grass to left of crags. Above, ease back right, still on grass, into the intriguing notch at 450m, shaped as though the Ghabhar goat had taken a great bite out of the Ceitlein cabbage. Its faultline leaps across Glen Etive to become one of the gullies in the Buachaille opposite.

The rise out of the notch is slightly rocky, so contour out left for 10 metres then head uphill. Just above, the slope eases, to the gentler climb southwest up the long ridge of **Beinn Ceitlein**. The ground at the top is knolly, with the summit of Beinn Ceitlein being just the highest knoll. The rocky pyramid of Stob Dubh, the higher summit and Corbett, makes itself obvious ahead and to the right.

Continue from Beinn Ceitlein summit southwest over another slight rise, then dip into a col and go straight up the steepish ridge (surprisingly composed of quartzite) to the summit of **Stob Dubh**. The view down into Glen Etive is spectacular.

Return through the col, and continue ahead (southeast) around the right-hand flank to drop into a slightly lower col. Here head down to the left, into **Coire Dubh-mor**. The stream in this steep re-entrant has waterfalls and small gorges: keep to open slopes to left of the stream. At the foot of Coire Dubh-mor cross the stream and then the wide tussocky valley of **Allt a' Chaorainn** ahead. Gain the long gentle spur directly opposite (NN 186482) that forms the right-hand rim of **Coire na Cloiche**. Keep to the crest to see the fine falls in the stream on the left. The spur rises to a very minor summit, where you cross a grassy col and head quite steeply onto **Meall Odhar**.

After all this tough ground, it's a treat to head east along the broad grassy ridge, down into Bealach Odhar, then gently up over **Stob a' Bruaich Leith**. From its right-hand (990m) summit, old fence posts lead along the ridge. This narrows enjoyably, then rises to the stony pyramid of **Stob Ghabhar**.

The **descent** starts by retracing steps. Head down northwest, curving to west, following the iron posts of the old fence. After 400 metres of level ridge, where the fencing swings down to the left, head northwest, along the wide and almost level ridge. After 300 metres

On Beinn Ceitlein, approaching its main summit Stob Dubh

Descending Sron a' Ghearrain. The ridge of Buachaille Mor lies ahead on the other side of Glen Etive; Ben Nevis is at the back.

it bends north, heading straight down the wide, gentle **Sron a' Ghearrain.**

The descent is easy to the 650m contour. Below there it steepens, so turn down left on steepish grass into **Coire Laoghan**. The stream at this point is a small gorge, so slant round to the right above it, dropping to join it below the gorge section. A small path on the opposite side leads downstream, and after 500 metres becomes a rather better stalkers' path.

This path runs above and to left of the lovely stream Allt Coire Laoghan. It drops in a zigzag, then contours across the steep slope of **Meall Ghiubhas**. Then it drops to cross **Allt Coire a' Chaolain** at a footbridge (NN 204486). The clear path continues around the base of **Aonach Mor**, through a gate, then drops to a narrow footbridge across the gorge of **Allt Coire Ghiubhasan** (NN 200500).

A carved rock ramp leads out of the gorge. The path beyond loses itself for a moment, but will be found again alongside the stream. It passes through a gate into a regeneration enclosure, then through another gate to **Alltchaorunn**.

88 Beinn nan Aighenan

Start/finish	Inveroran NN 270417
Distance	37.5km/23.5 miles
Ascent	1300m/4400ft
Approx time	12.5hr
Max altitude	Beinn nan Aighenan 957m
Terrain	Tracks, paths, grassy hill

Length

Difficulty

Beinn nan Aighenan is usually bagged as a slightly tiresome out-and-back on the way down Ben Starav (Route 73). Make it into a proper mountain, no longer tiresome but instead very tiring, by approaching it along the glen it lives in. In theory we all celebrate the long walk in. In practice one way to shorten it is to take a tent in as far as Loch Dochard, or overnight in the slightly sordid shed there. The track in could be cycled; it is challengingly rough. The track from Taynuilt (Route 89) is smooth and graded, but 21km each way.

Start on rough path out of the car park, rejoining the road to cross Victoria Bridge. Turn left, to left of two lodges, on the track up **Abhainn Shira**. In 2km keep ahead on the riverside path, swampy in parts (cyclists divert via Clashgour).

Take the footbridge over Allt Ghabhar, and turn right on a peaty path through the edge of forest. It crosses swamp to a footbridge and rejoins the track. Turn right, past **Loch Dochard** and down to River Kinglass. The bridge on maps is a disused suspension bridge; the new bridge is 400 metres downstream. In another 1km the

On the unfrequented east ridge of Beinn nan Aighenan

track joins the river; 300 metres later, look out for wheel-marks on the right up the line of an old path.

It runs above the ravine of **Eas a' Bhinnein** into Coire a' Bhinnein. Turn east, up gentle slopes, onto the corrie rim. A wide ridge of grass and rocky slabs runs north, then northwest, over a 744m top to **Beinn nan Aighenan**.

Descend north, on a gritty path over ledges and rocks, to a well-defined col at 618m. The path ahead continues to the 767m col east of Ben Starav, but turn down left into the valley of **Allt Hallater.** Slant down grassy slopes to join the stream, with a small path to its left. It runs down through a ravine into **Glen Kinglass**.

Turn left along the wide, smooth track. Opposite **Glenkinglass Lodge** keep ahead on an older track paved with rocks, after 1km rejoining the outward route.

89 Glen Kinglass

Start	Taynuilt NN 004312
Finish	Bridge of Orchy NN 297396
Distance	40km/25 miles
Ascent	750m/2500ft
Approx time	2 days (12hr going)
Max altitude	Kinglass Pass 290m; West Highland Way 330m
Terrain	Tracks, short soggy path
Sketch map	See overview map (page 15)

Length
■ ■ ■ ■ □

Difficulty
■ ■ □ □ □

A relatively easy route through some very tough country. With woodland regeneration Glen Kinglass should gradually get even prettier, but the pass at its head will always be bleak.

From Taynuilt station, **start** north through the village. Across River Nant, the road bends right, but a track ahead becomes path then rejoins the road. At once turn right beside the RC Church of the Visitation, and follow

*Loch Dochard.
A camp here breaks
the trek Route 89, or
takes several hours
off the long walk in to
Beinn nan Aighenan
(Route 88).*

a street through **Brochroy**. It becomes a track, forking left to pass alongside the Bonawe Ironworks. At the entrance gate to Bonawe House move across right onto the other track. Follow it through shady woods, and then between high shady hedges. After 800 metres it bends right; here take a kissing gate on the left, down to the **River Awe**.

Cross an impressive suspension bridge and the field beyond to a small gate beside brown huts. Pass between the huts, and up to the corner of the car park for **Inverawe Country Park**.

Turn left through the car park and right on the road beyond. After 800 metres turn left, up a forest track tarmacked for its first rise then gravel. After 500 metres, in a clear-felled valley, ignore a track right; 150 metres later ignore a fork left signed for Tigh na Ba. The main track ahead enters broadleaf woodland and passes a vehicle barrier and a disabled truck, then slants down to the side of Loch Etive beside a fish farm. After running out of the woodland, it passes two new-built houses (not on the map) then crosses River Noe. Keep on upstream to pass **Glennoe** farm.

The track runs across open moorland above Loch Etive, crossing first **River Liver**, and then the bridge at **Ardmaddy** (NN 079375; 12.5km/8 miles and 200m/700ft so far).

Turn right on a smooth track to left of River Kinglass, using an older track on the right if you spot it. **Narrachan** hut has been available for informal bothy use in the past. At **Glenkinglass Lodge** keep ahead on an older track paved with rocks. After 2.5km fork right to a sturdy bridge (NN 186399). Cross, and turn left up the riverbank to a disused footbridge (which is the bridge still marked on maps). Just beyond, pick up a very rough track. Follow it northeast, as it improves. At **Loch Dochard**, a former stable is an open but uncomfortable shelter.

In another 2km, turn left over a footbridge and cross peat swamp to a ladder stile and rough path between trees. A stout bridge crosses Allt Ghabhar. Now a riverside path is ahead, or a track via Clashgour if you prefer drier feet. The two rejoin to reach **Forest Lodge**.

Turn right past **Inveroran Hotel**, where the way-marked **West Highland Way** crosses the shoulder of Mam Carraigh then descends gradually to **Bridge of Orchy**.

PART TEN

BEN CRUACHAN AND OBAN

Oban bay at dusk

Oban is full of sailors and shoppers and people waiting for a ferry into the islands of the West. It's as busy as Fort William, but seems more of a real town – perhaps simply because of the smell of fish. And the circuit of Kerrera island is an offshore adventure that's a world away from the stony path up Ben Nevis.

But look back from Kerrera across the harbour, and high above the houses and the fanciful Colosseum rise the pointed summits of Ben Cruachan.

SUMMIT SUMMARY

Ben Cruachan

Cruachan is a hill of granite grandeur. Leaflets from the Forestry Commission list it as the highest in Argyll, and this usurping of Bidean nam Bian is not altogether presumptuous. (It is the highest in the Argyll and Bute district, but not in the old county of Argyll.) The super-steep northern slopes define its three triangular summits: Taynuilt Peak (Stob Dearg, 1104m); Cruachan summit; and Stob Diamh. These give its name – which means Hill of Stacks – and also its outline, so distinctive in views from Glen Coe and Ben Nevis.

Cruachan has two Munros, and a granite ridge between that offers a moment of scrambling. The best circuit is clockwise, with the awkward ascent by Bealach an Lochain in the easier uphill direction; the same for scrambling the 'Granny-stopper'; and so that, at the final col, you can decide whether there's time to include the bonus peak Beinn a' Bhuiridh. That circuit is Route 90; the final diversion over the bonus Corbett Beinn a' Bhuiridh is Route 92.

If that's a Munro classic, the lesser classic is the Dalmally Horseshoe. This approaches from the east, taking only the second Munro but adding the Corbett, so that it lacks scrambling as well as the main summit of Cruachan. Instead it offers sharp but grassy ridges and a delightful descent.

For romantics, Route 96 is a back way in under that impressive northern side, offering a little extra scrambling and a small arête to Drochaid Ghlas. For the even more romantic, *Scrambles in Lochaber* (see Appendix 3) offers two wild but easy scrambles, the North Ridge of Taynuilt Peak and the East Ridge of Stob Garbh, both Grade 1.

Ben Cruachan
Summit Summary

Taynuilt Peak

Ben Cruachan

Meall Cuanail

Stob Diamh

Beinn a' Bhuiridh

Loch Awe

0 1 2 km

N

BEN CRUACHAN ROUTES

90	Cruachan Horseshoe	93	Cruachan Ridge in Reverse
91	Meall Cuanail	94	Dalmally Horseshoe
92	Beinn a' Bhuiridh add-on	95	Stob Garbh Southeast Ridge
92A	Descent North from Beinn a' Bhuiridh	96	Drochaid Ghlas Northeast Ridge
		97	Cruachan Reservoir

90 Cruachan Horseshoe

Length

Difficulty

Start/finish	Cruachan Power Station NN 078268
Distance	13km/8 miles
Ascent	1400m/4600ft
Approx time	7hr
Terrain	Steep paths, bouldery and rocky ridges with a short scramble (Grade 1)

The Cruachan horsehoe is one of the classic hill circuits of Scotland.

Parking at the Power Station Visitor Centre isn't for walkers. Informal parking is opposite on the north side of the road, also pull-ins 200 metres further east, and a larger space 800 metres west.

Paths run up on either side of the Cruachan falls (for more details see Route 97). **Start** up the western one, at a tarred lane opposite the entrance to the power station proper (not the Visitor Centre, 100 metres further east). (The eastern path is signed for the railway station; it passes under the rails in a narrow tunnel, then heads left towards the stream.)

The track becomes rough and crosses the railway. A path continues uphill, with steep zigzags through the wood, to a ladder stile. With the stream on your right, continue to a track below the **Cruachan dam**. Turn left up the base of the dam, until steep steps lead up onto its top.

Turn left to the dam end, and up to a track just above. Turn right, and follow the track above the reservoir. At the reservoir end, look out for a cairn where a path turns off left; the path is initially undefined across wet ground. It becomes clear, first to left of a stream, then crossing it to run up on its right. As the path runs up the steep back wall of **Coire Dearg** it is steep and eroded, but the craggy surroundings are compensation.

The path arrives at the small pass Bealach an Lochain, with a small pool and the posts and stile of a former fence. Turn up right, on a path that's still steep and eroded, and then up a boulderfield to **Cruachan summit**. The trig point, a concrete cylinder, has been broken off.

> The **out-and-back to Taynuilt Peak** gives an extra bit of scrambly ridge and a superb view. Taynuilt Peak (Stob Dearg) is only a Munro Top, not a fully independent Munro. The ridge path leads down gently, avoiding some slabby crest by keeping left. After a short rise, the ridge steepens downwards; here is a well-scrambled groove-line down the crest, with exposure on the right. The groove can be avoided by dropping left then contouring across, on mossy rocks that aren't much easier than the crest line.
>
> The ridge continues gently downwards, then up **Taynuilt Peak**, a fairly steep cone of stones, boulders and grass. Return the same way to **Cruachan summit**.

The bouldery ridgeline descends gently east – this section could be avoided by a path a few metres down on the right (south). After a steeper descent, a col (NN 072304) is below the scrambling obstacle, nicknamed (by guidebook writer Ralph Storer) as the **Granny-stopper**. Many grannies will find it nothing but fun; on the other hand, in wind, wet or flying snow, even the youngest and most vigorous may pause here. There are three ways at it.

• The direct line up the crest is easy, on good rock, but is exposed, with big drops nearby on the left. From the col, a steep move to right of a 2m pinnacle leads onto slabs. Continue straight up. The lower section of slabs has good handholds; the upper part has less holds, but is easier angled.

The 'Granny-stopper'
scrambling moment on
Cruachan's main ridge

- Alternatively, if you like delicacy rather than strain, contour out right from the col along a line of sloping footholds. The final steps, which lack handholds, are protected by a sort of rock trench just below. From the end of the traverse, a rocky groove leads up for 20 metres to the ridge crest above the obstacle.

- The obstacle can be avoided altogether on steep grass, though in winter or spring this may be snow-covered. From the col, a steep and rather nasty path descends to the right (south). After 50 metres it descends more gently to the left, and soon crosses a narrow run of stones, often with a trickle of water. Although the path continues beyond, turn left up the stony strip, soon to enter a steep grass gully between low rock walls. It leads up to the ridge crest above the obstacle.

Continue along the ridge, which is narrow and boul-dery, with a path. It turns northwest and rises gradually towards the midpoint summit Drochaid Ghlas. At a tiny col (NN 0834 3070) the right fork is the continuing ridge-line towards Stob Diamh, but first you could take the left fork for a few metres to the small cairn on **Drochaid Ghlas** (the 'grey bridge') between the two Munros. It is a true bridge, as water gathered from Glen Noe passes below it into Cruachan Reservoir.

Return to the continuing ridgeline path. The ridge descends then climbs to the second Munro, **Stob Diamh**;

the final ascent to this is steep, and the path heads out right, to approach the summit from the south.

Leaving the summit, the path is initially unclear. Head down south; 50 metres from the cairn a path appears, running down a shapely ridge that dips then climbs to **Stob Garbh**.

About 100 metres after this summit, you might be drawn round left onto the top of its east ridge, but as this narrows to an unpathed mossy arête you realise your mistake. Instead keep south, to a wide grassy col with two small pools 200 metres from the summit. Beyond is a slight rise to 947m; the main path bears right to bypass this. ▶ Now a broad ridge descends gently south to **Lairig Torran** col below Beinn a' Bhuiridh.

To descend the Southeast Ridge (Route 95) head up onto the top of this rise.

Now decide whether to include Beinn a' Bhuiridh (Route 92). It's not much extra ascent, and its evening views are quite magical as the sun sinks at the end of Loch Awe (in winter) or (in summer) considerably further round to the north.

From Lairig Torran, descend to right of the small gorge towards **Cruachan Reservoir**. At 550m as the

Approaching Stob Diamh on the Cruachan Horseshoe

ground steepens, a path forms at the top of a slight spur 50 metres to right of the ravine. The path drops to cross the stream at the foot of the ravine at the 450m contour, and runs gently around the slope down to a track end near the **Cruachan dam**.

Follow the track past the dam end, to a junction; here turn right for 50 metres to the stream. Just across the stream is the path used for the ascent; but go down to left of the stream, to a high ladder stile and a clear path. This descends grassy slopes with views of some of the waterfalls, then goes down steeply through the woods to emerge past **Falls of Cruachan station**.

91 Meall Cuanail

Difficulty
■■■□□

Start	Cruachan Power Station
	NN 078268
Distance	12.5km/8 miles (full horseshoe)
Ascent	1200m/4000ft
Approx time	
(full circuit)	6hr
Terrain	Pathless slope of grass and stones

This route avoids the eroded steep path in Coire Dearg, exchanging its craggy enclosure for more open views. It adds 100m of ascent, and a minor Munro Top.

Start as Route 90 up to **Cruachan Dam**. From the dam's left end head up to a track just above and follow it to the left for 50 metres. Head straight up (left of outcrops) onto **Meall Cuanail**. A decaying fence along the south ridgeline leads up (with long Loch Awe views) to the summit, which is a Munro Top by 2m (Landranger) or 4m (Explorer).

The fence line leads onward, down quite steeply into the Bealach an Lochain col, where continue as Route 90 on the steep path ahead to **Cruachan summit**.

92 Beinn a' Bhuiridh add-on

Start	Cruachan Power Station	
	NN 078268	
Distance	13.5km/8.5 miles (full horseshoe)	
Ascent	1300m/4300ft	
Approx time (without		
Taynuilt Peak)	6.5hr	
Terrain	Steep slopes with small outcrops	

Difficulty

Extend the classic Cruachan circuit by adding its Corbett and the very best Loch Awe views.

Follow Route 90 (or 91) over both Cruachan Munros and down to the Lairig Torran pass below Beinn a' Bhuiridh.

From **Lairig Torran** the slope of Beinn a' Bhuiridh ahead is rather steep, with stonefields at the bottom and outcrops above, then a fringe of broken crag along the top edge. Starting from the right-hand end of the pass, a slight spur gives a break in the initial stonefields. Then

Setting off up Meall Cuanail, with Beinn a' Bhuiridh behind. Route 92 descends the lesser spur immediately above the walker.

head up, zigzagging among the outcrops. If no clear way shows through the final crag, slant to the right below it for 300 metres. You can now round the end of the crag to arrive at once at a summit cairn. **Beinn a' Bhuiridh** has three summit cairns in a 50-metre triangle: you have arrived at the northwest one (NN 0939 2833), but the south one has the really Awe-some views.

From that south cairn head south, descending steeply for 100m to a flatter platform. Here turn right, directly towards the Cruachan dam, and descend steepish grass; a line of crag is above on the right, flanking the west spur of Beinn a' Bhuiridh (that spur itself would make an unattractive descent as it becomes steep and cragged at the bottom). The ridge has a final hump where you can continue ahead to the dam end or drop left to join the track just below.

Follow the track down left to its junction below the dam and turn right for 50 metres. Just before a stream, take a path down left to a high ladder stile, and down through woods to **Falls of Cruachan station** and the road just below.

92A Descent North from Beinn a' Bhuiridh

If you want to do the Cruachan Ridge westbound (Route 93), you first have to get up Stob Diamh. **Ascent**s from the east will be Routes 94 and 95, but the simplest is to reverse Route 90, or else Route 92. The difficulty there is to descend north from Beinn a' Bhuiridh to Lairig Torran – tricky, especially in mist.

Difficulty

The best descent is not quite the same as the ascent line described in **Route 92**. Instead, from the three summit cairns, head east along the plateau for 300 metres to a small pool (NN 0962 2845). Follow its trickle to the steep northern slope top, and slant down to the right (northeast) to near drops on the right. Then double back left onto open ground above the **Lairig Torran**.

Now the slope below is steep but without large crags. Heading straight down should take you to right of the lower stonefields.

93 Cruachan Ridge in Reverse

Start	Stob Diamh NN 094308
Distance (circuit from Power Station)	13km/8 miles
Ascent	1400m/4600ft
Approx time (with Taynuilt Peak)	7hr
Terrain	Steep paths, bouldery and rocky ridges with a short down-scramble (Grade 1)

Various route combinations may have you crossing the main ridge westbound (rather than the easier eastbound direction of Route 90). This direction does have even finer views, featuring the sea.

Head down **Stob Diamh**'s south ridge for 20 or 30 metres, then turn sharp right to slant down below the steep ground to gain the westward ridgeline. The well-defined ridge runs down west, with drops on the right (north). After a drop and rise, and 2km from Stob Diamh, a small diversion back sharp right leads to the precipice-poised summit **Drochaid Ghlas**.

The most striking section of ridge follows, with drops on the right sometimes vertical. It runs down southwest, then turns just north of west and ascends gently to a sharp drop. This is the so-called **Granny-stopper** (NN 072304). A metre-long arête passes above a grass gully down left. At this point there are three onward routes.

- For the classic crest, continue up a slight rise, and take slabs down alongside a fierce drop on the

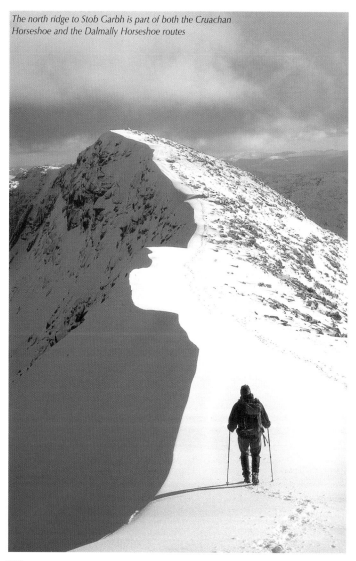

The north ridge to Stob Garbh is part of both the Cruachan Horseshoe and the Dalmally Horseshoe routes

right. The slabs are gentle but holdless, then slightly steeper but with holds. A steep step alongside a small detached pinnacle leads to the col below the Granny-stopper.

- Alternatively, if your climbing is subtle rather than strenuous, from the one-metre arête descend left for 20 metres in a rocky groove. Then turn right and contour across slabs, with trodden footholds. The first steps are without handholds and you must simply step confidently on the sloping footholds; a rock trench below provides security. Continue with a similar move without the rock trench below, then across easier slabs with handholds, to the col below the Granny-stopper.

- In windy weather, you may prefer to avoid the rocks altogether, although this grass option may be snow-covered in winter or spring. From the 1-metre arete, descend left, but instead of taking the rock groove, fork slightly further left into a grass gully between low rock walls. After 50 metres, with the rock walls opened out, a small path crosses. Turn right up this, slanting uphill then straight up a rather eroded path to the col below the Granny-stopper.

The ridge ahead is stony, then develops into a bouldery crest with a path a few metres down left if you prefer. Either way soon leads to **Cruachan summit**. ▶

    Descent southwards is tricky in mist, as the boulder-field below the summit does not show the path, so keep the compass handy. After the first drop the path becomes clear, and indeed rather eroded, with the spur line defined by a steep drop on the left. After a steep descent, the col Bealach an Lochain is marked by a small pool and the posts of a dead fence. Here turn left to descend **Route 90** – the easiest continuation with its clear, if steep and eroded, path.

For out-and-back to Taynuilt Peak see Route 90.

94 Dalmally Horseshoe

Length
■ ■ ■ □ □

Difficulty
■ ■ ■ □ □

Start/finish	Stronmilchan road end B8077 meets A85 NN 132283
Distance	14km/8.5 miles
Ascent	1300m/4200ft
Approx time	7hr
Terrain	Grassy ridges

The easier but still satisfying circuit that misses out Cruchan's main summit.

Parking is 100 metres along the A85 east from its junction with the B8077.

Start along a track that leaves the B8077 at the road junction. After 1km, stop at a gate to survey the ridge ahead. In another 200 metres, the main track bends left uphill, with a fainter track contouring ahead; here turn off right, aiming for the bridge at NN 127297 – the bridge is out of sight, but the eroded ground on the further bank can be seen.

Cross the wide bridge, and head up to the base of **Sron an Isean**. The steep ridge rises in bracken, with a worn path up the ill-defined crest. At 250m the slope eases slightly: here the path contours left for 20 metres before continuing straight up through more bracken.

Above the bracken, slant up right, to the foot of outcrops. A grassy gap runs up and right; or head further right to bypass the outcrops, then back left to reach the grassy crest above. The slope is now less steep, with a small path along the crest. Ever pleasanter grassy ridge-walking leads to the summit of **Sron an Isean**.

The ridge now narrows, with boulders and grass, running southwest above Coire Lochain (a remote hollow that must reward its very infrequent visitors). **Stob Diamh** top is stony with a cairn.

Leaving the summit requires some care as the path is initially unclear. Head down south, ignoring paths turning off right (formed by those arriving from the west, zigzagging to avoid the final steep of Stob Diamh). By 50 metres from the cairn a path has formed running down a definite ridge that rises to **Stob Garbh**.

Keep south, to a wide grassy col with two small pools 200 metres from the summit. Beyond is a slight rise; the path bears right to bypass this. ▶

The ridge now broadens and swings south, down to the broad pass Lairig Torran below **Beinn a' Bhuiridh**. The slope of Beinn a' Bhuiridh ahead is rather steep, with stonefields at the bottom and outcrops above, and a fringe of broken crag along the top edge. Starting from the right-hand end of the pass, a slight spur gives a break in the initial stonefields. Above them, zigzag up among the outcrops. If no clear way shows through the final crag, slant to the right below it for 300 metres. You can now round the end of the crag to arrive at once at a summit cairn. **Beinn a' Bhuiridh** has three summit cairns in a 50-metre triangle: you have arrived at the northwest one (NN 0939 2833), but the south one has the really Awe-some views.

The descent of Beinn a' Bhuiridh is gentle pleasure. Head east past the rock knoll of Beinn a' Bhuiridh's east top, and down a broad gentle ridge with drops on the left. The ridge rises slightly to the flat plateau of **Monadh Driseig**; a visit to the trig point, out right, is worthwhile for

A useful escape here is to descend Route 95, the southeast ridge, from the top of the 947m knoll.

Looking across the Dalmally Horseshoe: Beinn a' Bhuiridh from Sron an Isean's east ridge

more views. The ridge down east is decorated with granite erratics, poised in textbook style on outcrops of schist.

At 450m the ridge turns northeast and steepens down to a col at 350m. From here a direct descent down right is steep and bracken-infested, so instead turn down left (north) on gentler slopes. After passing to left of a rocky outcrop, head right, to find the old quarries. Traces of old path, to left of the workings, lead down to lower quarries, with the track of the upward route just below.

95 Stob Garbh Southeast Ridge

Difficulty

Start	Stronmilchan road end (NN 132283)
Distance (Meall a' Bhuiridh circuit)	11.5km/7 miles
Ascent	900m/3000ft
Approx time	5.5hr
Terrain	Grassy ridge

The most comfortable way onto the Cruachan Ridge, with no steepness, scrambling, bog or shaggy vegetation. Combine it with the end of Route 94 for a half-day over the Corbett Beinn a' Bhuiridh. In descent, it's a useful escape halfway around the full Route 94, Dalmally Horseshoe.

There's parking on the A85, 100 metres east of the Stronmilchan road end. **Start** at that road end, where a track heads north, under power lines and below disused quarries to a stout footbridge (NN 120295). Turn left, on a path above and alongside **Allt Coire Ghlais**, for 400 metres to a small ruin. Here turn up right onto the ridgeline towards Stob Garbh.

The ridge ascends grassily and gently. Sometimes there is a small path. A small col at 450m has a pool. Two thirds of the way up keep ahead for Stob Garbh and Stob Diamh, or else aim off left for Beinn a' Bhuiridh.

- For **Stob Diamh** the ascent is uncomplicated. Keep up the ridge, which steepens with drops on the right, and becomes a featureless steep slope to a knoll at 947m with a couple of cairns. Turn right, northwest, soon joining the ridge path to **Stob Diamh**.

- If you are aiming for Lairig Torran and **Beinn a' Bhuiridh**, ascend the ridge to the 700m contour only. In mist, try to find a marking boulder, with a W-shape excised from its left corner (NN 1029 2969). From here a grassy shelf runs to the left, with steeper ground above and below. In mist, contouring along this shelf needs concentration. Finally climb slightly to avoid slabby ground ahead, and reach the rise (750m) immediately north of Lairig Torran. ▶ Continue over **Beinn a' Bhuiridh** as on **Route 94.**

The rise has a boulder shaped like the smile on a crocodile, a striking-off point for those reversing this line in mist.

Descent of Southeast Ridge from Stob Diamh Keep south for 200 metres, to a wide grassy col with two small pools. Beyond is a slight rise to 947m; the main path bears right to bypass this, but head up onto its top (NN 0972 2997 – in mist beware a cairn 50 metres SW, which isn't a good place to find the ridgeline from). Descend south-southeast, down steep grass, with even steeper grass on the left. There is a trace of path, but compass is the best way down here in mist. At 750m the slope eases and the ridgeline becomes apparent.

96 Drochaid Ghlas Northeast Ridge

Start	Castles farm track NN 136288
Distance	10km/6 miles (to Cruachan summit)
Ascent	1200m/4000ft
Approx time up	5.5hr
Terrain	Pathless ridge, short scramble Grade 1

Difficulty
■ ■ ■ ■ ■

*The steep and little-visited north side of
Ben Cruachan, seen along Loch Etive*

The romantic back way onto Ben Cruachan.

There are two small parking pull-offs at the bridge over
Allt Mhoille. There is another pull-off 500 metres east
(NN 141290), and on the A85 just east of its junction
with the B8077.

There are two entrances to the track system towards
Castles farm. At the eastern one (by a brown bungalow)
enter and turn left on track for 150 metres, then turn
right. At the western entrance (marked Castles Estate)
enter across a cattle grid, and keep ahead.

At NN 1297 3064,
270m, a small cairn
and path on the right
are the 'standard'
route up Beinn
Eunaich.

Follow the main track ahead to a junction near
Castles farm. Turn left through a gate, onto the track,
with traces of tarmac, climbing up across the flank of
Beinn Eunaich. ◀

The track crosses **Allt Lairig Ianachain** and passes a
side-track on the right. This side-track is where Route 98
descends from Beinn a' Chochuill. Then it runs almost
level to pass below a locked hut. Just before the next stream
crossing, six tall marker poles mark the way up to **Lairig
Noe**. The apparent track on Explorer maps here is actually
a tunnel. (From the pass, steep grass slopes give access to
Sron an Isean and Beinn a' Chochuill on either side.)

Two more tall posts guide through the pass and more are on the descent to the isolated track stretch across the head of **Glen Noe**. Turn left to go past a water-tunnel entry, and follow the track, green and little used, to its end at the foot of a slabby stream. Crossing the stream is usually easy as the water is gathered just above and taken away under the mountain!

Head up to right of the slabby stream until the slope eases into a shallow corrie at 550m. Bear up right onto the ridgeline, and go up it with drops on the right. The ridge bends from southwest to south and steepens; then at the 900m contour steepens even more into a rocky tower. This is overcome by a gritty narrow gully slanting right, with a scrambling moment. For descenders with GPS, the top of this gully is at NN 0843 3109. Regain the crest above, for a little easy scrambling over boulders and easy slabs, until the ridge levels to a charming arête with small path. A tiny gendarme (obstacle) is teetered past on the left. The ridge rises slightly to the small cairn on **Drochaid Ghlas**.

97 Cruachan Reservoir

Start/finish	Cruachan Power Station
	NN 077268
Distance	7km/4.5 miles
Ascent	400m/1300ft
Approx time	3hr
Max altitude	450m
Terrain	Steep rough paths

Length

Difficulty

This is a tough little walk, so allow more time than the distance and height gain alone would suggest. The views all the way up are fine, and the reservoir at the top is most attractive unless it's been emptied to power the UK's electric toasters and kettles (it provides quick power for surges like the ones in breaks of popular TV programmes). Afterwards, you can view the same terrain from underneath, on a tour of the power station inside Cruachan mountain. The walk is also the start of routes onto Cruachan's granite ridge, high above the reservoir.

Parking at the Power Station Visitor Centre is not intended for walkers and is locked at the end of the afternoon. Parking is opposite its entrance on the north side of the road; there are also small pull-ins further east, and a larger space 800 metres west.

Two paths run up, on either side of the Cruachan falls. Both are initially rough and steep through woodland. The eastern one is signed for the railway station. This route ascends the left-hand (western) one and comes down the other. **Start** at a tarred lane opposite the entrance to the power station proper (not the Visitor Centre entrance, 100 metres further west).

The track soon becomes rough and crosses the railway. A path continues uphill, with steep zigzags through the wood, to a high ladder stile over a deer fence at the wood's top. With the stream on your right, continue up the small path, to a track below the **Cruachan dam**. Turn left, up to the base of the dam. Steps on the left lead up below the dam, until steep iron steps lead to its top.

Turn right, and cross the dam. ▶ For the full walk, turn left to a tunnel outlet, and continue on a well-used path that slants gradually uphill above the reservoir. It reaches and crosses a stream just below its small ravine (NN 085286, 450m). Now the path turns uphill, but keep ahead, gradually slanting down pathless grass to the head of the reservoir, crossing several small streams.

The big stream flowing into the reservoir head is often impassable, but don't worry: head upstream to find that it, too, flows out of a tunnel. Pass across the top of the outlet to a track starting beyond. Follow this along the western shore of the reservoir and back to the **dam**, which is crossed for the second time back to its eastern end.

Turn right down a track for 300 metres to a junction. Turn right for 50 metres. You could now cross the

At the track at its eastern end, you could turn right for an immediate descent.

Loch Awe from the path above Falls of Cruachan

stream ahead and descend by the route used for coming up. Probably slightly easier is to descend to left of the stream, with no path defined, to a high (and when I crossed it very wobbly) ladder stile. Below this there is a clear path that descends grassy slopes with views of some of the Falls of Cruachan down on the right. Once inside the wood it's a steep and rough descent to **Falls of Cruachan station**. The path turns left to a tunnel under the railway line, and reaches the A85 just below.

98 Eunuch and Cockle

Length

Difficulty

Start	Stronmilchan road end
	NN 133284
Finish	Taynuilt NN 004312
Alternate	
start/finish	Bridge of River Strae NN 145294
Distance	24km/15 miles
Ascent	1500m/5000ft
Approx time	10hr
Max altitude	Beinn Eunaich 989m
Terrain	Paths, grassy ridges, tracks
Transport	Rail or Citylink coach Taynuilt –
	Dalmally (three of each daily)

Beinn Eunaich and Beinn a' Chochuill are usually considered as just two more to bag at the back of Ben Cruachan. Up the track behind Castles farm to a small cairn (NN 1297 3064); up Eunuch; then use this route and its opt-out descent back to Castles farm.

But the ridge linking the two extends above 600m for 8km. Instead of doing just the little bit in the middle between the two Munros, how much better to do it all. East of Beinn Eunaich is narrow green ridgewalking of the best sort, and almost pathless. A descent westwards to Loch Etive gives a long linear outing with return by bus or train; or there is a less 'ridge-it' option to descend back to a car in Glen Orchy.

'Eunaich' is birdish, with 'Eunuch' a nickname bestowed by mountaineer Ivan Waller. He thought 'Cockle' was another nickname, but in fact 'Cochuill' already means a seashell.

The Citylink bus will let you off near the Stronmilchan road end; from Lochawe station there's an extra 1km of verge to walk. For the non-linear walk, there's a small pull-in on the north side of the Stronmilchan road (NN 141290), or at the start of the Glen Strae track.

Start northeast along B8077, to a bridge over the **River Strae**, where a track turns off left. There's a sign to 'Old Village' and a white arrow. After 500 metres, the track forks. Right is signed for Duiletter and Glen Strae, but take the track left past a building. A pool is on the right, then the track passes through a deer fence to a junction. Keep ahead on the main track which has returned from

Duilettir bridge. After 1km, the track reaches a bridge over the **Allt Dhoirrean**.

Before the bridge, turn left up through a field gate, on faint quad-bike tracks. The path to right of the stream could be used initially, but it turns aside onto the spur of Beinn Lurachan. The wheelmark track is very faint, but if you lose it the going is rough grassland, comfortable enough. This track replaces an older stalkers' path.

The faint quad track, and the even fainter old stalkers' path, head up to left of the stream. After the crossing of the side-stream Allt Raineach, a few cairns mark the old path line into the col **Lairig Dhoireann**, with a pair of cairns to pass between at the high point. Route 77 to Glen Etive uses this as a true pass and continues ahead here.

Turn left, with rocky outcrops to thread among, then a stony slope to the summit of **Meall Copagach**. Now a lovely ridge with a very faint path leads west over two minor humps to **Beinn Eunaich**.

Lairig Dhoireann, on the back way up Beinn Eunaich

Here make a sharp right turn, to descend northwest, soon finding a trodden baggers' path. It leads down across a col (Lairig Ianachain) then up a quite sharp ridge, to a very minor top at 896m. Behind this is a slight drop to a col where the ridge turns slightly to the right. ▶

Keep ahead, along a pleasingly narrow level ridge, then a short steeper climb to the summit of **Beinn a' Chochuill**. From here both tops of Cruachan appear pointy and the main one positively Matterhorned.

Here is a 1.2m long haggis-shaped boulder which marks the turn-off point if you later want to descend to Strath of Orchy.

• **To return to Strath of Orchy**, retrace steps to the haggis-shaped boulder (NN 1181 3252). Bear right, southeast, to find within a few steps a path leading down a forming spur. The path fades, but follow the spur down until a track crosses it. This track should be downhill to the right (if it's slightly downhill left, you've come down west of the track junction, and need to turn *left*). Turn right, the downhill direction, to a junction, then left on a more-used track with traces of tarmac. It leads around the flank of Beinn Eunaich, to turn right near **Castles farm** and reach B8077.

• For the **long route to Taynuilt**, continue from Beinn a' Chochuill northwest down a ridge defined by the drop on the right. After 1.5km comes a sharp dip across the ridgeline just before **Aonach Breac** (Point 730m). The faultline groove down to the left harbours the beginning of the guiding stream Allt nan Gillean. Cross the dip to go down the spur to right of Allt nan Gillean, marked with some old iron fence posts. At 400m the spur levels to wet grassland. Here slant down its left edge to the bend in Allt nan Gillean where it leaves the faultline. To right of the stream (NN 073340) find quad-bike wheelmarks, which run down westwards.

The wheelmarks lead onto grassland pasture below **Creag an Fhithich**, with green humps of old lazybed cultivation. Head down to the waterfalls marked on maps, with the top end of the track at a quarry nearby.

Follow the track out past **Glennoe** farm to join a bigger track running alongside Loch Etive. Turn left, on a smooth track that after 400 metres crosses the **River Noe**, and then reaches the side of **Loch Etive**. It runs into pleasant woodland, and (4km from Glennoe) arrives at the lane, the Old Military Road, near Inverawe house.

Turn right, signed for **Inverawe Country Park**. After 400 metres turn left to the far corner of the country park's car park. Beside the shop, a sign marks a path for the Riverside Walk. Follow it down, between a couple of brown huts, to a riverside field. Cross to a large imposing footbridge over the **River Awe**.

Head up the field beyond to a kissing gate, to turn right along a tree-lined track to Bonawe Furnace. The track and street beyond lead into the north edge of Taynuilt. At the Catholic church cross into a path that rejoins street below. Follow this ahead, over the River Nant, to **Taynuilt station**.

99 Kerrera Island

Length

Difficulty

Start/finish	Kerrera ferry pier NM 830286
Distance	18km/12.5 miles (or shorter)
Ascent	300m/1000ft
Approx time	Up to 7hr
Max altitude	50m
Terrain	Tracks, fairly comfortable pathless grassland
Map	Landranger 49 (Oban) or Explorers 376 and 359
Transport	First ferry 8.45am; technically next 10.30am but timetable flexible

Kerrera is a low-lying basalt island of great character. It has an impressive castle, a tea garden, and no real roads. The island's standard route, referred to below as the 'Classic Track', is a circuit by Barnabuck and Ardmore to

Gylen Castle and along the east coast back to the ferry. It's an easy and rather busy walk of 11km/7 miles. The present route extends that by diverting to the island's northern end, and then forking off for a walk along the west coast along raised beach and clifftops. This is rather rougher and much quieter than the standard track, but even so not very rough. Castle and tea garden do still get in on the act, and the time given includes proper attention to both.

The northern part, to the busy yacht harbour, is a slightly urban introduction to the total island walk. A shortened start is at the end of the description.

From the ferry you can spot the old path running along the shoreline. From the slipway **start** through a field gate on the right, and turn uphill a few metres past a red diamond post (marking an underwater power line). Just above it, the old path runs to the right under bracken, becoming clearer. Follow it along the shoreline, sometimes hidden under bracken but mostly good. It develops into tractor wheelmarks and, 1km from the jetty, into a track. This slants left away from the shore below a basalt crag line, then drops to a field gate near Ardantrive (NM 837298). The track runs down a field, joined by another at the field foot – that track will be the return journey. Continue ahead to pass through **Ardantrive** farmyard with its five species of domestic fowl (including peacock and guinea).

The track continues to the busy yacht harbour. Either pass through the harbour or take a track just behind the

Walking above raised beaches on the northwest coast of Kerrera

buildings. Just beyond, the track, now green, divides
into two parallel ones. Where these rejoin, turn up left
through a wooden kissing gate to the stone **monument**
to Mr Hutcheson, who greatly improved steam
transport among the islands in the 1850s,
as manager of what later became
CalMac Ferries.

Return through
Ardantrive farm-
yard, and

take the track
forking right. It runs
below basalt outcrops,
and along the northern shoreline, to a shingle bay **Oitir Mhor**
with a small island Eilean nan Eun (Isle
of Birds) just offshore. ▶

The shortened route joins here: see below.

As the track bears left, keep ahead along
the shoreline. A faint path trace leads to Rubha
Redegich point. Continue along the shoreline,
over some bracken and bog but mostly fairly comfortable going, to reach the sandy **Slatrach Bay**.

At the bay's western end is a ruined boathouse.
Here a grass track continues along the shoreline, which
develops into a raised beach backed by low basalt cliffs.
The track follows the top of the cliffs, though the former
beach below is short-cropped grass for walking as well.
After 1km the track ends at a fence gate. Here turn down
right to the shoreline, beside a former sea cave Uamh
Rubha na Lice (Cave of the Point of Slabs). Floored with
sheep droppings and old bones, it's not a suitable wet-
weather picnic spot.

Continue along the shoreline, above wave-cut platforms of basalt, and past former sea stack pinnacles sticking out of the grass. In 400 metres the cliff projects towards the sea, with a rocky little path. Around this corner, a little sheep path passes up left by a rock ledge, for a continuation along the tops of the low cliffs. The going gets a bit rougher, with long grass and soft ground. A wheelmark track forms below the cliff line, leading to the next bay, **Barr-nam-boc**, below Barnabuck house.

From the bay's west corner, cross grass to a track behind a broken wall. Just up back left is the 'Classic Track' of the island's standard walk, but turn right instead, passing around the base of a headland, then round to the left. The track disappears, but keep ahead (southeast) to find the Classic Track just before it passes through a gate.

This is the best bit of the Classic Track. It follows a wandering path south, across a flat little valley and through a pass, to descend to **Ardmore**. On the right, a textbook-style basalt dyke sticks up out of the grass. In 400 metres the track reaches the corner of a rocky bay: ahead through a little col can be seen the top of Gylen Castle. Here turn off right on a faint green track through a gate. It crosses wet ground, then goes through the narrow little col. Pass around the head of Port a' Chaisteil bay, and take a path up through a rock gap to **Gylen Castle**. ◀

Gylen Castle is open to human visitors; please keep the wooden gate closed to exclude those visitors who are sheep.

Return through the rock gap to the head of Port a' Chaisteil, and take a path alongside a stream to a gate. A green track leads up to join the Classic Track circuit beside **Upper Gylen** tea garden.

Turn right, on tarmac track that reverts to gravel at the slope top. It descends past a couple of houses to the eastern shoreline, and follows it for 2km to the ferry slipway.

To leave out the northern part of the island This slightly shortened walk saves 3.5km (1hr). From the ferry slipway, follow the track ahead for 250 metres, past a red phone box. Take a track forking up right past the old schoolhouse. After the farm at **Balliemore**, a gate on the left with a wide track is signed for Gylen Castle and Tea Garden – that is the 'Classic Track' route.

Keep ahead, ignoring the track left, and passing through the col of the island watershed. After 300 metres, a track forks off right signed 'Shell Bay'. The track descends, turns right, and passes through a bracken col, before descending again to **Oitir Mhor** bay. Here turn left around the bay to Rubha Redegich point, now continuing on the main walk.

Glyen Castle and its bay, which was formerly the ferry terminal for the Western Isles

The **Classic Track** is a pleasant and easy 6.5-mile walk whose drawbacks are that it is mostly away from the shoreline, and is very busy and popular. Follow the 'leave out the north' route just above to the side-track signed for Gylen Castle. Take this track to pass just below **Barnabuck**, and up between two basalt craglets to a gate. Now a wide path, the route runs south across a flat little valley and through a pass, to descend to **Ardmore**. It passes to right of the house to reach the shore. Short-cut to Gylen Castle (as on the main route) or follow the clear track ahead to **Upper Gylen** Tea Garden. A signed gate on the right is the side-path to **Gylen Castle**. Return to **Upper Gylen**, and continue on the main track to the east coast and the slipway.

100 Beinn Lora

Length

■ ☐ ☐ ☐ ☐

Difficulty

■ ■ ☐ ☐ ☐

Start/finish	Benderloch NM 905381
Distance	6km/4 miles
Ascent	400m/1300ft
Approx time	2.5hr
Max altitude	Beinn Lora 308m
Terrain	Paths, good but steep, then peaty and small
Map	Landranger 49 or Explorer 376 (both 'Oban') or FC walk leaflet

Although Beinn Lora only just makes it to the 1000ft contour, its quality is indicated by the way various institutions in Benderloch below have adopted its name; notably the Beinn Lora café, convenient and comfortable (no muddy boots). The walk is short and on mostly good paths, but surprisingly steep. The hill itself is basalt, the views have a lot of intermixed sea and landscape, and the broadleaf woods at the bottom are pleasant.

There's a Forestry Commission car park on the east side
of the A828 road, or village parking (with café, and path
to the 1km-long sandy beach) on the west side of the
A828. A Forestry Commission map is available locally,
and on a board at the **start**.

Just inside the wood the path divides. To use the
steeper path for the ascent, turn left here, following
red/blue waymarks. A broad,
smooth path runs
along the foot

of the wood,
then turns right and
steeply uphill. At the 100m
contour it levels into a col, now in evergreen plantations.
At a fork, the right branch, downhill, has a viewpoint
bench and will be the return route. For now, fork left,
with blue waymarks, climbing gently and then more
steeply alongside a stream ravine (its waterfalls invisible
in summer behind beech leaves). As the slope eases at the
200m contour, a branch path left leads to a viewpoint.

Loch Etive from Connel Bridge below Beinn Lora

It's worth visiting for its steep view down on Benderloch.

Return to the main path and continue uphill. The path passes around **Ron's Lochan** (Lochan nan Ron, not named after me). It's just a reedbed swamp. About 200 metres later the path reaches the forest edge at a picnic table.

A kissing gate leads onto open hill. A peaty path, slightly downhill to start, leads through some boggy ground – its wet patches are reinforced with stones, so go across rather than around them. Around 500 metres and 70m of ascent lead to **Beinn Lora**'s summit with its trig pillar. Continue 100 metres south for a sub-summit with downward views.

Descend the same way, back into the forest, to the path junction at 100m altitude. Turn sharp left (red and blue waymarks) past a viewpoint bench and down into beech woods. The path divides, with a branch path ahead (red waymark) leading only to an unsatisfactory viewpoint with obstructing brushwood (probably not worth the bother). The Uamh Caillich, Witch's Cave, isn't on this path but somewhere in the steep ground below. So ignore it and fork down left, soon regaining the car park. ◄

For the beach, cross the A828 into the car park opposite, and find a path from its back left corner.

THE LONG ROUTES

West Highland Way

The territory of this book is where the WH Way finally escapes the traffic noise of the A82 and sets out into open country. Even so, it remains a broad pathway or track, busy and very hard to get lost off. As the first wild hill since Conic Hill, the short crossing between Bridge of Orchy and Inveroran is enjoyable. The edge of Rannoch Moor is crossed on a comfortable track, below the great hill face of the Black Mount; as the map suggests, this can be used as the return leg of a crossing of that high hill ridge (Route 86).

The crossing of the Devil's Staircase to Kinlochleven, on a well-graded and mostly smooth path, gives very fine views and beautiful woodland; it is not part of any plausible day walk. The Lairig Mor has more fine views

Buachaille Etive Mor from the West Highland Way

on the high track above Loch Leven, but ends through forest. The final roadwalk along Glen Nevis can be mitigated by a riverside path (Route 4).

According to your temperament, the crossing of the Devil's Staircase is the 'bad bit' or the 'good bit' of the West Highland Way. If the latter, then you should enjoy the more challenging, wilder, and very much quieter 'through routes' here.

Through Routes

The through routes are mapped on the overview maps at the beginning of the book (pages 12–15). In the Introduction I've tried to persuade you that if you haven't tried this strenuous but satisfying form of hill fun this area is a good one to start off in.

Even more strenuous and satisfying is the game of hauling the heavy rucksack, with the tent and so on, right up onto the tops. Any high ridgeline that looks plausible on the overview maps will usually be covered by day-walk routes in the book, though you may have to reverse

Wild camp in Glen Nevis – such lightweight, no-trace camping is now a legal right in Scotland

some of the route description. Here I'll mention specifically just two high passes. Walking from Dalmally to Loch Etive, after the first high pass of Route 77 (Dalmally variant), a splendid continuation on fairly good paths runs through the pass immediately east of Ben Starav (Routes 88 and 73). From Kinlochleven to Fort William an even higher pass crosses the Mamores, again on good paths, crossing Sgurr an Iubhair (Routes 37 and 28).

Dalmally or Taynuilt to Fort William in three or four days: good. If you don't want to stop there, the overview maps indicate where you could be going next. The first escape off the overview map is at Bridge of Orchy, where a track along Auch Glen leads into Glen Lyon. The continuing walk will be on quiet roads more than paths, through the great green hills of Highland Perthshire.

From Kings House, a rough peaty crossing of Rannoch Moor is more challenging. After Rannoch station and the Black Wood of Rannoch, walkers could head for Blair Atholl and the path network centred on Pitlochry.

From Corrour station a very fine pass north of Ben Alder, the Bealach Dubh, leads to Culra bothy on well-maintained paths through very remote country. The continuation to Dalwhinnie is on a rather harsh Landrover track alongside Loch Ericht.

Fort William is the start of the Great Glen Way to Inverness – a smooth and waymarked way, with too much track and towpath for my taste. However, at Gairlochy it leads naturally into the foot of Gleann Cia-aig, a fine crossing to Glen Garry, with onward paths to Knoydart (see below) or Cluanie Inn, Loch Affric and Wester Ross.

The better way out of William is by the passenger ferry across Loch Linnhe, when a good track by Cona Glen leads by a high path to Glenfinnan station. Stop there, or continue under the 'Hogwarts' viaduct for some really wild and rough country through to Glen Dessarry and Knoydart. In the far west, Inverie is reached only on foot, or by the ferry that takes you out to Mallaig. For those with the legs, this is what Scottish backpacking is all about!

The Three Ridges

Of the area's 44 Munro summits, 27 lie along three 'super-ridges' – these are easily seen on the two overview maps, where Munros are marked by solid triangles. Each of them makes a superb high-level traverse for any extremely fit walker.

Nevis to Grey Corries (8 summits) is possibly the best of all. The long haul up Ben Nevis can be taken in the dark, for sunrise on the summit. After getting the thrilling Carn Mor Dearg Arête all to yourself, the serious descents and reclimbs on either side of the Aonachs are the make-or-break section of the day. Then you get the whole of the Grey Corries without any of the preliminary forest trudge. Carry overnight gear and end at Lairig Leacach bothy, or else hike out under the moon to Spean Bridge. (Glen Nevis to Lairig Leacach: 25km/3100m or 15.5 miles/10,000ft – about 14 hours. If you think this is too long, the walker pictured doing just this with a big pack on page 56 is not, you'll note, extremely youthful.)

The Mamores (10 summits) – though it has the most Munros – is possibly the least excessive of the three. Once two loose hills at the eastern end are sorted out, it's just narrow ridges down a bit, along a bit, and up a bit, all the rest of the way. The range even allows a circular walk, returning to a start-point in either Glen Nevis or Kinlochleven. Just don't get caught in the dark in the forest above Polldubh! (Start and end Glen Nevis, 35.5km/3400m or 22 miles/11,500ft – 17 hours).

Etive to Black Mount (6–9 summits) is the wildest and least frequented of the three. It's also the most inconvenient; I approached it from Dalmally by way of Loch Etive side. In parts it's pathless, and needs skilful route-finding. A descent of Sron na Creise leaves the outcome in doubt right to the end. (Etive Shore to Kings House, 6 Munros without outliers, 30km/3000m or 19 miles/10,000ft, 15 hours).

Completing any of these ridges, in a day or as a self-suffi-cient trip with tent or bivvy bag, is something to be proud of. At the same time – modesty! The first two of them are linked into Tranter's Walk, the UK's ultimate one-day trek. That's 18 Munro summits, starting and finishing in Glen Nevis, between midnight and midnight. Too much? Well, the Tranter Walk has been attempted several times in winter conditions, though not yet completed within the day. Hill runners attempt to go 5 Munros further (Beinn na Lap, Chno Dearg, Stob Coire Sgriodain, Stob a' Choire Mheadhoin and Stob Coire Easain) in a 24-hour circuit of 90km/8250m of ascent. Though the distance and climb are similar to England's Bob Graham Round, the length of the individual climbs, together with the rough terrain, mean that this is a bit more than a standard superfit human can actually manage, and only a couple of dozen have achieved it.

A runner called John Fleetwood has extended the Etive–Blackmount ridge by adding in the Appin Munros and all of Glen Coe, including the Aonach Eagach and several other scrambles. He crossed 16 Munros and a Corbett (Beinn Maol Chaluim), 83km/8500m of ascent, in just under 29 hours.

Runner Paul McClintock (in blue top) and supporters on the Grey Corries during a successful Ramsay Round

297

APPENDIX 1

Access (in particular during the deer-stalking season)

Since 2005 Scotland has a legal right of access to almost all open country and farmland (the main exceptions being growing crops and land around buildings). Footbridges are explicitly included in the access rights, as are non-damaging cycling, and wild camping – though this doesn't mean roadside camping. Access must be taken 'responsibly', which basically means with consideration and care for other hill-users, land managers and the environment. Full text of the Scottish Access Code is at www.outdooraccess-scotland.com (or from Scottish Natural Heritage).

The long linear routes are on established customary paths, marked on Scotways' Hill Tracks map (apart from the Leum Uilleim variant on Route 46). Most of these are rights of way, with an absolute right of access. On Route 77, the Lairig Dhoireann north of Dalmally and the Etive shore path north of Glen Kinglass are not actually listed as rights of way, but it shouldn't make any difference. Scotways, formerly the Scottish Rights of Way Society, kept these lines alive during the long century before the Scottish Land Reform Act and erected the green 'SRWS' signposts on several routes in this book (www.scotways.com; 24 Annandale Street, Edinburgh EH7 4AN).

In parts of this area, from August (sometimes July) to 21 October, responsible access includes avoiding disturbance to deer stalking. (Stalking does not take place on Sundays.) The boundaries of the estates listed below are on the overview maps on pages 12 and 14.

Grey Corries Mamores West (GCM West)

There are no limitations on access on Ben Nevis, the Aonachs and the Mamores.

Grey Corries Mamores East (GCM East)

Including Grey Corries, Sgurr Eilde Mor: 14 August–20 October, consult hill-phone: 01397 732362. The general advice is to use normal paths, tracks and ridgelines and avoid corries. Redwells Estate, Fort William, tel: 01397 702433.

Corrour

Including Leum Uilleim: stalking 1 July–20 October and non-commercial stalking through winter to reduce overpopulation. Estate asks walkers to keep to established valley paths and hill ridges, and to avoid entering corries.

Black Corries

Including Beinn a' Chrulaiste: the estate is intensively stalked during the short period 1–21 October. Head Stalker, tel: 01855 851272.

National Trust for Scotland, Glencoe (NTS)
No restrictions.

Forestry Commission (FC)
No restrictions. Take particular care not to start fires.

Glencreran
Including Beinn Sgulaird: stalking 1 August–20 October, tel: 01631 563093.

Blackmount Partnership
Map boards at car parks and path ends show requested routes, which are the popular routes to the Munros (see above) during stalking (August–20 October). Ranger, Forest Lodge, tel: 01838 400562.

Castles Farm
Most routes on Ben Cruachan: no information offered.

APPENDIX 2
Information and Accommodation

Accommodation

Hotels, B&Bs www.visitscotland.com 0845 22 55 121 (or individual Tourist Information Centres below) also www.lochaber.com

Scottish Youth Hostels Association www.syha.org.uk, central bookings 08701 55 32 55

Independent Hostels www.hostel-scotland.co.uk, or for the free Blue Guide send stamped envelope to Scottish Independent Hostels, PO Box 7024, Fort William PH33 6YX

Campsites www.UKcampsite.co.uk

Travel

Journey planner www.travelinescotland.com 0871 200 22 33

Trains www.firstscotrail.com 08457 55 00 33

Coaches four daily each way Glasgow – Bride of Orchy – Kings House – Ballachulish – Fort William, also Glasgow – Oban, www.citylink.co.uk tel: 08705 505050

Buses Highland Country Buses 01463 710555 www.rapsons.co.uk

Ferries, chairlifts and so on See below

Weather and snow

Best weather forecast is at www.mwis.org.uk, posted at youth hostels etc daily. The site has links for snow conditions on Ben Nevis, Aonachs.

Avalanche forecast www.sais.gov.uk and posted locally.

Snow conditions (for skiers but useful for walkers and climbers too):
Nevis Range (Aonach Mor) www.nevisrange.co.uk
White Corries (Glencoe) www.glencoemountain.com

Webcams Ben Nevis http://visit-fortwilliam.co.uk/webcam
Glen Coe (Buachaille Mor) www.kingy.com

Ben Cruachan seen from a bivvy bag on Stob Ghabhar during a two-day traverse of the Etive range (Etive to Black Mount, page 296)

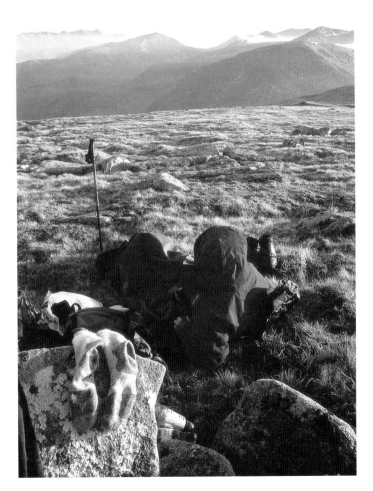

Summit panoramas computer views from Nevis, Bidean, Cruachan and 3 others
www.viewfinderpanoramas.org

Fort William and Glen Nevis

Tourist Information 19 High Street, Fort William PH33 6DH 01397 701801
www.visitscotland.com; Glen Nevis Visitor Centre PH33 6PF 01397 705922;
www.discover-fortwilliam.com, www.visit-fortwilliam.co.uk

Pubs and restaurants many in Fort William. Nevisport has a hearty café and a
bar underneath. Ben Nevis Inn at the foot of the Mountain Track (NN 125729)
has great food, atmosphere and views, even if only one real ale (also bunkhouse)

Supplies etc Morrisons supermarket, many gear shops and all other services.
Small interesting West Highland Museum, Cameron Square

SYHA Glen Nevis (year round) 01397 702 336

Independent hostels six, including Ben Nevis Inn

Camping Glen Nevis

Local transport Jacobite steam train mid-May – Sept bookings 0845 128 4681
www.steamtrain.info

Glas Bheinn Mhor from Allt Mheuran (Route 75)

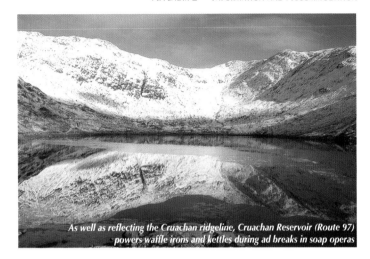

As well as reflecting the Cruachan ridgeline, Cruachan Reservoir (Route 97) powers waffle irons and kettles during ad breaks in soap operas

Spean Bridge

Pubs and restaurants café and chip shop. Bar meals at the unassuming Aonach Mor Hotel

Supplies Spar shop

Independent hostels Station Lodge Tulloch; Grey Corries Lodge Roy Bridge

Local transport Nevis Range gondola 01397 705825 www.nevisrange.co.uk

Corrour Station

Supplies etc Corrour Station bunkhouse has closed but there is still a restaurant and B&B 01397 732236

SYHA Loch Ossian 01397 732 207 Apr–Oct

Kinlochleven

Tourist Information at public library 01855 831663; walks leaflets 01855 831779 or download at www.kinlochleven.co.uk

Pubs and restaurants several including late-opening café at the Ice Factor and chip shop. Tailrace Inn is on the West Highland Way and very walker-friendly,

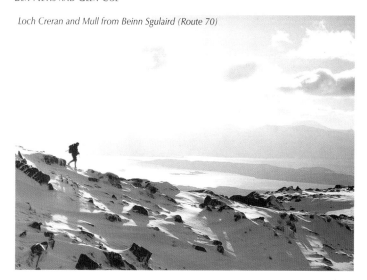

Loch Creran and Mull from Beinn Sgulaird (Route 70)

with singing of 'Loch Lomond' on Thursday and Friday nights in summer; Mamore Lodge serves afternoon tea

Supplies late-opening Co-op; hill gear at Ice Factor

Indoor climbing Ice Factor, UK's only indoor winter climbing wall 01855 831100 www.ice-factor.co.uk

Independent hostel comfortable Blackwater Hostel 01855 831253/402 www.blackwaterhostel.co.uk

Local transport buses to Ballachulish and Fort William

Glen Coe

Tourist Information Ballachulish Information Centre 01855 811866; The National Trust for Scotland Glencoe Visitors Centre 0844 493 2222 www.glencoe-nts.org.uk

Pubs and restaurants east of Glencoe village, Clachaig Inn with its big and busy bar serves good food and beer until 9pm (www.clachaig.com 01855 811252). At the top end of Glen Coe, the Kings House, even more historic than the Clachaig, has a smaller and less noisy bar but equally good food and drink (01855 851259 www.kingy.com).

Supplies etc grocer's in Glencoe village, late-opening Co-op at Ballachulish village, and a tiny folk museum.

SYHA Glencoe (01855 811 219)

Independent hostels Glencoe Hostel & Bunkhouse (01855 811906 www.glencoehostel.co.uk).

Camping Invercoe camp site 01855 811210; Glencoe camp site (at Visitor Centre on A82) 01844 811397; Red Squirrel Camp Site (east of Glencoe Village, open all year) 01855 811256; informal camping at Kings House and along Glen Etive opposite.

Orchy and Inveroran

Pubs and restaurants Good bar meals at Inveroran Hotel www.inveroran.com 01838 400220 and at Bridge of Orchy Hotel. Tyndrum has three contrasted eating experiences: Tyndrum Lodge Hotel (carvery and grill); Green Welly Stop (quiche and coffee), and Real Food Café (chip shop – with hippie ambiance, odd but excellent).

Glencoe village and Loch Leven from Sgorr nam Fiannaidh (Route 52)

Supplies etc two well-stocked shops at Tyndrum

Independent hostels West Highland Way sleeper, Bridge of Orchy cosy hostel on the station platform (01838 400548 www.westhighlandwaysleeper.co.uk), bunkhouse at Bridge of Orchy Hotel (www.bridgeoforchy.co.uk), and By the Way at Tyndrum (01838 400333 www.tyndrumbytheway.com).

Camping By the Way, Tyndrum; informal camping across the river at Bridge of Orchy, and bridge north of, Inveroran Hotel.

Dalmally and Taynuilt

Pubs and restaurants bar meals and reasonably-priced B&B Glenorchy Lodge Hotel, Dalmally 01838 200312 and Taynuilt Hotel (both at 01838 200251 www.glhotels.co.uk); Hollow Mountain Café at Cruachan Power Station

Supplies etc small grocers Glenview Stores, Dalmally and in Taynuilt

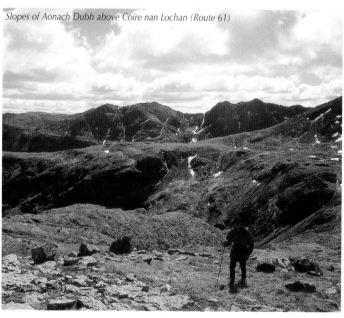

Slopes of Aonach Dubh above Coire nan Lochan (Route 61)

On the east ridge of Stob Ban, approaching the summit (Routes 38, 25)

Oban

Tourist Information 01631 563122

Supplies etc in abundance

SYHA in seafront villa (01631 562025)

Independent hostels three in Oban; Kerrera Bunkhouse at Lower Gylen www.kerrerabunkhouse.co.uk 01631 570223

Camping two camp/caravan sites south-west of town and one at Benderloch

Local transport ferry timetables: www.argyll-bute.gov.uk 01546 604360; Lismore Appin 01631 730686 (see www.calmac.co.uk); Lismore Oban www.calmac.co.uk 01631 566688; Kerrera 01631 563665

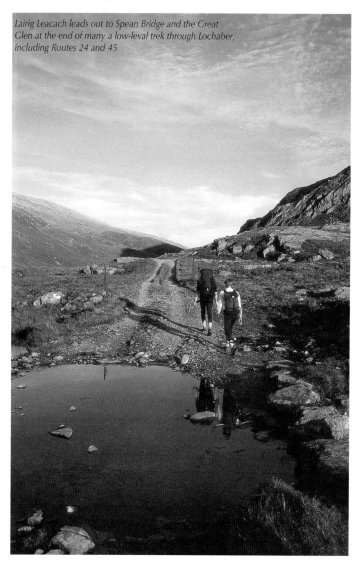

Lairig Leacach leads out to Spean Bridge and the Great
Glen at the end of many a low-leval trek through Lochaber,
including Routes 24 and 45

APPENDIX 3
Further Reading

Walking the Munros Vol 1 Southern by Steve Kew,
p/b Cicerone ISBN 978 1 85284 402 8 (2004)
If you simply wanted the convenient route up each of the Munros you should
have bought Kew's book rather than the one you're reading now.

Scrambles in Lochaber by Noel Williams,
p/b Cicerone 2nd edition ISBN 978 1 85284 234 5 (1996)
Covers 72 routes, many of them down to the author's own explorations. Good
routes lucidly described, with the occasional geological insight as a bonus.

SMC *Ben Nevis Rock and Ice Climbs* from the Scottish Mountaineering Club,
SMT ISBN 978 0 907521 73 0
Includes the Aonachs and areas east.

Climbing Guide – Glen Coe from the Scottish Mountaineering Club,
p/b SMT ISBN 978 0 907521 70 9

Winter Climbs Ben Nevis and Glen Coe by Alan Kimber,
p/b Cicerone 6th edition ISBN 978 1 85284 348 9 (2002)
The routes graded 1 are accessible to competent walkers with ice axe and crampons (or look at the pictures and get scared!)

Lochaber Geotrails: Glen Nevis and *Glen Coe* by Lochaber Geopark Association
These two leaflets (from TICs) are good introductions to the 'collapsing caldera'
formation special to Ben Nevis and Glen Coe.

Appin Munros and Stob Dubh from Stob Ghabhar (Route 85)

Buachaille Etive Mor from Kings House (Route 55)

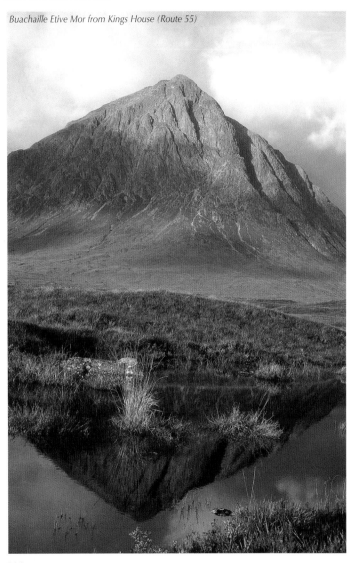

Ben Nevis – Britain's Highest Mountain by Ken Crocket,
p/b SMT ISBN 978 0 907521 16 7 (1986)
The history of climbing on Ben Nevis; new edition in preparation.

Glencoe by John Prebble, Penguin ISBN 978 0 14 002897 3
A passionate but scholarly account of the massacre without any of the usual easy myths, placing it in context as the first chapter in the destruction of the Highland way of life. Skip the visitor centre, or go in there just to buy this book.

Mountaineering in Scotland by W.H. Murray,
Bâton Wicks ISBN 978 1 898573 23 4 (1947)
Bidean and the Buachaille should not just be walked up! Places hillwalking in its wider context of rock, snow and ice-climbing, while being the greatest work so far of Scottish landscape appreciation.

Hostile Habitats: Scotland's Mountain Environment
p/b SMT ISBN 978 0 907521 93 8 (2006)
Takes your knowledge a bit further on everything from rhyolite to ravens.

NOTES

LISTING OF CICERONE GUIDES

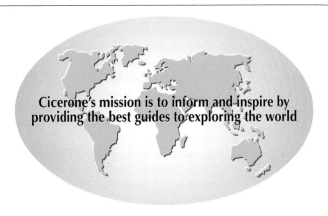

Cicerone's mission is to inform and inspire by providing the best guides to exploring the world

Since its foundation 40 years ago, Cicerone has specialised in publishing guidebooks and has built a reputation for quality and reliability. It now publishes nearly 300 guides to the major destinations for outdoor enthusiasts, including Europe, UK and the rest of the world.

Written by leading and committed specialists, Cicerone guides are recognised as the most authoritative. They are full of information, maps and illustrations so that the user can plan and complete a successful and safe trip or expedition – be it a long face climb, a walk over Lakeland fells, an alpine cycling tour, a Himalayan trek or a ramble in the countryside.

With a thorough introduction to assist planning, clear diagrams, maps and colour photographs to illustrate the terrain and route, and accurate and detailed text, Cicerone guides are designed for ease of use and access to the information.

If the facts on the ground change, or there is any aspect of a guide that you think we can improve, we are always delighted to hear from you.

Cicerone Press
2 Police Square Milnthorpe Cumbria LA7 7PY
Tel: 015395 62069 Fax: 015395 63417
info@cicerone.co.uk www.cicerone.co.uk

CICERONE